Anthony Trollope

NORTH AMERICA
---

in two volumes

VOLUME I

GRANVILLE PUBLISHING

The Angel Bookshop
102 Islington High Street
London N1 8EG

© Notes and editing, Granville Publishing, 1986
All rights reserved
Type (10½/12 Linotron Baskerville) set by Fakenham Photosetting Ltd,
Fakenham, Norfolk
Printed by Biddles Ltd, Guildford for
GRANVILLE PUBLISHING
The Angel Bookshop, 102 Islington High Street
London, N1 8EG

9 8 7 6 5 4 3 2 1

ISBN Vol. I   o 948 21404 X (boards)
             o 948 21406 6 (paper)
      Vol. II   o 948 21405 8 (boards)
             o 948 21407 4 (paper)

British Library Cataloguing in Publication Data

Trollope, Anthony
   North America.
   Vol. 1
   1. North America—Description and travel
   I. Title
   917'.044   E41

   ISBN 0–948214–04–X
   ISBN 0–948214–06–6 Pbk

NORTH AMERICA

Contents

A Note on the Text

The text used for this edition is that of the third English edition of *North America* of 1862, published by Chapman and Hall. This third edition would now more usually be called a third impression, for the only changes from the first edition, which appeared earlier in the same year, were the correction of some errors and the introduction of a few others.

The original editions of *North America* also included three appendixes, which contained the Declaration of Independence, the Articles of Confederation, and the United States' Constitution. These are not included in this edition, and to avoid confusion, three sentences that referred to the presence of those appendixes have been altered.

Errors in the text have been silently corrected. Where necessary, the text has been checked against the first edition and the Tauchnitz edition.

I

Introduction

IT has been the ambition of my literary life to write a book about the United States, and I had made up my mind to visit the country with this object before the intestine troubles of the United States Government had commenced. I have not allowed the division among the States and the breaking out of civil war to interfere with my intention; but I should not purposely have chosen this period either for my book or for my visit. I say so much, in order that it may not be supposed that it is my special purpose to write an account of the struggle as far as it has yet been carried. My wish is to describe as well as I can the present social and political state of the country. This I should have attempted, with more personal satisfaction in the work, had there been no disruption between the North and South; but I have not allowed that disruption to deter me from an object which, if it were delayed, might probably never be carried out. I am therefore forced to take the subject in its present condition, and being so forced I must write of the war, of the causes which have led to it, and of its probable termination. But I wish it to be understood that it was not my selected task to do so, and is not now my primary object.

Thirty years ago my mother wrote a book about the Americans, to which I believe I may allude as a well known and successful work without being guilty of any undue family conceit. That was essentially a woman's book. She saw with a woman's keen eye, and described with a woman's light but graphic pen, the social defects and absurdities which our near relatives had adopted into their domestic life. All that she told was worth the telling, and the telling, if done successfully, was sure to produce a good result. I am satisfied that it did so. But she did not regard it as a part of her work to dilate on the nature and operation of those political arrangements which had produced the social absurdities which she saw, or to explain that though such absurdities were the natural result of those arrangements in their newness, the defects would certainly pass away, while the political arrangements, if good, would remain. Such a work is fitter for a man than for a woman. I am very far from thinking that it is a task which I can perform with satisfaction either to myself or to others. It is a work which some man will do who has earned a right by education, study, and success to rank himself among the political sages of his age. But I may perhaps be able to add something to the familiarity of Englishmen with Americans. The writings which have been most popular in England on the subject of the United States have hitherto dealt chiefly with social details; and though in most cases true and useful, have created laughter on one side of the Atlantic, and soreness on the other. If I could do anything to mitigate the soreness, if I could in any small degree add to the good feeling which should exist between two nations which ought to love each other so well, and which do hang upon each other so constantly, I should think that I had cause to be proud of my work.

But it is very hard to write about any country a book that does not represent the country described in a more or less ridiculous point of view. It is hard at least to do so in such a book as I must write. A De Tocqueville may do it. It may be done by any philosophico-political or politico-statistical, or statistico-scientific writer; but it can hardly be done by a man who professes to use a light pen, and to manufacture his article for the use of general readers. Such a writer may tell all that he sees of the beautiful; but he must also tell, if not all that he sees of the ludicrous, at any rate the most piquant part of it. How to do this without being offensive is the problem which a man with such a task before him has to solve. His first duty is owed to his readers, and consists mainly in this: that he shall tell the truth, and shall so tell that truth that what he has written may be readable. But a second duty is due to those of whom he writes; and he does not perform that duty well if he gives offence to those, as to whom, on the summing up of the whole evidence for and against them in his own mind, he intends to give a favourable verdict. There are of course those against whom a writer does not intend to give a favourable verdict;—people and places whom he desires to describe on the peril of his own judgment, as bad, ill-educated, ugly, and odious. In such cases his course is straightforward enough. His judgment may be in great peril, but his volume or chapter will be easily written. Ridicule and censure run glibly from the pen, and form themselves into sharp paragraphs which are pleasant to the reader. Whereas eulogy is commonly dull, and too frequently sounds as though it were false. There is much difficulty in expressing a verdict which is intended to be favourable; but which, though favourable, shall not be falsely eulogistic; and though true, not offensive.

Who has ever travelled in foreign countries without meeting excellent stories against the citizens of such countries? And how few can travel without hearing such stories against themselves? It is impossible for me to avoid telling of a very excellent gentleman whom I met before I had been in the United States a week, and who asked me whether lords in England ever spoke to men who were not lords. Nor can I omit the opening address of another gentleman to my wife. "You like our institutions, ma'am?" "Yes, indeed," said my wife,—not with all that eagerness of assent which the occasion perhaps required. "Ah," said he, "I never yet met the down-trodden subject of a despot who did not hug his chains." The first gentleman was certainly somewhat ignorant of our customs, and the second was rather abrupt in his condemnation of the political principles of a person whom he only first saw at that moment. It comes to me in the way of my trade to repeat such incidents; but I can tell stories which are quite as good against Englishmen. As for instance, when I was tapped on the back in one of the galleries of Florence by a countryman of mine, and asked to show him where stood the medical Venus. Nor is anything that one can say of the inconveniences attendant upon travel in the United States to be beaten by what foreigners might truly say of us. I shall never forget the look of a Frenchman whom I found on a wet afternoon in the best inn of a provincial town in the west of England. He was seated on a horsehair-covered chair in the middle of a small dingy ill-furnished private sitting-room. No eloquence of mine could make intelligible to a Frenchman or an American the utter desolation of such an apartment. The world as then seen by that Frenchman offered him solace of no description. The air without was heavy, dull, and thick. The street beyond the window was dark and narrow. The room contained mahogany chairs covered with horsehair, a mahogany table ricketty in its legs, and a mahogany sideboard ornamented with inverted glasses and old cruet-stands. The Frenchman had come to the house for shelter and food, and had been asked whether he was commercial. Whereupon he shook his head. "Did he want a sitting-room?" Yes, he did. "He was a leetle tired and vanted to seet." Whereupon he was presumed to have ordered a private room, and was shown up to the Eden I have described. I found him there at death's door. Nothing that I can say with reference to the social habits of the Americans can tell more against them than the story of that Frenchman's fate tells against those of our country.

From which remarks I would wish to be understood as deprecating offence from my American friends, if in the course of my book should be found aught which may seem to argue against the excellence of their institutions, and the grace of their social life. Of this at any rate I can assure them in sober earnestness that I admire what they have done in the world and for the world with a true and hearty admiration; and that whether or no all their institutions be at present excellent, and their social life all graceful, my wishes are that they should be so, and my convictions are that that improvement will come for which there may perhaps even yet be some little room.

And now touching this war which had broken out between the North and South before I left England. I would wish to explain what my feelings were; or rather what I believe the general feelings of England to have been, before I found myself among the people by whom it was being waged. It is very difficult for the people of any one nation to realize the political relations of another, and to chew the cud and digest the bearings of those external politics. But it is unjust in the one to decide upon the political aspirations and doings of that other without such understanding. Constantly as the name of France is in our mouth, comparatively few Englishmen understand the way in which France is governed;—that is, how far absolute despotism prevails, and how far the power of the one ruler is tempered, or, as it may be, hampered by the voices and influence of others. And as regards England, how seldom is it that in common society a foreigner is met who comprehends the nature of her political arrangements! To a Frenchman,—I do not of course include great men who have made the subject a study,—but to the ordinary intelligent Frenchman the thing is altogether incomprehensible. Language, it may be said, has much to do with that. But an American speaks English; and how often is an American met, who has combined in his mind the idea of a monarch, so called, with that of a republic, properly so named,—a combination of ideas which I take to be necessary to the understanding of English politics? The gentleman who scorned my wife for hugging her chains had certainly not done so, and yet he conceived that he had studied the subject. The matter is one most difficult of comprehension. How many Englishmen have failed to understand accurately their own constitution, or the true bearing of their own politics! But when this knowledge has been attained, it has generally been filtered into the mind slowly, and has come from the unconscious study of many years. An Englishman handles a newspaper for a quarter of an hour daily, and daily exchanges some few words in politics with those around him, till drop by drop the pleasant springs of his liberty creep into his mind and water his heart; and thus, earlier or later in life according to the nature of his intelligence, he understands why it is that he is at all points a free man. But if this be so of our own politics; if it be so rare a thing to find a foreigner who understands them in all their niceties, why is it that we are so confident in our remarks on all the niceties of those of other nations?

I hope that I may not be misunderstood as saying that we should not discuss foreign politics in our press, our parliament, our public meetings, or our private houses. No man could be mad enough to preach such a doctrine. As regards our Parliament, that is probably the best British school of foreign politics, seeing that the subject is not there often taken up by men who are absolutely ignorant, and that mistakes when made are subject to a correction which is both rough and ready. The press, though very liable to error, labours hard at its vocation in teaching foreign politics, and spares no expense in letting in daylight. If the light let in be sometimes moonshine, excuse may easily be made. Where so much is attempted, there must necessarily be some failure. But even the moonshine does good, if it be not offensive moonshine. What I would deprecate is, that aptness at reproach which we assume;—the readiness with scorn, the quiet words of insult, the instant judgment and condemnation with which we are so inclined to visit, not the great outward acts, but the smaller inward politics of our neighbours.

And do others spare us, will be the instant reply of all who may read this. In my counter reply I make bold to place myself and my country on very high ground, and to say that we, the older and therefore more experienced people as regards the United States, and the better governed as regards France, and the stronger as regards all the world beyond, should not throw mud again even though mud be thrown at us. I yield the path to a small chimney-sweeper as readily as to a lady; and forbear from an interchange of courtesies with a Billingsgate heroine, even though at heart I may have a proud consciousness that I should not altogether go to the wall in such an encounter.

I left England in August last—August 1861. At that time, and for some months previous, I think that the general English feeling on the American question was as follows. "This wide-spread nationality of the United States, with its enormous territorial possessions and increasing population, has fallen asunder, torn to pieces by the weight of its own discordant parts,—as a congregation when its size has become unwieldy will separate, and reform itself into two wholesome wholes. It is well that this should be so, for the people are not homogeneous, as a people should be who are called to live together as one nation. They have attempted to combine free-soil sentiments with the practice of slavery, and to make these two antagonists live together in peace and unity under the same roof; but, as we have long expected, they have failed. Now has come the period for separation; and if the people would only see this, and act in accordance with the circumstances which Providence and the inevitable hand of the world's ruler has prepared for them, all would be well. But they will not do this. They will go to war with each other. The South will make her demands for secession with an arrogance and instant pressure which exasperates the North; and the North, forgetting that an equal temper in such matters is the most powerful of all weapons, will not recognize the strength of its own position. It allows itself to be exasperated, and goes to war for that which if regained would only be injurious to it. Thus millions on millions sterling will be spent. A heavy debt will be incurred; and the North, which divided from the South might take its place among the greatest of nations, will throw itself back for half a century, and perhaps injure the splendour of its ultimate prospects. If only they would be wise, throw down their arms, and agree to part! But they will not."

This was, I think, the general opinion when I left England. It would not, however, be necessary to go back many months to reach the time when Englishmen were saying how impossible it was that so great a national power should ignore its own greatness, and destroy its own power by an internecine separation. But in August last all that had gone by, and we in England had realized the probability of actual secession. .

To these feelings on the subject may be added another, which was natural enough though perhaps not noble. "These western cocks have crowed loudly," we said, "too loudly for the comfort of those who live after all at no such great distance from them. It is well that their combs should be clipped. Cocks who crow so very loudly are a nuisance. It might have gone so far that the clipping would become a work necessarily to be done from without. But it is ten times better for all parties that it should be done from within; and as the cocks are now clipping their own combs, in God's name let them do it and the whole world will be the quieter." That, I say, was not a very noble idea; but it was natural enough, and certainly has done somewhat in mitigating that grief which the horrors of civil war and the want of cotton have caused to us in England.

Such certainly had been my belief as to the country. I speak here of my opinion as to the ultimate success of secession and the folly of the war,—repudiating any concurrence of my own in the ignoble but natural sentiment alluded to in the last paragraph. I certainly did think that the Northern States, if wise, would have let the Southern States go. I had blamed Buchanan as a traitor for allowing the germ of secession to make any growth;—and as I thought him a traitor then, so do I think him a traitor now. But I had also blamed Lincoln, or rather the government of which Mr. Lincoln in this matter is no more than the exponent, for his efforts to avoid that which is inevitable. In this I think that I—or as I believe I may say we, we Englishmen— were wrong. I do not see how the North, treated as it was and had been, could have submitted to secession without resistance. We all remember what Shakespere says of the great armies which were led out to fight for a piece of ground not large enough to cover the bodies of those who would be slain in the battle; but I do not remember that Shakespere says that the battle was on this account necessarily unreasonable. It is the old point of honour, which, till it had been made absurd by certain changes of circumstances, was always grand and usually beneficent. These changes of circumstances have altered the manner in which appeal may be made, but have not altered the point of honour. Had the Southern States sought to obtain secession by constitutional means, they might or might not have been successful; but if successful there would have been no war. I do not mean to brand all the Southern States with treason, nor do I intend to say that having secession at heart they could have obtained it by constitutional means. But I do intend to say that acting as they did, demanding secession not constitutionally but in opposition to the constitution, taking upon themselves the right of breaking up a nationality of which they formed only a part, and doing that without consent of the other part, opposition from the North and war was an inevitable consequence.

It is, I think, only necessary to look back to the revolution by which the United States separated themselves from England to see this. There is hardly to be met, here and there, an Englishman who now regrets the loss of the revolted American colonies;—who now thinks that civilization was retarded and the world injured by that revolt; who now conceives that England should have expended more treasure and more lives in the hope of retaining those colonies. It is agreed that the revolt was a good thing; that those who were then rebels became patriots by success, and that they deserved well of all coming ages of mankind. But not the less absolutely necessary was it that England should endeavour to hold her own. She was as the mother bird when the young bird will fly alone. She suffered those pangs which Nature calls upon mothers to endure.

As was the necessity of British opposition to American independence, so was the necessity of Northern opposition to Southern secession. I do not say that in other respects the two cases were parallel. The States separated from us because they would not endure taxation without representation—in other words because they were old enough and big enough to go alone. The South is seceding from the North because the two are not homogeneous. They have different instincts, different appetites, different morals, and a different culture. It is well for one man to say that slavery has caused the separation; and for another to say that slavery has not caused it. Each in so saying speaks the truth. Slavery has caused it, seeing that slavery is the great point on which the two have agreed to differ. But slavery has not caused it, seeing that other points of difference are to be found in every circumstance and feature of the two people. The North and the South must ever be dissimilar. In the North labour will always be honourable, and because honourable successful. In the South labour has ever been servile,—at least in some sense, and therefore dishonourable; and because dishonourable has not, to itself, been successful. In the South, I say, labour ever has been dishonourable; and I am driven to confess that I have not hitherto seen a sign of any change in the Creator's fiat on this matter. That labour will be honourable all the world over, as years advance and the millennium draws nigh, I for one never doubt.

So much for English opinion about America in August last. And now I will venture to say a word or two as to American feeling respecting this English opinion at that period. It will of course be remembered by all my readers that at the beginning of the war Lord Russell, who was then in the lower house, declared as Foreign Secretary of State that England would regard the North and South as belligerents, and would remain neutral as to both of them. This declaration gave violent offence to the North, and has been taken as indicating British sympathy with the cause of the seceders. I am not going to explain—indeed it would be necessary that I should first understand—the laws of nations with regard to blockaded ports, privateering, ships and men and goods contraband of war, and all those semi-nautical semi-military rules and axioms which it is necessary that all Attorneys-General and such like should at the present moment have at their fingers' end. But it must be evident to the most ignorant in those matters, among which large crowd I certainly include myself, that it was essentially necessary that Lord John Russell should at that time declare openly what England intended to do. It was essential that our seamen should know where they would be protected and where not, and that the course to be taken by England should be defined. Reticence in the matter was not within the power of the British Government. It behoved the Foreign Secretary of State to declare openly that England intended to side either with one party or with the other, or else to remain neutral between them.

I had heard this matter discussed by Americans before I left England, and I have of course heard it discussed very frequently in America. There can be no doubt that the front of the offence given by England to the Northern States was this declaration of Lord John Russell's. But it has been always made evident to me that the sin did not consist in the fact of England's neutrality,—in the fact of her regarding the two parties as belligerents,—but in the open declaration made to the world by a Secretary of State that she did intend so to regard them. If another proof were wanting, this would afford another proof of the immense weight attached in America to all the proceedings and to all the feelings of England on this matter. The very anger of the North is a compliment paid by the North to England. But not the less is that anger unreasonable. To those in America who understand our constitution, it must be evident that our Government cannot take official measures without a public avowal of such measures. France can do so. Russia can do so. The Government of the United States can do so, and could do so even before this rupture. But the Government of England cannot do so. All men connected with the Government in England have felt themselves from time to time more or less hampered by the necessity of publicity. Our statesmen have been forced to fight their battles with the plan of their tactics open before their adversaries. But we, in England, are inclined to believe, that the general result is good, and that battles so fought and so won will be fought with the honestest blows, and won with the surest results. Reticence in this matter was not possible, and Lord John Russell in making the open

avowal which gave such offence to the Northern States only did that
which, as a·servant of England, England required him to do.

"What would you in England have thought," a gentleman of much
weight in Boston said to me, "if when you were in trouble in India, we
had openly declared that we regarded your opponents there as belligerents on equal terms with yourselves?" I was forced to say that, as far
as I could see, there was no analogy between the two cases. In India an
army had mutinied, and that an army composed of a subdued, if not a
servile race. The analogy would have been fairer had it referred to any
sympathy shown by us to insurgent negroes. But, nevertheless, had the
army which mutinied in India been in possession of ports and seaboard; had they held in their hands vast commercial cities and great
agricultural districts; had they owned ships and been masters of a
wide-spread trade, America could have done nothing better towards
us than have remained neutral in such a conflict, and have regarded
the parties as belligerents. The only question is whether she would
have done so well by us. "But," said my friend in answer to all this,
"we should not have proclaimed to the world that we regarded you
and them as standing on an equal footing." There again appeared the
true gist of the offence. A word from England such as that spoken by
Lord John Russell was of such weight to the South, that the North
could not endure to have it spoken. I did not say to that gentleman,
—but here I may say, that had such circumstances arisen as those
conjectured, and had America spoken such a word, England would
not have felt herself called upon to resent it.

But the fairer analogy lies between Ireland and the Southern States.
The monster meetings and O'Connell's triumphs are not so long gone
by but that many of us can remember the first demand for secession
made by Ireland, and the line which was then taken by American
sympathies. It is not too much to say that America then believed that
Ireland would secure secession, and that the great trust of the Irish
repealers was in the moral aid which she did and would receive from
America. "But our Government proclaimed no sympathy with Ireland," said my friend. No. The American Government is not called on
to make such proclamations; nor had Ireland ever taken upon herself
the nature and labours of a belligerent.

That this anger on the part of the North is unreasonable I cannot
doubt. That it is unfortunate, grievous, and very bitter I am quite sure.
But I do not think that it is in any degree surprising. I am inclined to
think that did I belong to Boston as I do belong to London, I should
share in the feeling, and rave as loudly as all men there have raved

against the coldness of England. When men have on hand such a job of work as the North has now undertaken they are always guided by their feelings rather than their reason. What two men ever had a quarrel in which each did not think that all the world, if just, would espouse his own side of the dispute? The North feels that it has been more than loyal to the South, and that the South has taken advantage of that over-loyalty to betray the North. "We have worked for them, and fought for them, and paid for them," says the North. "By our labour we have raised their indolence to a par with our energy. While we have worked like men, we have allowed them to talk and bluster. We have warmed them in our bosom, and now they turn against us and sting us. The world sees that this is so. England, above all, must see it, and seeing it should speak out her true opinion." The North is hot with such thoughts as these, and one cannot wonder that she should be angry with her friend, when her friend, with an expression of certain easy good wishes, bids her fight out her own battles. The North has been unreasonable with England;—but I believe that every reader of this page would have been as unreasonable had that reader been born in Massachusetts.

Mr. and Mrs. Jones are the dearly beloved friends of my family. My wife and I have lived with Mrs. Jones on terms of intimacy which have been quite endearing. Jones has had the run of my house with perfect freedom, and in Mrs. Jones' drawing-room I have always had my own arm-chair, and have been regaled with large breakfast-cups of tea, quite as though I were at home. But of a sudden Jones and his wife have fallen out, and there is for a while in Jones' Hall a cat and dog life that may end—in one hardly dare to surmise what calamity. Mrs. Jones begs that I will interfere with her husband, and Jones entreats the good offices of my wife in moderating the hot temper of his own. But we know better than that. If we interfere, the chances are that my dear friends will make it up and turn upon us. I grieve beyond measure in a general way at the temporary break up of the Jones' Hall happiness. I express general wishes that it may be temporary. But as for saying which is right or which is wrong,—as to expressing special sympathy on either side in such a quarrel,—it is out of the question. "My dear Jones, you must excuse me. Any news in the City to-day? Sugars have fell; how are teas?" Of course Jones thinks that I'm a brute; but what can I do?

I have been somewhat surprised to find the trouble that has been taken by American orators, statesmen, and logicians to prove that this secession on the part of the South has been revolutionary;—that is to

say, that it has been undertaken and carried on not in compliance with
the constitution of the United States, but in defiance of it. This has
been done over and over again by some of the greatest men of the
North, and has been done most successfully. But what then? Of course
the movement has been revolutionary and anti-constitutional. Nobody, no single Southerner, can really believe that the Constitution of
the United States as framed in 1787, or altered since, intended to give
to the separate States the power of seceding as they pleased. It is surely
useless going through long arguments to prove this, seeing that it is
absolutely proved by the absence of any clause giving such licence to
the separate States. Such licence would have been destructive to the
very idea of a great nationality. Where would New England have been
as a part of the United States, if New York, which stretches from the
Atlantic to the borders of Canada, had been endowed with the power
of cutting off the six Northern States from the rest of the Union? No
one will for a moment doubt that the movement was revolutionary,
and yet infinite pains are taken to prove a fact that is patent to
every one.

It is revolutionary, but what then? Have the Northern States of the
American Union taken upon themselves in 1861 to proclaim their
opinion that revolution is a sin? Are they going back to the divine right
of any sovereignty? Are they going to tell the world that a nation or a
people is bound to remain in any political status, because that status is
the recognized form of government under which such a people have
lived? Is this to be the doctrine of United States' citizens,—of all
people? And is this the doctrine preached now, of all times, when the
King of Naples and the Italian dukes have just been dismissed from
their thrones with such enchanting nonchalance, because their people
have not chosen to keep them? Of course the movement is revolutionary; and why not? It is agreed now among all men and all nations that
any people may change its form of government to any other, if it wills
to do so,—and if it can do so.

There are two other points on which these Northern statesmen and
logicians also insist, and these two other points are at any rate better
worth an argument than that which touches the question of revolution.
It being settled that secession on the part of the Southerners is revolution, it is argued, firstly, that no occasion for revolution had been given
by the North to the South; and, secondly, that the South has been
dishonest in its revolutionary tactics. Men certainly should not raise a
revolution for nothing; and it may certainly be declared that whatever
men do, they should do honestly.

But in that matter of the cause and ground for revolution, it is so very easy for either party to put in a plea that shall be satisfactory to itself! Mr. and Mrs. Jones each had a separate story. Mr. Jones was sure that the right lay with him: but Mrs. Jones was no less sure. No doubt the North had done much for the South;—had earned money for it; had fed it;—and had moreover in a great measure fostered all its bad habits. It had not only been generous to the South, but over-indulgent. But also it had continually irritated the South by meddling with that which the Southerners believed to be a question absolutely private to themselves. The matter was illustrated to me by a New Hampshire man who was conversant with black bears. At the hotels in the New Hampshire mountains it is customary to find black bears chained to poles. These bears are caught among the hills, and are thus imprisoned for the amusement of the hotel guests. "Them South-erners," said my friend, "are jist as one as that 'ere bear. We feeds him and gives him a house and his belly is ollers full. But then, jist becase he's a black bear, we're ollers a poking him with sticks, and a' course the beast is kinder riled. He wants to be back to the mountains. He wouldn't have his belly filled, but he'd have his own way. It's jist so with them Southerners."

It is of no use proving to any man or to any nation that they have got all they should want, if they have not got all that they do want. If a servant desires to go, it is of no avail to show him that he has all he can desire in his present place. The Northerners say that they have given no offence to the Southerners, and that therefore the South is wrong to raise a revolution. The very fact that the North is the North, is an offence to the South. As long as Mr. and Mrs. Jones were one in heart and one in feeling having the same hopes and the same joys, it was well that they should remain together. But when it is proved that they cannot so live without tearing out each other's eyes, Sir Cresswell Cresswell, the revolutionary institution of domestic life, interferes and separates them. This is the age of such separations. I do not wonder that the North should use its logic to show that it has received cause of offence but given none. But I do think that such logic is thrown away. The matter is not one for argument. The South has thought that it can do better without the North than with it; and if it has the power to separate itself, it must be conceded that it has the right.

And then as to that question of honesty. Whatever men do they certainly should do honestly. Speaking broadly one may say that the rule applies to nations as strongly as to individuals, and should be observed in politics as accurately as in other matters. We must, however, confess that men who are scrupulous in their private dealings do too constantly drop those scruples when they handle public affairs,—and especially when they handle them at stirring moments of great national changes. The name of Napoleon III stands fair now before Europe, and yet he filched the French empire with a falsehood. The union of England and Ireland is a successful fact, but nevertheless it can hardly be said that it was honestly achieved. I heartily believe that the whole of Texas is improved in every sense by having been taken from Mexico and added to the southern States, but I much doubt whether that annexation was accomplished with absolute honesty. We all reverence the name of Cavour, but Cavour did not consent to abandon Nice to France with clean hands. When men have political ends to gain they regard their opponents as adversaries, and then that old rule of war is brought to bear, Deceit or Valour,—either may be used against a foe. Would it were not so! The rascally rule—rascally in reference to all political contests—is becoming less universal than it was. But it still exists with sufficient force to be urged as an excuse; and while it does exist it seems almost needless to show that a certain amount of fraud has been used by a certain party in a revolution. If the South be ultimately successful, the fraud of which it may have been guilty will be condoned by the world.

The Southern or democratic party of the United States had, as all men know, been in power for many years. Either Southern Presidents had been elected, or Northern Presidents with Southern politics. The South for many years had had the disposition of military matters, and the power of distributing military appliances of all descriptions. It is now alleged by the North that a conspiracy had long been hatching in the South with the view of giving to the southern States the power of secession whenever they might think fit to secede; and it is further alleged that President after President for years back has unduly sent the military treasure of the nation away from the North down to the South, in order that the South might be prepared when the day should come. That a President with southern instincts should unduly favour the South, that he should strengthen the South, and feel that arms and ammunition were stored there with better effect than they could be stored in the North, is very probable. We all understand what is the bias of a man's mind, and how strong that bias may become when the man is not especially scrupulous. But I do not believe that any President previous to Buchanan sent military materials to the South with the self-acknowledged purpose of using them against the Union. That

Buchanan did so, or knowingly allowed this to be done, I do believe, and I think that Buchanan was a traitor to the country whose servant he was and whose pay he received.

And now, having said so much in the way of introduction, I will begin my journey.

II

Newport—Rhode Island

WE—the we consisting of my wife and myself—left Liverpool for Boston on the 24th August, 1861, in the 'Arabia,' one of Cunard's North American mail packets. We had determined that my wife should return alone at the beginning of winter, when I intended to go to a part of the country in which, under the existing circumstances of the war, a lady might not feel herself altogether comfortable. I proposed staying in America over the winter, and returning in the spring; and this programme I have carried out with sufficient exactness.

The 'Arabia' touched at Halifax; and as the touch extended from 11 A.M. to 6 P.M. we had an opportunity of seeing a good deal of that colony;—not quite sufficient to justify me at this critical age in writing a chapter of travels in Nova Scotia, but enough perhaps to warrant a paragraph. It chanced that a cousin of mine was then in command of the troops there, so that we saw the fort with all the honours. A dinner on shore was, I think, a greater treat to us even than this. We also inspected sundry specimens of the gold which is now being found for the first time in Nova Scotia,—as to the glory and probable profits of which the Nova Scotians seemed to be fully alive. But still, I think, the dinner on shore took rank with us as the most memorable and meritorious of all that we did and saw at Halifax. At seven o'clock on the morning but one after that, we were landed at Boston.

At Boston I found friends ready to receive us with open arms, though they were friends we had never known before. I own that I felt myself burdened with much nervous anxiety at my first introduction to men and women in Boston. I knew what the feeling there was with reference to England, and I knew also how impossible it is for an Englishman to hold his tongue and submit to dispraise of England. As for going among a people whose whole minds were filled with affairs of the war, and saying nothing about the war,—I knew that no resolution to such an effect could be carried out. If one could not trust oneself to speak, one should have stayed at home in England. I will here state that I always did speak out openly what I thought and felt, and that though I encountered very strong—sometimes almost fierce— opposition, I never was subjected to anything that was personally disagreeable to me.

In September we did not stay above a week in Boston, having been fairly driven out of it by the mosquitoes. I had been told that I should find nobody in Boston whom I cared to see, as everybody was habitually out of town during the heat of the latter summer and early autumn; but this was not so. The war and attendant turmoils of war had made the season of vacation shorter than usual, and most of those for whom I asked were back at their posts. I know no place at which an Englishman may drop down suddenly among a pleasanter circle of acquaintance, or find himself with a more clever set of men, than he can do at Boston. I confess that in this respect I think that but few towns are at present more fortunately circumstanced than the capital of the Bay State, as Massachusetts is called, and that very few towns make a better use of their advantages. Boston has a right to be proud of what it has done for the world of letters. It is proud; but I have not found that its pride was carried too far.

Boston is not in itself a fine city, but it is a very pleasant city. They say that the harbour is very grand and very beautiful. It certainly is not so fine as that of Portland in a nautical point of view, and as certainly it is not as beautiful. It is the entrance from the sea into Boston of which people say so much; but I did not think it quite worthy of all I had heard. In such matters, however, much depends on the peculiar light in which scenery is seen. An evening light is generally the best for all landscapes; and I did not see the entrance to Boston harbour by an evening light. It was not the beauty of the harbour of which I thought the most; but of the tea that had been sunk there, and of all that came of that successful speculation. Few towns now standing have a right to be more proud of their antecedents than Boston.

But as I have said, it is not specially interesting to the eye—what new town, or even what simply adult town, can be so? There is an Athenæum, and a State Hall, and a fashionable street,—Beacon Street, very like Piccadilly as it runs along the Green Park,—and there is the Green Park opposite to this Piccadilly, called Boston Common. Beacon Street and Boston Common are very pleasant. Excellent houses there are, and large churches, and enormous hotels; but of such things as these a man can write nothing that is worth the reading. The traveller who desires to tell his experience of North America must write of people rather than of things.

As I have said, I found myself instantly involved in discussions on American politics, and the bearing of England upon those politics. "What do you think, you in England—what do you all believe will be the upshot of this war?" That was the question always asked in those or other words. "Secession, certainly," I always said, but not speaking quite with that abruptness. "And you believe, then, that the South will beat the North?" I explained that I, personally, had never so thought, and that I did not believe that to be the general idea. Men's opinions in England, however, were too divided to enable me to say that there was any prevailing conviction on the matter. My own impression was, and is, that the North will, in a military point of view, have the best of the contest,—will beat the South; but that the Northerners will not prevent secession, let their success be what it may. Should the North prevail after a two years' conflict, the North will not admit the South to an equal participation of good things with themselves, even though each separate rebellious State should return suppliant, like a prodigal son, kneeling on the floor of Congress, each with a separate rope of humiliation round its neck. Such was my idea as expressed then, and I do not know that I have since had much cause to change it.

"We will never give it up," one gentleman said to me—and, indeed, many have said the same, "till the whole territory is again united from the Bay to the Gulf! It is impossible that we should allow of two nationalities within those limits." "And do you think it possible," I asked, "that you should receive back into your bosom this people which you now hate with so deep a hatred, and receive them again into your arms as brothers on equal terms? Is it in accordance with experience that a conquered people should be so treated—and that, too, a people whose every habit of life is at variance with the habits of their presumed conquerors? When you have flogged them into a return of fraternal affection, are they to keep their slaves or are they to abolish them?" "No," said my friend; "it may not be practical to put those rebellious States at once on an equality with ourselves. For a time they will probably be treated as the Territories are now treated." (The Territories are vast outlying districts belonging to the Union, but not as yet endowed with State governments, or a participation in the United States Congress.) "For a time they must, perhaps, lose their full privileges; but the Union will be anxious to readmit them at the earliest possible period." "And as to the slaves?" I asked again. "Let them emigrate to Liberia: back to their own country." I could not say that I thought much of the solution of the difficulty. It would, I suggested, overtask even the energy of America to send out an emigration of four million souls, to provide for their wants in a new and uncultivated country, and to provide after that for the terrible gap made in the labour market of the Southern States. "The Israelites went back from bondage," said my friend. But a way was opened for them by a miracle across the sea, and food was sent to them from heaven, and they had among them a Moses for a leader and a Joshua to fight their battles. I could not but express my fear that the days of such immigrations were over. This plan of sending back the negroes to Africa did not reach me only from one or from two mouths; and it was suggested by men whose opinions respecting their country have weight at home and are entitled to weight abroad. I mention this merely to show how insurmountable would be the difficulty of preventing secession, let which side win that may.

"We will never abandon the right to the mouth of the Mississippi." That in all such arguments is a strong point with men of the northern States;—perhaps the point to which they all return with the greatest firmness. It is that on which Mr. Everett insists in the last paragraph of the oration which he made in New York on 4th of July, 1861. "The Missouri and the Mississippi rivers," he says, "with their hundred tributaries give to the great central basin of our continent its character and destiny. The outlet of this system lies between the States of Tennessee and Missouri, of Mississippi and Arkansas, and through the State of Louisiana. The ancient province so called, the proudest monument of the mighty monarch whose name it bears, passed from the jurisdiction of France to that of Spain in 1763. Spain coveted it; not that she might fill it with prosperous colonies and rising States, but that it might stretch as a broad waste barrier, infested with warlike tribes, between the Anglo-American power and the silver mines of Mexico. With the independence of the United States, the fear of a still more dangerous neighbour grew upon Spain; and in the insane expectation of checking the progress of the Union westward, she threatened, and at times attempted, to close the mouth of the Mississippi on the rapidly increasing trade of the West. The bare suggestion of such a policy roused the population upon the banks of the Ohio, then inconsiderable, as one man. Their confidence in Washington scarcely restrained them from rushing to the seizure of New Orleans, when the treaty of San Lorenzo El Real, in 1795, stipulated for them a precarious right of navigating the noble river to the sea, with a right of deposit at New Orleans. This subject was for years the turning-point of the politics of the West; and it was perfectly well understood that, sooner or later, she would be content with nothing less than the sovereign control of the mighty stream from its head-spring to its outlet in the Gulf. *And that is as true now as it was then.*"

This is well put. It describes with force the desires, ambition, and necessities of a great nation, and it tells with historical truth the story of the success of that nation. It was a great thing done when the purchase of the whole of Louisiana was completed by the United States,—that cession by France, however, having been made at the instance of Napoleon, and not in consequence of any demand made by the States. The district then called Louisiana included the present State of that name, and the States of Missouri and Arkansas;— included also the right to possess, if not the absolute possession of, all that enormous expanse of country running from thence back to the Pacific; a huge amount of territory of which the most fertile portion is watered by the Mississippi and its vast tributaries. That river and those tributaries are navigable through the whole centre of the American continent up to Wisconsin and Minnesota. To the United States the navigation of the Mississippi was, we may say, indispensable; and to the States when no longer united the navigation will be equally indispensable. But the days are gone when any country, such as Spain was, can interfere to stop the highways of the world with the all but avowed intention of arresting the progress of civilization. It may be that the North and the South can never again be friends as the component parts of one nation. Such I take it is the belief of all politicians in Europe, and of many of those who live across the water. But as separate nations they may yet live together in amity, and share between them the great water-ways which God has given them for their enrichment. The Rhine is free to Prussia and to Holland. The Danube is not closed against Austria. It will be said that the Danube has in fact been closed against Austria, in spite of treaties to the contrary. But the faults of bad and weak governments are made known as cautions to the world, and not as facts to copy. The free use of the waters of a common river between two nations is an affair for treaty; and it has not yet come to that that treaties must necessarily be null and void through the falseness of politicians.

"And what will England do for cotton? Is it not the fact that Lord John Russell with his professed neutrality intends to express sympathy with the South, intends to pave the way for the advent of Southern cotton?" "You ought to love us," so say men in Boston, "because we have been with you in heart and spirit for long, long years. But your trade has eaten into your souls, and you love American cotton better than American loyalty and American fellowship." This I found to be unfair, and in what politest language I could use I said so. I had not any special knowledge of the minds of English statesmen on this matter; but I knew as well as Americans could do what our statesmen had said and done respecting it. That cotton, if it came from the South, would be made very welcome in Liverpool, of course, I knew. If private enterprise could bring it, it might be brought. But the very declaration made by Lord John Russell was the surest pledge that England as a nation would not interfere, even to supply her own wants. It may easily be imagined what eager words all this would bring about; but I never found that eager words led to feelings which were personally hostile.

All the world has heard of Newport in Rhode Island as being the Brighton, and Tenby, and Scarborough of New England. And the glory of Newport is by no means confined to New England, but is shared by New York and Washington, and in ordinary years by the extreme South. It is the habit of Americans to go to some watering place every summer,—that is, to some place either of sea water or of inland waters. This is done much in England; more in Ireland than in England; but, I think, more in the States than even in Ireland. But of all such summer haunts, Newport is supposed to be in many ways the most captivating. In the first place it is certainly the most fashionable, and in the next place it is said to be the most beautiful. We decided on going to Newport,—led thither by the latter reputation rather than the former. As we were still in the early part of September we expected to find the place full, but in this we were disappointed;—disappointed, I say, rather than gratified, although a crowded house at such a place is certainly a nuisance. But a house which is prepared to make up six hundred beds, and which is called on to make up only twenty-five becomes, after a while, somewhat melancholy. The natural depression of the landlord communicates itself to his servants, and from the servants it descends to the twenty-five guests, who wander about the long passages and deserted balconies like the ghosts of those of the summer visitors, who cannot rest quietly in their graves at home.

In England we know nothing of hotels prepared for six hundred visitors, all of whom are expected to live in common. Domestic architects would be frightened at the dimensions which are needed, and at the number of apartments which are required to be clustered under one roof. We went to the Ocean Hotel at Newport, and fancied, as we first entered the hall under a verandah as high as the house, and made our way into the passage, that we had been taken to a well-arranged barrack. "Have you rooms?" I asked, as a man always does ask on first reaching his inn. "Rooms enough," the clerk said. "We have only fifty here." But that fifty dwindled down to twenty-five during the next day or two.

We were a melancholy set, the ladies appearing to be afflicted in this way worse than the gentlemen, on account of their enforced abstinence from tobacco. What can twelve ladies do scattered about a drawing-room, so-called, intended for the accommodation of two hundred? The drawing-room at the Ocean Hotel, Newport, is not as big as Westminster Hall, but would, I should think, make a very good House of Commons for the British nation. Fancy the feelings of a lady when she walks into such a room intending to spend her evening there, and finds six or seven other ladies located on various sofas at terrible distances,—all strangers to her. She has come to Newport probably to enjoy herself; and as, in accordance with the customs of the place, she has dined at two, she has nothing before her for the evening but the society of that huge furnished cavern. Her husband, if she have one, or her father, or her lover, has probably entered the room with her. But a man has never the courage to endure such a position long. He sidles out with some muttered excuse, and seeks solace with a cigar. The lady, after half an hour of contemplation, creeps silently near some companion in the desert, and suggests in a whisper that Newport does not seem to be very full at present.

We stayed there for a week, and were very melancholy; but in our melancholy we still talked of the war. Americans are said to be given to bragging, and it is a sin of which I cannot altogether acquit them. But I have constantly been surprised at hearing the Northern speak of their own military achievements with anything but self-praise. "We've been whipped, sir; and we shall be whipped again before we've done; uncommon well whipped we shall be." "We began cowardly, and were afraid to send our own regiments through one of our own cities."

This alluded to a demand that had been made on the Government, that troops going to Washington should not be sent through Baltimore, because of the strong feeling for rebellion which was known to exist in that city. President Lincoln complied with this request, thinking it well to avoid a collision between the mob and the soldiers. "We began cowardly, and now we're going on cowardly, and darn't attack them. Well; when we've been whipped often enough, then we shall learn the trade." Now all this,—and I heard much of such a nature,—could not be called boasting. But yet with it all there was a substratum of confidence. I have heard northern gentlemen complaining of the President, complaining of all his ministers one after another, complaining of the contractors who were robbing the army, of the commanders who did not know how to command the army, and of the army itself which did not know how to obey; but I do not remember that I have discussed the matter with any Northerner who would admit a doubt as to ultimate success.

We were certainly rather melancholy at Newport, and the empty house may perhaps have given its tone to the discussions on the war. I confess that I could not stand the drawing-room—the ladies' drawing-room as such-like rooms are always called at the hotels, and that I basely deserted my wife. I could not stand it either here or elsewhere, and it seemed to me that other husbands,—ay, and even lovers,— were as hard pressed as myself. I protest that there is no spot on the earth's surface so dear to me as my own drawing-room, or rather my wife's drawing-room at home; that I am not a man given hugely to clubs, but one rather rejoicing in the rustle of petticoats. I like to have women in the same room with me. But at these hotels I found myself driven away,—propelled as it were by some unknown force,—to absent myself from the feminine haunts. Anything was more palatable than them; even "liquoring up" at a nasty bar, or smoking in a comfortless reading-room among a deluge of American newspapers. And I protest also,—hoping as I do so that I may say much in these volumes to prove the truth of such protestation,—that this comes from no fault of the American women. They are as lovely as our own women. Taken generally, they are better instructed—though perhaps not better educated. They are seldom troubled with *mauvaise honte*,—I do not say it in irony, but begging that the words may be taken at their proper meaning. They can always talk, and very often can talk well. But when assembled together in these vast, cavernous, would-be luxurious, but in truth horribly comfortless hotel drawing-rooms,— they are unapproachable. I have seen lovers, whom I have known to be lovers, unable to remain five minutes in the same cavern with their beloved ones.

And then the music? There is always a piano in an hotel drawing-room, on which, of course, some one of the forlorn ladies is generally employed. I do not suppose that these pianos are in fact, as a rule, louder and harsher, more violent and less musical, than other instruments of the kind. They seem to be so, but that, I take it, arises from the exceptional mental depression of those who have to listen to them. Then the ladies, or probably some one lady, will sing, and as she hears her own voice ring and echo through the lofty corners and round the empty walls, she is surprised at her own force, and with increased efforts sings louder and still louder. She is tempted to fancy that she is suddenly gifted with some power of vocal melody unknown to her before, and filled with the glory of her own performance shouts till the whole house rings. At such moments she at least is happy, if no one else is so. Looking at the general sadness of her position, who can grudge her such happiness?

And then the children,—babies, I should say if I were speaking of English bairns of their age; but seeing that they are Americans, I hardly dare to call them children. The actual age of these perfectly civilized and highly educated beings may be from three to four. One will often see five or six such seated at the long dinner-table of the hotel, breakfasting and dining with their elders, and going through the ceremony with all the gravity, and more than all the decorum of their grandfathers. When I was three years old I had not yet, as I imagine, been promoted beyond a silver spoon of my own wherewith to eat my bread and milk in the nursery, and I feel assured that I was under the immediate care of a nursemaid, as I gobbled up my minced mutton mixed with potatoes and gravy. But at hotel life in the States the adult infant lisps to the waiter for everything at table, handles his fish with epicurean delicacy, is choice in his selection of pickles, very particular that his beefsteak at breakfast shall be hot, and is instant in his demand for fresh ice in his water. But perhaps his, or in this case her, retreat from the room when the meal is over, is the *chef d'œuvre* of the whole performance. The little precocious, full-blown beauty of four signifies that she has completed her meal,—or is "through" her dinner, as she would express it,—by carefully extricating herself from the napkin which has been tucked around her. Then the waiter, ever attentive to her movements, draws back the chair on which she is seated, and the young lady glides to the floor. A little girl in Old England would scramble down, but little girls in New England never scramble. Her father and mother, who are no more than her chief ministers, walk before her out of the saloon, and then she,—swims after them. But swimming is not the proper word. Fishes in making their way through the water assist, or rather impede, their motion with no dorsal riggle. No animal taught to move directly by its Creator adopts a gait so useless, and at the same time so graceless. Many women, having received their lessons in walking from a less eligible instructor, do move in this way, and such women this unfortunate little lady has been instructed to copy. The peculiar step to which I allude is to be seen often on the Boulevards in Paris. It is to be seen more often in second rate French towns, and among fourth rate French women. Of all signs in women betokening vulgarity, bad taste, and aptitude to bad morals, it is the surest. And this is the gait of going which American mothers,—some American mothers I should say,—love to teach their daughters! As a comedy at an hotel, it is very delightful, but in private life I should object to it.

To me Newport could never be a place charming by reason of its own charms. That it is a very pleasant place when it is full of people and the people are in spirits and happy, I do not doubt. But then the visitors would bring, as far as I am concerned, the pleasantness with them. The coast is not fine. To those who know the best portions of the coast of Wales or Cornwall,—or better still, the western coast of Ireland, of Clare and Kerry for instance,—it would not be in any way remarkable. It is by no means equal to Dieppe or Biarritz, and not to be talked of in the same breath with Spezzia. The hotels, too, are all built away from the sea; so that one cannot sit and watch the play of the waves from one's window. Nor are there pleasant rambling paths down among the rocks, and from one short strand to another. There is excellent bathing for those who like bathing on shelving sand. I don't. The spot is about half a mile from the hotels, and to this the bathers are carried in omnibuses. Till one o'clock ladies bathe;—which operation, however, does not at all militate against the bathing of men, but rather necessitates it as regards those men who have ladies with them. For here ladies and gentlemen bathe in decorous dresses, and are very polite to each other. I must say, that I think the ladies have the best of it. My idea of sea-bathing for my own gratification is not compatible with a full suit of clothing. I own that my tastes are vulgar and perhaps indecent; but I love to jump into the deep clear sea from off a rock, and I love to be hampered by no outward impediments as I do so. For ordinary bathers, for all ladies, and for men less savage in their instincts than I am, the bathing at Newport is very good.

The private houses—villa residences as they would be termed by an auctioneer in England—are excellent. Many of them are, in fact, large mansions, and are surrounded with grounds, which, as the shrubs grow up, will be very beautiful. Some have large, well-kept lawns, stretching down to the rocks, and these to my taste give the charm to Newport. They extend about two miles along the coast. Should my lot have made me a citizen of the United States, I should have had no objection to become the possessor of one of these "villa residences," but I do not think that I should have "gone in" for hotel life at Newport.

We hired saddle-horses, and rode out nearly the length of the island. It was all very well, but there was little in it remarkable either as regards cultivation or scenery. We found nothing that it would be possible either to describe or remember. The Americans of the United States have had time to build and populate vast cities, but they have not yet had time to surround themselves with pretty scenery. Outlying grand scenery is given by nature; but the prettiness of home scenery is a work of art. It comes from the thorough draining of land, from the planting and subsequent thinning of trees, from the controlling of waters, and constant use of minute patches of broken land. In another hundred years or so Rhode Island may be, perhaps, as pretty as the Isle of Wight. The horses which we got were not good. They were unhandy and badly mouthed, and that which my wife rode was altogether ignorant of the art of walking. We hired them from an Englishman, who had established himself at New York as a riding-master for ladies, and who had come to Newport for the season on the same business. He complained to me with much bitterness of the saddle-horses which came in his way,—of course thinking that it was the special business of a country to produce saddle-horses,—as I think it the special business of a country to produce pens, ink, and paper of good quality. According to him, riding has not yet become an American art, and hence the awkwardness of American horses. "Lord bless you, sir! they don't give an animal a chance of a mouth." In this he alluded only, I presume, to saddle-horses. I know nothing of the trotting-horses, but I should imagine that a fine mouth must be an essential requisite for a trotting-match in harness. As regards riding at Newport, we were not tempted to repeat the experiment. The number of carriages which we saw there,—remembering as I did that the place was comparatively empty,—and their general smartness, surprised me very much. It seemed that every lady with a house of her own had also her own carriage. These carriages were always open, and the law of the land imperatively demands that the occupants shall cover their knees with a worked worsted apron of brilliant colours. These aprons at first, I confess, seemed tawdry; but the eye soon becomes used to bright colours, in carriage aprons as well as in architecture, and I soon learned to like them.

Rhode Island, as the State is usually called, is the smallest State in the Union. I may perhaps best show its disparity to other States by saying that New York extends about 250 miles from north to south and the same distance from east to west; whereas the State called Rhode Island is about forty miles long by twenty broad, independently of certain small islands. It would, in fact, not form a considerable addition, if added on to many of the other States. Nevertheless, it has all the same powers of self-government as are possessed by such nationalities as the States of New York and Pennsylvania; and sends two senators to the Senate at Washington, as do those enormous States. Small as the State is, Rhode Island itself forms but a small portion of it. The authorized and proper name of the State is Providence Plantation and Rhode Island. Roger Williams was the first founder of the colony, and he established himself on the mainland at a spot which he called Providence. Here now stands the city of Providence, the chief town of the State; and a thriving, comfortable town it seems to be, full of banks, fed by railways and steamers, and going ahead quite as quickly as Roger Williams could in his fondest hopes have desired.

Rhode Island, as I have said, has all the attributes of government in common with her stouter and more famous sisters. She has a governor, and an upper house, and a lower house of legislature; and she is somewhat fantastic in the use of these constitutional powers, for she calls on them to sit now in one town and now in another. Providence is the capital of the State; but the Rhode Island parliament sits sometimes at Providence and sometimes at Newport. At stated times also it has to collect itself at Bristol, and at other stated times at Kingston, and at others at East Greenwich. Of all legislative assemblies it is the most peripatetic. Universal suffrage does not absolutely prevail in this State, a certain property qualification being necessary to confer a right to vote even for the State Representatives. I should think it would be well for all parties if the whole State could be swallowed up by Massachusetts or by Connecticut, either of which lie conveniently for the feat; but I presume that any suggestion of such a nature would be regarded as treason by the men of Providence Plantation.

We returned back to Boston by Attleborough, a town at which in ordinary times the whole population is supported by the jewellers' trade. It is a place with a speciality, upon which speciality it has thriven well and become a town. But the speciality is one ill-adapted for times of war; and we were assured that the trade was for the present at an end. What man could now-a-days buy jewels, or even what woman, seeing that everything would be required for the war? I do not say that such abstinence from luxury has been begotten altogether by a feeling of patriotism. The direct taxes which all Americans will now be called on to pay, have had, and will have much to do with such abstinence. In the mean time the poor jewellers of Attleborough have gone altogether to the wall.

III

Maine, New Hampshire, and Vermont

Perhaps I ought to assume that all the world in England knows that that portion of the United States called New England consists of the six States of Maine, New Hampshire, Vermont, Massachusetts, Connecticut, and Rhode Island. This is especially the land of Yankees, and none can properly be called Yankees but those who belong to New England. I have named the States as nearly as may be in order from the North downwards. Of Rhode Island, the smallest State in the Union, I have already said what little I have to say. Of these six States Boston may be called the capital. Not that it is so in any civil or political sense;—it is simply the capital of Massachusetts. But as it is the Athens of the Western world; as it was the cradle of American freedom; as everybody of course knows that into Boston harbour was thrown the tea which George III would tax, and that at Boston, on account of that and similar taxes, sprang up the new revolution; and as it has grown in wealth, and fame, and size beyond other towns in New England, it may be allowed to us to regard it as the capital of these six Northern States, without guilt of *lèse majesté* towards the other five. To me, I confess, this Northern division of our once unruly colonies is, and always has been, the dearest. I am no Puritan myself, and fancy that had I lived in the days of the Puritans, I should have been anti-Puritan to the full extent of my capabilities. But I should have been so through ignorance and prejudice, and actuated by that love of existing rights and wrongs which men call loyalty. If the Canadas were to rebel now, I

29

should be for putting down the Canadians with a strong hand; but not the less have I an idea that it will become the Canadas to rebel and assert their independence at some future period;—unless it be conceded to them without such rebellion. Who, on looking back, can now refuse to admire the political aspirations of the English Puritans, or decline to acknowledge the beauty and fitness of what they did? It was by them that these States of New England were colonized. They came hither stating themselves to be pilgrims, and as such they first placed their feet on that hallowed rock at Plymouth, on the shore of Massachusetts. They came here driven by no thirst of conquest, by no greed for gold, dreaming of no Western empire such as Cortez had achieved and Raleigh had meditated. They desired to earn their bread in the sweat of their brow, worshipping God according to their own lights, living in harmony under their own laws, and feeling that no master could claim a right to put a heel upon their necks. And be it remembered that here in England, in those days, earthly masters were still apt to put their heels on the necks of men. The Star Chamber was gone, but Jeffreys had not yet reigned. What earthly aspirations were ever higher than these, or more manly? And what earthly efforts ever led to grander results?

We determined to go to Portland, in Maine, from thence to the White Mountains in New Hampshire—the American Alps, as they love to call themselves,—and then on to Quebec and up through the two Canadas to Niagara; and this route we followed. From Boston to Portland we travelled by railroad,—the carriages on which are in America always called cars. And here I beg, once for all, to enter my protest loudly against the manner in which these conveyances are conducted. The one grand fault—there are other smaller faults—but the one grand fault is that they admit but one class. Two reasons for this are given. The first is that the finances of the companies will not admit of a divided accommodation; and the second is that the republican nature of the people will not brook a superior or aristocratic classification of travelling. As regards the first, I do not in the least believe in it. If a more expensive manner of railway travelling will pay in England, it would surely do so here. Were a better class of carriages organized, as large a portion of the population would use them in the United States as in any country in Europe. And it seems to be evident that in arranging that there shall be only one rate of travelling, the price is enhanced on poor travellers exactly in proportion as it is made cheap to those who are not poor. For the poorer classes, travelling in America is by no means cheap,—the average rate being, as far as I can judge, fully three-halfpence a mile. It is manifest that dearer rates for one class would allow of cheaper rates for the other; and that in this manner general travelling would be encouraged and increased.

But I do not believe that the question of expenditure has had anything to do with it. I conceive it to be true that the railways are afraid to put themselves at variance with the general feeling of the people. If so the railways may be right. But then, on the other hand, the general feeling of the people must in such case be wrong. Such a feeling argues a total mistake as to the nature of that liberty and equality for the security of which the people is so anxious, and that mistake is the very one which has made shipwreck so many attempts at freedom in other countries. It argues that confusion between social and political equality which has led astray multitudes who have longed for liberty fervently, but who have not thought of it carefully. If a first-class railway carriage should be held as offensive, so should a first-class house, or a first-class horse, or a first-class dinner. But first-class houses, first-class horses, and first-class dinners are very rife in America. Of course it may be said that the expenditure shown in these last-named objects is private expenditure, and cannot be controlled; and that railway travelling is of a public nature, and can be made subject to public opinion. But the fault is in that public opinion which desires to control matters of this nature. Such an arrangement partakes of all the vice of a sumptuary law, and sumptuary laws are in their very essence mistakes. It is well that a man should always have all for which he is willing to pay. If he desires and obtains more than is good for him, the punishment, and thus also the preventive, will come from other sources.

It will be said that the American cars are good enough for all purposes. The seats are not very hard, and the room for sitting is sufficient. Nevertheless I deny that they are good enough for all purposes. They are very long, and to enter them and find a place often requires a struggle and almost a fight. There is rarely any person to tell a stranger which car he should enter. One never meets an uncivil or unruly man, but the women of the lower ranks are not courteous. American ladies love to lie at ease in their carriages, as thoroughly as do our women in Hyde Park, and to those who are used to such luxury, travelling by railroad in their own country must be grievous. I would not wish to be thought a Sybarite myself, or to be held as complaining because I have been compelled to give up my seat to women with babies and bandboxes who have accepted the courtesy with very scanty grace. I have borne worse things than these, and have roughed

it much in my days from want of means and other reasons. Nor am I
yet so old but what I can rough it still. Nevertheless I like to see things
as well done as is practicable, and railway travelling in the States is not
well done. I feel bound to say as much as this, and now I have said it,
once for all.

Few cities, or localities for cities, have fairer natural advantages
than Portland—and I am bound to say that the people of Portland
have done much in turning them to account. This town is not the
capital of the State in a political point of view. Augusta, which is
further to the North, on the Kenebee river, is the seat of the State
Government for Maine. It is very generally the case that the States do
not hold their legislatures and carry on their Government at their chief
towns. Augusta and not Portland is the capital of Maine. Of the State
of New York, Albany is the capital, and not the city which bears the
State's name. And of Pennsylvania, Harrisburg and not Philadelphia
is the capital. I think the idea has been that old-fashioned notions were
bad in that they were old-fashioned; and that a new people, bound by
no prejudices, might certainly make improvement by choosing for
themselves new ways. If so the American politicians have not been the
first in the world who have thought that any change must be a change
for the better. The assigned reason is the centrical position of the
selected political capitals: but I have generally found the real
commercial capital to be easier of access than the smaller town in
which the two legislative houses are obliged to collect themselves.

What must be the natural excellence of the harbour of Portland will
be understood when it is borne in mind that the Great Eastern can
enter it at all times, and that it can lie along the wharves at any hour of
the tide. The wharves which have been prepared for her—and of
which I will say a word further by-and-by—are joined to and in fact
are a portion of the station of the Grand Trunk Railway, which runs
from Portland up to Canada. So that passengers landing at Portland
out of a vessel so large even as the Great Eastern can walk at once on
shore, and goods can be passed on to the railway without any of the
cost of removal. I will not say that there is no other harbour in the
world that would allow of this, but I do not know any other that would
do so.

From Portland a line of railway, called as a whole by the name of the
Canada Grand Trunk line, runs across the State of Maine through the
Northern parts of New Hampshire and Vermont, to Montreal, a
branch striking from Richmond, a little within the limits of Canada, to
Quebec, and down the St. Lawrence to Rivière du Loup. The main

line is continued from Montreal, through Upper Canada to Toronto, and from thence to Detroit in the State of Michigan. The total distance thus traversed is in a direct line about 900 miles. From Detroit there is railway communication through the immense North-Western States of Michigan, Wisconsin, and Illinois, than which perhaps the surface of the globe affords no finer districts for purposes of agriculture. The produce of the two Canadas must be poured forth to the Eastern world, and the men of the Eastern world must throng into these lands, by means of this railroad,—and, as at present arranged, through the harbour of Portland. At present the line has been opened, and they who have opened are sorely suffering in pocket for what they have done. The question of the railway is rather one applying to Canada than to the State of Maine, and I will therefore leave it for the present.

But the Great Eastern has never been to Portland, and as far as I know has no intention of going there. She was, I believe, built with that object. At any rate it was proclaimed during her building that such was her destiny, and the Portlanders believed it with a perfect faith. They went to work and built wharves expressly for her; two wharves prepared to fit her two gangways, or ways of exit and entrance. They built a huge hotel to receive her passengers. They prepared for her advent with a full conviction that a millennium of trade was about to be wafted to their happy port. "Sir, the town has expended two hundred thousand dollars in expectation of that ship, and that ship has deceived us." So was the matter spoken of to me by an intelligent Portlander. I explained to that intelligent gentleman that two hundred thousand dollars would go a very little way towards making up the loss which the ill-fortuned vessel had occasioned on the other side of the water. He did not in words express gratification at this information, but he looked it. The matter was as it were a partnership without deed of contract between the Portlanders and the shareholders of the vessel, and the Portlanders, though they also have suffered their losses, have not had the worst of it.

But there are still good days in store for the town. Though the Great Eastern has not gone there, other ships from Europe, more profitable if less in size, must eventually find their way thither. At present the Canada line of packets runs to Portland only during those months in which it is shut out from the St. Lawrence and Quebec by ice. But the St. Lawrence and Quebec cannot offer the advantages which Portland enjoys, and that big hotel and those new wharves will not have been built in vain.

I have said that a good time is coming, but I would by no means wish to signify that the present times in Portland are bad. So far from it, that I doubt whether I ever saw a town with more evident signs of prosperity. It has about it every mark of ample means, and no mark of poverty. It contains about 27,000 people, and for that population covers a very large space of ground. The streets are broad and well built, the main streets not running in those absolutely straight parallels which are so common in American towns, and are so distressing to English eyes and English feelings. All these, except the streets devoted exclusively to business, are shaded on both sides by trees—generally, if I remember rightly, by the beautiful American elm, whose drooping boughs have all the grace of the willow without its fantastic melancholy. What the poorer streets of Portland may be like I cannot say. I saw no poor street. But in no town of 30,000 inhabitants did I ever see so many houses which must require an expenditure of from six to eight hundred a year to maintain them.

The place too is beautifully situated. It is on a long promontory, which takes the shape of a peninsula;—for the neck which joins it to the mainland is not above half a mile across. But though the town thus stands out into the sea, it is not exposed and bleak. The harbour again is surrounded by land, or so guarded and locked by islands as to form a series of salt-water lakes running round the town. Of those islands there are, of course, 365. Travellers who write their travels are constantly called upon to record that number, so that it may now be considered as a superlative in local phraseology, signifying a very great many indeed. The town stands between two hills, the suburbs or outskirts running up on to each of them. The one looking out towards the sea is called Mountjoy—though the obstinate Americans will write it Munjoy on their maps. From thence the view out to the harbour and beyond the harbour to the islands is, I may not say unequalled, or I shall be guilty of running into superlatives myself; but it is, in its way, equal to anything I have seen. Perhaps it is more like Cork harbour, as seen from certain heights over Passage than anything else I can remember; but Portland harbour, though equally landlocked, is larger; and then from Portland harbour there is as it were a river outlet, running through delicious islands, most unalluring to the navigator, but delicious to the eyes of an uncommercial traveller. There are in all four outlets to the sea, one of which appears to have been made expressly for the Great Eastern. Then there is the hill looking inwards. If it has a name I forget it. The view from this hill is also over the water on each side, and though not so extensive is perhaps as pleasing as the other.

The ways of the people seemed to be quiet, smooth, orderly, and republican. There is nothing to drink in Portland of course, for, thanks to Mr. Neal Dow, the Father Mathew of the State of Maine, the Maine Liquor Law is still in force in that State. There is nothing to drink, I should say, in such orderly houses as that I selected. "People do drink some in the town, they say," said my hostess to me; "and liquor is to be got. But I never venture to sell any. An ill-natured person might turn on me, and where should I be then?" I did not press her, and she was good enough to put a bottle of porter at my right hand at dinner, for which I observed she made no charge. "But they advertise beer in the shop-windows," I said to a man who was driving me—"Scotch ale, and bitter beer. A man can get drunk on them." "Wa'al, yes. If he goes to work hard, and drinks a bucketfull," said the driver, "perhaps he may." From which and other things I gathered that the men of Maine drank pottle deep before Mr. Neal Dow brought his exertions to a successful termination.

The Maine Liquor Law still stands in Maine, and is the law of the land throughout New England; but it is not actually put in force in the other States. By this law no man may retail wine, spirits, or, in truth, beer, except with a special license, which is given only to those who are presumed to sell them as medicines. A man may have what he likes in his own cellar for his own use—such at least is the actual working of the law—but may not obtain it at hotels and public-houses. This law, like all sumptuary laws, must fail. And it is fast failing even in Maine. But it did appear to me from such information as I could collect that the passing of it had done much to hinder and repress a habit of hard drinking which was becoming terribly common, not only in the towns of Maine, but among the farmers and hired labourers in the country.

But if the men and women of Portland may not drink they may eat, and it is a place, I should say, in which good living on that side of the question is very rife. It has an air of supreme plenty, as though the agonies of an empty stomach were never know there. The faces of the people tell of three regular meals of meat a day, and of digestive powers in proportion. Oh happy Portlanders, if they only knew their own good fortune! They get up early, and go to bed early. The women are comely and sturdy, able to take care of themselves without any fal-lal of chivalry; and the men are sedate, obliging, and industrious. I saw the young girls in the streets, coming home from their tea-parties at nine o'clock, many of them alone, and all with some basket in their hands which betokened an evening not passed absolutely in idleness. No fear there of unruly questions on the way, or of insolence from the ill-conducted of the other sex! All was, or seemed to be, orderly, sleek, and unobtrusive. Probably of all modes of life that are allotted to man by his Creator, life such as this is the most happy. One hint, however, for improvement I must give, even to Portland! It would be well if they could make their streets of some material harder than sand.

I must not leave the town without desiring those who may visit it to mount the Observatory. They will from thence get the best view of the harbour and of the surrounding land; and, if they chance to do so under the reign of the present keeper of the signals, they will find a man there able and willing to tell them everything needful about the State of Maine in general, and the harbour in particular. He will come out in his shirt sleeves, and, like a true American, will not at first be very smooth in his courtesy; but he will wax brighter in conversation, and if not stroked the wrong way will turn out to be an uncommonly pleasant fellow. Such I believe to be the case with most of them.

From Portland we made our way up to the White Mountains, which lay on our route to Canada. Now I would ask any of my readers who are candid enough to expose their own ignorance whether they ever heard, or at any rate whether they know anything of the White Mountains. As regards myself I confess that the name had reached my ears; that I had an indefinite idea that they formed an intermediate stage between the Rocky Mountains and the Alleghenies, and that they were inhabited either by Mormons, Indians, or simply by black bears. That there was a district in New England containing mountain scenery superior to much that is yearly crowded by tourists in Europe, that this is to be reached with ease by railways and stage-coaches, and that it is dotted with huge hotels, almost as thickly as they lie in Switzerland, I had no idea. Much of this scenery, I say, is superior to the famed and classic lands of Europe. I know nothing, for instance, on the Rhine equal to the view from Mount Willard, down the mountain pass called the Notch.

Let the visitor of these regions be as late in the year as he can, taking care that he is not so late as to find the hotels closed. October, no doubt, is the most beautiful month among these mountains, but according to the present arrangement of matters here, the hotels are shut up by the end of September. With us, August, September, and October are the holiday months; whereas our rebel children across the Atlantic love to disport themselves in July and August. The great beauty of the autumn, or fall, is in the brilliant hues which are then

taken by the foliage. The autumnal tints are fine with us. They are
lovely and bright wherever foliage and vegetation form a part of the
beauty of scenery. But in no other land do they approach the brilliancy
of the fall in America. The bright rose colour, the rich bronze which is
almost purple in its richness, and the glorious golden yellows must be
seen to be understood. By me at any rate they cannot be described.
These begin to show themselves in September, and perhaps I might
name the latter half of that month as the best time for visiting the
White Mountains.

I am not going to write a guide-book, feeling sure that Mr. Murray
will do New England, and Canada, including Niagara and the Hudson
river, with a peep into Boston and New York before many more
seasons have passed by. But I cannot forbear to tell my countrymen
that any enterprising individual with a hundred pounds to spend on
his holiday,—a hundred and twenty would make him more comfortable in regard to wine, washing, and other luxuries,—and an absence
of two months from his labours, may see as much and do as much here
for the money as he can see or do elsewhere. In some respects he may
do more; for he will learn more of American nature in such a journey than
he can ever learn of the nature of Frenchmen or Italians by such an
excursion among them. Some three weeks of the time, or perhaps a day
or two over, he must be at sea, and that portion of his trip will cost him
fifty pounds,—presuming that he chooses to go in the most comfortable and costly way;—but his time on board ship will not be lost. He
will learn to know much of Americans there, and will perhaps form
acquaintances of which he will not altogether lose sight for many a
year. He will land at Boston, and staying a day or two there will visit
Cambridge, Lowell, and Bunker Hill; and, if he be that way given, will
remember that here live, and occasionally are to be seen alive, men
such as Longfellow, Emerson, Hawthorne, and a host of others whose
names and fames have made Boston the throne of Western Literature.
He will then,—if he take my advice and follow my track,—go by
Portland up into the White Mountains. At Gorham, a station on the
Grand Trunk line, he will find an hotel as good as any of its kind, and
from thence he will take a light waggon, so called in these
countries;—and here let me presume that the traveller is not alone; he
has his wife or friend, or perhaps a pair of sisters,—and in his waggon
he will go up through primeval forests to the Glen House. When there
he will ascend Mount Washington on a pony. That is *de rigueur*, and I
do not, therefore, dare to recommend him to omit the ascent. I did not
gain much myself by my labour. He will not stay at the Glen House,

but will go on to—Jackson's I think they call the next hotel; at which he will sleep. From thence he will take his waggon on through the Notch to the Crawford House, sleeping there again; and when here let him of all things remember to go up Mount Willard. It is but a walk of two hours, up and down, if so much. When reaching the top he will be startled to find that he looks down into the ravine without an inch of fore-ground. He will come out suddenly on a ledge of rock, from whence, as it seems, he might leap down at once into the valley below. Then going on from the Crawford House he will be driven through the woods of Cherry Mount, passing, I fear without toll of custom, the house of my excellent friend Mr. Plaistead, who keeps an hotel at Jefferson. "Sir," said Mr. Plaistead, "I have everything here that a man ought to want; air, sir, that ain't to be got better nowhere; trout, chickens, beef, mutton, milk,—and all for a dollar a day. A top of that hill, sir, there's a view that ain't to be beaten this side of the Atlantic, or I believe the other. And an echo, sir!—We've an echo that comes back to us six times, sir; floating on the light wind, and wafted about from rock to rock till you would think the angels were talking to you. If I could raise that echo, sir, every day at command I'd give a thousand dollars for it. It would be worth all the money to a house like this." And he waved his hand about from hill to hill, pointing out in graceful curves the lines which the sounds would take. Had destiny not called on Mr. Plaistead to keep an American hotel, he might have been a poet.

My traveller, however, unless time were plenty with him, would pass Mr. Plaistead, merely lighting a friendly cigar, or perhaps breaking the Maine Liquor Law if the weather be warm, and would return to Gorham on the railway. All this mountain district is in New Hampshire, and presuming him to be capable of going about the world with his mouth, ears, and eyes open, he would learn much of the way in which men are settling themselves in this still sparsely populated country. Here young farmers go into the woods, as they are doing far down west in the Territories, and buying some hundred acres at perhaps six shillings an acre, fell and burn the trees and build their huts, and take the first steps, as far as man's work is concerned, towards accomplishing the will of the Creator in those regions. For such pioneers of civilization there is still ample room even in the long settled States of New Hampshire and Vermont.

But to return to my traveller, whom having brought so far, I must send on. Let him go on from Gorham to Quebec, and the heights of Abraham, stopping at Sherbrooke that he might visit from thence the lake of Memphra Magog. As to the manner of travelling over this ground I shall say a little in the next chapter, when I come to the progress of myself and my wife. From Quebec he will go up the St. Lawrence to Montreal. He will visit Ottawa, the new capital, and Toronto. He will cross the Lake to Niagara, resting probably at the Clifton House on the Canada side. He will then pass on to Albany, taking the Trenton falls on his way. From Albany he will go down the Hudson to West-Point. He cannot stop at the Catskill Mountains, for the hotel will be closed. And then he will take the river boat, and in a few hours will find himself at New York. If he desires to go into American city society, he will find New York agreeable; but in that case he must exceed his two months. If he do not so desire, a short sojourn at New York will show him all that there is to be seen, and all that there is not to be seen in that great city. That the Cunard line of steamers will bring him safely back to Liverpool in about eleven days, I need not tell to any Englishman, or, as I believe, to any American. So much, in the spirit of a guide, I vouchsafe to all who are willing to take my counsel,—thereby anticipating Murray, and leaving these few pages as a legacy to him or to his collaborateurs.

I cannot say that I like the hotels in those parts, or indeed the mode of life at American hotels in general. In order that I may not unjustly defame them, I will commence these observations by declaring that they are cheap to those who choose to practise the economy which they encourage, that the viands are profuse in quantity and wholesome in quality, that the attendance is quick and unsparing, and that travellers are never annoyed by that grasping greedy hunger and thirst after francs and shillings which disgrace in Europe many English and many continental inns. All this is, as must be admitted, great praise; and yet I do not like the American hotels.

One is in a free country and has come from a country in which one has been brought up to hug one's chains,—so at least the English traveller is constantly assured—and yet in an American inn one can never do as one likes. A terrific gong sounds early in the morning, breaking one's sweet slumbers, and then a second gong sounding some thirty minutes later, makes you understand that you must proceed to breakfast, whether you be dressed or no. You certainly can go on with your toilet and obtain your meal after half an hour's delay. Nobody actually scolds you for so doing, but the breakfast is, as they say in this country, "through." You sit down alone, and the attendant stands immediately over you. Probably there are two so standing. They fill your cup the instant it is empty. They tender you fresh food before that

which has disappeared from your plate has been swallowed. They
begrudge you no amount that you can eat or drink; but they begrudge
you a single moment that you sit there neither eating nor drinking.
This is your fate if you're too late, and therefore as a rule you are not
late. In that case you form one of a long row of eaters who proceed
through their work with a solid energy that is past all praise. It is
wrong to say that Americans will not talk at their meals. I never met
but few who would not talk to me, at any rate till I got to the far west;
but I have rarely found that they would address me first. Then the
dinner comes early; at least it always does so in New England, and the
ceremony is much of the same kind. You came there to eat, and the
food is pressed on you almost *ad nauseam*. But as far as one can see there
is no drinking. In these days, I am quite aware, that drinking has
become improper, even in England. We are apt at home to speak of
wine as a thing tabooed, wondering how our fathers lived and swilled.
I believe that as a fact we drink as much as they did; but nevertheless
that is our theory. I confess, however, that I like wine. It is very
wicked, but it seems to me that my dinner goes down better with a
glass of sherry than without it. As a rule I always did get it at hotels in
America. But I had no comfort with it. Sherry they do not understand
at all. Of course I am only speaking of hotels. Their claret they get
exclusively from Mr. Gladstone, and looking at the quality, have a
right to quarrel even with Mr. Gladstone's price. But it is not the
quality of the wine that I hereby intend to subject to ignominy, so
much as the want of any opportunity for drinking it. After dinner, if all
that I hear be true, the gentlemen occasionally drop into the hotel bar
and "liquor up." Or rather this is not done specially after dinner, but
without prejudice to the hour at any time that may be found desirable.
I also have "liquored up," but I cannot say that I enjoy the process. I
do not intend hereby to accuse Americans of drinking much, but I
maintain that what they do drink, they drink in the most uncomfortable manner that the imagination can devise.

    The greatest luxury at an English inn is one's tea, one's fire, and
one's book. Such an arrangement is not practicable at an American
hotel. Tea, like breakfast, is a great meal, at which meat should be
eaten, generally with the addition of much jelly, jam, and sweet
preserve; but no person delays over his tea-cup. I love to have my
tea-cup emptied and filled with gradual pauses, so that time for
oblivion may accrue, and no exact record be taken. No such meal is
known at American hotels. It is possible to hire a separate room and
have one's meals served in it; but in doing so a man runs counter to all

the institutions of the country, and a woman does so equally. A stranger does not wish to be viewed askance by all around him; and the rule which holds that men at Rome should do as Romans do, if true anywhere, is true in America. Therefore I say that in an American inn one can never do as one pleases.

In what I have here said I do not intend to speak of hotels in the largest cities, such as Boston or New York. At them meals are served in the public room separately, and pretty nearly at any or at all hours of the day; but at them also the attendant stands over the unfortunate eater, and drives him. The guest feels that he is controlled by laws adapted to the usages of the Medes and Persians. He is not the master on the occasion, but the slave; a slave well treated and fattened up to the full endurance of humanity; but yet a slave.

From Gorham we went on to Island Pond, a station on the same Canada Trunk Railway, on a Saturday evening, and were forced by the circumstances of the line to pass a melancholy Sunday at the place. The cars do not run on Sundays, and run but once a day on other days over the whole line; so that in fact the impediment to travelling spreads over two days. Island Pond is a lake with an island in it, and the place which has taken the name is a small village, about ten years old, standing in the midst of uncut forests, and has been created by the railway. In ten years more there will no doubt be a spreading town at Island Pond; the forests will recede, and men rushing out from the crowded cities will find here food and space and wealth. For myself I never remain long in such a spot without feeling thankful that it has not been my mission to be a pioneer of civilization.

The farther that I got away from Boston the less strong did I find the feeling of anger against England. There, as I have said before, there was a bitter animosity against the mother country in that she had shown no open sympathy with the North. In Maine and New Hampshire I did not find this to be the case to any violent degree. Men spoke of the war as openly as they did at Boston, and in speaking to me generally connected England with the subject. But they did so simply to ask questions as to England's policy. What will she do for cotton when her operatives are really pressed? Will she break the blockade? Will she insist on a right to trade with Charlestown and New Orleans? I always answered that she would insist on no such right, if that right were denied to others and the denial enforced. England, I took upon myself to say, would not break a veritable blockade, let her be driven to what shifts she might in providing for her operatives. "Ah; that's what we fear," a very stanch patriot said to me, if words may be taken as a

proof of stanchness. "If England allies herself with the Southerners, all
our trouble is for nothing." It was impossible not to feel that all that
was said was complimentary to England. It is her sympathy that the
Northern men desire, to her co-operation that they would willingly
trust, on her honesty that they would choose to depend. It is the same
feeling whether it shows itself in anger or in curiosity. An American
whether he be embarked in politics, in literature, or in commerce,
desires English admiration, English appreciation of his energy, and
English encouragement. The anger of Boston is but a sign of its
affectionate friendliness. What feeling is so hot as that of a friend when
his dearest friend refuses to share his quarrel or to sympathize in his
wrongs? To my thinking the men of Boston are wrong and unreasonable in their anger; but were I a man of Boston I should be as wrong
and as unreasonable as any of them. All that, however, will come right.
I will not believe it possible that there should in very truth be a quarrel
between England and the northern States.

In the guidance of those who are not quite *au fait* at the details of
American Government, I will here in a few words describe the outlines
of State Government as it is arranged in New Hampshire. The States
in this respect are not all alike, the modes of election of their officers
and periods of service being different. Even the franchise is different in
different States. Universal suffrage is not the rule throughout the
United States; though it is I believe very generally thought in England
that such is the fact. I need hardly say that the laws in the different
States may be as various as the different legislatures may choose to
make them.

In New Hampshire universal suffrage does prevail; which means
that any man may vote who lives in the State, supports himself, and
assists to support the poor by means of poor rates. A governor of the
State is elected for one year only, but it is customary or at any rate not
uncustomary to re-elect him for a second year. His salary is a thousand
dollars a year, or 200*l*. It must be presumed therefore that glory and
not money is his object. To him is appended a council, by whose
opinions he must in a great degree be guided. His functions are to the
State what those of the President are to the country, and for the short
period of his reign he is as it were a Prime Minister of the State with
certain very limited regal attributes. He however by no means enjoys
the regal attribute of doing no wrong. In every State there is an
Assembly, consisting of two houses of elected representatives; the
Senate, or upper house, and the House of Representatives so called. In
New Hampshire this Assembly, or Parliament, is styled The General

Court of New Hampshire. It sits annually; whereas the legislature in many States sits only every other year. Both Houses are re-elected every year. This Assembly passes laws with all the power vested in our Parliament, but such laws apply of course only to the State in question. The Governor of the State has a veto on all bills passed by the two Houses. But, after receipt of his veto, any bill so stopped by the Governor can be passed by a majority of two thirds in each House. The General Court generally sits for about ten weeks. There are in the State eight judges, three Supreme who sit at Concord, the capital, as a court of appeal both in civil and criminal matters; and then five lesser judges, who go circuit through the State. The salaries of these lesser judges do not exceed from 250*l*. to 300*l*. a year; but they are, I believe, allowed to practise as lawyers in any counties except those in which they sit as judges,—being guided in this respect by the same law as that which regulates the work of assistant barristers in Ireland. The assistant barristers in Ireland are attached to the counties as judges at Quarter Sessions, but they practise or may practise as advocates in all counties except that to which they are so attached. The judges in New Hampshire are appointed by the Governor with the assistance of his Council. No judge in New Hampshire can hold his seat after he has reached seventy years of age.

So much at the present moment with reference to the Government of New Hampshire.

IV

Lower Canada

T HE Grand Trunk Railway runs directly from Portland to
  Montreal, which latter town is, in fact, the capital of Canada,
though it never has been so exclusively, and, as it seems, never is to be
so, as regards authority, government, and official name. In such
matters authority and government often say one thing while
commerce says another; but commerce always has the best of it and
wins the game whatever Government may decree. Albany in this way
is the capital of the State of New York, as authorized by the State
Government; but New York has made herself the capital of America,
and will remain so. So also Montreal has made herself the capital of
Canada. The Grand Trunk Railway runs from Portland to Montreal;
but there is a branch from Richmond, a township within the limits of
Canada, to Quebec; so that travellers to Quebec, as we were, are not
obliged to reach that place *viâ* Montreal.

Quebec is the present seat of Canadian Government, its turn for
that honour having come round some two years ago; but it is about to
be deserted in favour of Ottawa, a town which is, in fact, still to be built
on the river of that name. The public edifices are, however, in a state of
forwardness; and if all goes well the Governor, the two Councils, and
the House of Representatives will be there before two years are over
whether there be any town to receive them or no. Who can think of
Ottawa without bidding his brothers to row, and reminding them that
the stream runs fast, that the rapids are near and the daylight past? I

asked, as a matter of course, whether Quebeć was much disgusted at the proposed change, and I was told that the feeling was not now very strong. Had it been determined to make Montreal the permanent seat of government Quebec and Toronto would both have been up in arms.

I must confess that in going from the States into Canada, an Englishman is struck by the feeling that he is going from a richer country into one that is poorer, and from a greater country into one that is less. An Englishman going from a foreign land into a land which is in one sense his own, of course finds much in the change to gratify him. He is able to speak as the master, instead of speaking as the visitor. His tongue becomes more free, and he is able to fall back to his national habits and national expressions. He no longer feels that he is admitted on sufferance, or that he must be careful to respect laws which he does not quite understand. This feeling was naturally strong in an Englishman in passing from the States into Canada at the time of my visit. English policy at that moment was violently abused by Americans, and was upheld as violently in Canada. But, nevertheless, with all this, I could not enter Canada without seeing, and hearing, and feeling that there was less of enterprise around me there than in the States—less of general movement, and less of commercial success. To say why this is so would require a long and very difficult discussion, and one which I am not prepared to hold. It may be that a dependent country, let the feeling of dependence be ever so much modified by powers of self-governance, cannot hold its own against countries which are in all respects their own masters. Few, I believe, would now maintain that the Northern States of America would have risen in commerce as they have risen, had they still remained attached to England as colonies. If this be so, that privilege of self-rule which they have acquired, has been the cause of their success. It does not follow as a consequence that the Canadas fighting their battle alone in the world could do as the States have done. Climate, or size, or geographical position might stand in their way. But I fear that it does follow, if not as a logical conclusion at least as a natural result, that they never will do so well unless some day they shall so fight their battle. It may be argued that Canada has in fact the power of self-governance; that she rules herself and makes her own laws as England does; that the Sovereign of England has but a veto on those laws, and stands in regard to Canada exactly as she does in regard to England. This is so, I believe, by the letter of the Constitution, but is not so in reality, and cannot, in truth, be so in any colony, even of Great Britain. In England the political power of the Crown is nothing. The Crown has no such power, and now-a-days makes no attempt at having any. But the political power of the Crown, as it is felt in Canada, is everything. The Crown has no such power in England because it must change its ministers whenever called upon to do so by the House of Commons. But the Colonial Minister in Downing Street is the Crown's Prime Minister as regards the Colonies, and he is changed not as any Colonial House of Assembly may wish, but in accordance with the will of the British Commons. Both the Houses in Canada—that, namely, of the Representatives, or Lower House, and of the Legislative Council, or Upper House— are now elective, and are filled without direct influence from the Crown. The power of self-government is as thoroughly developed as perhaps may be possible in a colony. But after all it is a dependent form of government, and as such may perhaps not conduce to so thorough a development of the resources of the country as might be achieved under a ruling power of its own, to which the welfare of Canada itself would be the chief if not the only object.

I beg that it may not be considered from this that I would propose to Canada to set up for itself at once and declare itself independent. In the first place I do not wish to throw over Canada; and in the next place I do not wish to throw over England. If such a separation shall ever take place, I trust that it may be caused, not by Canadian violence but by British generosity. Such a separation, however, never can be good till Canada herself shall wish it. That she does not wish it yet is certain. If Canada ever should wish it, and should ever press for the accomplishment of such a wish, she must do so in connection with Nova Scotia and New Brunswick. If at any future time there be formed such a separate political power, it must include the whole of British North America.

In the meantime, I return to my assertion, that in entering Canada from the States one clearly comes from a richer to a poorer country. When I have said so, I have heard no Canadian absolutely deny it; though in refraining from denying it, they have usually expressed a general conviction, that in settling himself for life, it is better for a man to set up his staff in Canada than in the States. "I do not know that we are richer," a Canadian says, "but on the whole we are doing better and are happier." Now, I regard the golden rules against the love of gold, the "*aurum irrepertum et sic melius situm*," and the rest of it, as very excellent when applied to individuals. Such teaching has not much effect, perhaps, in inducing men to abstain from wealth,—but such effect as it may have will be good. Men and women do, I suppose, learn to be happier when they learn to disregard riches. But such a doctrine is absolutely false as regards a nation. National wealth produces education and progress, and through them produces plenty of food, good morals, and all else that is good. It produces luxury also, and certain evils attendant on luxury. But I think it may be clearly shown, and that it is universally acknowledged, that national wealth produces individual well-being. If this be so, the argument of my friend the Canadian is nought.

To the feeling of a refined gentleman, or of a lady whose eye loves to rest always on the beautiful, an agricultural population that touches its hat, eats plain victuals, and goes to church is more picturesque and delightful than the thronged crowd of a great city by which a lady and gentleman is hustled without remorse, which never touches its hat, and perhaps also never goes to church. And as we are always tempted to approve of that which we like, and to think that that which is good to us is good altogether, we—the refined gentlemen and ladies of England I mean—are very apt to prefer the hat-touchers to those who are not hat-touchers. In doing so we intend, and wish, and strive to be philanthropical. We argue to ourselves that the dear, excellent lower classes receive an immense amount of consoling happiness from that ceremony of hat-touching, and quite pity those who, unfortunately for themselves, know nothing about it. I would ask any such lady or gentleman whether he or she does not feel a certain amount of commiseration for the rudeness of the town-bred artisan, who walks about with his hands in his pockets as though he recognized a superior in no one.

But that which is good and pleasant to us, is often not good and pleasant altogether. Every man's chief object is himself; and the philanthropist should endeavour to regard this question, not from his own point of view, but from that which would be taken by the individuals for whose happiness he is anxious. The honest, happy rustic makes a very pretty picture; and I hope that honest rustics are happy. But the man who earns two shillings a day in the country would always prefer to earn five in the town. The man who finds himself bound to touch his hat to the squire would be glad to dispense with that ceremony, if circumstances would permit. A crowd of greasy-coated town artisans with grimy hands and pale faces, is not in itself delectable; but each of that crowd has probably more of the goods of life than any rural labourer. He thinks more, reads more, feels more, sees more, hears more, learns more, and lives more. It is through great

cities that the civilization of the world has progressed, and the charms
of life been advanced. Man in his rudest state begins in the country,
and in his most finished state may retire there. But the battle of the
world has to be fought in the cities; and the country that shows the
greatest city population is ever the one that is going most ahead in the
world's history.

If this be so, I say that the argument of my Canadian friend was
nought. It may be that he does not desire crowded cities with dirty,
independent artisans; that to his view small farmers, living sparingly
but with content on the sweat of their brows, are surer signs of a
country's prosperity than hives of men and smoking chimneys. He has,
probably, all the upper classes of England with him in so thinking, and
as far as I know the upper classes of all Europe. But the crowds
themselves, the thick masses of which are composed those
populations which we count by millions, are against him. Up in those
regions which are watered by the great lakes, Lake Michigan, Lake
Huron, Lake Erie, Lake Ontario, and by the St. Lawrence, the country
is divided between Canada and the States. The cities in Canada were
settled long before those in the States. Quebec and Montreal were
important cities before any of the towns belonging to the States had
been founded. But taking the population of three of each, including the
three largest Canadian towns, we find they are as follows:—In
Canada, Quebec has 60,000; Montreal, 85,000; Toronto, 55,000. In
the States, Chicago has 120,000; Detroit, 70,000, and Buffalo, 80,000.
If the population had been equal, it would have shown a great
superiority in the progress of those belonging to the States, because the
towns of Canada had so great a start. But the numbers are by no means
equal, showing instead a vast preponderance in favour of the States.
There can be no stronger proof that the States are advancing faster
than Canada,—and in fact doing better than Canada.

Quebec is a very picturesque town,—from its natural advantages
almost as much so as any town I know. Edinburgh, perhaps, and
Innspruck may beat it. But Quebec has very little to recommend it
beyond the beauty of its situation. Its public buildings and works of art
do not deserve a long narrative. It stands at the confluence of the St.
Lawrence and St. Charles rivers; the best part of the town is built high
upon the rock,—the rock which forms the celebrated plains of Abram;
and the view from thence down to the mountains which shut in the St.
Lawrence is magnificent. The best point of view is, I think, from the
esplanade, which is distant some five minutes' walk from the hotels.
When that has been seen by the light of the setting sun, and seen again,

if possible, by moonlight, the most considerable lion of Quebec may be regarded as "done," and may be ticked off from the list.

The most considerable lion according to my taste. Lions which roar merely by the force of association of ideas are not to me very valuable beasts. To many the rock over which Wolfe climbed to the plains of Abram, and on the summit of which he fell in the hour of victory, gives to Quebec its chiefest charm. But I confess to being somewhat dull in such matters. I can count up Wolfe, and realize his glory, and put my hand as it were upon his monument, in my own room at home as well as I can at Quebec. I do not say this boastingly or with pride; but truly acknowledging a deficiency. I have never cared to sit in chairs in which old kings have sat, or to have their crowns upon my head.

Nevertheless, and as a matter of course, I went to see the rock, and can only say, as so many have said before me, that it is very steep. It is not a rock which I think it would be difficult for any ordinarily active man to climb,—providing, of course, that he was used to such work. But Wolfe took regiments of men up there at night—and that in face of enemies who held the summits. One grieves that he should have fallen there and have never tasted the sweet cup of his own fame. For fame is sweet, and the praise of one's brother men the sweetest draught which a man can drain. But now, and for coming ages, Wolfe's name stands higher than it probably would have done had he lived to enjoy his reward.

But there is another very worthy lion near Quebec,—the Falls, namely, of Montmorency. They are eight miles from the town, and the road lies through the suburb of St. Roch, and the long straggling French village of Beauport. These are in themselves very interesting, as showing the quiet, orderly, unimpulsive manner in which the French Canadians live. Such is their character, although there have been such men as Papineau, and although there have been times in which English rule has been unpopular with the French settlers. As far as I could learn there is no such feeling now. These people are quiet, contented; and as regards a sufficiency of the simple staples of living, sufficiently well to do. They are thrifty;—but they do not thrive. They do not advance, and push ahead, and become a bigger people from year to year as settlers in a new country should do. They do not even hold their own in comparison with those around them. But has not this always been the case with colonists out of France; and has it not always been the case with Roman Catholics when they have been forced to measure themselves against Protestants? As to the ultimate fate in the world of this people, one can hardly form a speculation. There are, as nearly as I could learn, about 800,000 of them in Lower Canada; but it seems that the wealth and commercial enterprise of the country is passing out of their hands: Montreal, and even Quebec are, I think, becoming less and less French every day; but in the villages and on the small farms the French remain, keeping up their language, their habits, and their religion. In the cities they are becoming hewers of wood and drawers of water. I am inclined to think that the same will ultimately be their fate in the country. Surely one may declare as a fact that a Roman Catholic popoulation can never hold its ground against one that is Protestant. I do not speak of numbers, for the Roman Catholics will increase and multiply, and stick by their religion, although their religion entails poverty and dependence; as they have done and still do in Ireland. But in progress and wealth the Romanists have always gone to the wall when the two have been made to compete together. And yet I love their religion. There is something beautiful and almost divine in the faith and obedience of a true son of the Holy Mother. I sometimes fancy that I would fain be a Roman Catholic,—if I could; as also I would often wish to be still a child, if that were possible.

All this is on the way to the Falls of Montmorency. These falls are placed exactly at the mouth of the little river of the same name, so that it may be said absolutely to fall into the St. Lawrence. The people of the country, however, declare that the river into which the waters of the Montmorency fall is not the St. Lawrence, but the Charles. Without a map I do not know that I can explain this. The river Charles appears to, and in fact does, run into the St. Lawrence just below Quebec. But the waters do not mix. The thicker, browner stream of the lesser river still keeps the north-eastern bank till it comes to the island of Orleans, which lies in the river five or six miles below Quebec. Here or hereabouts are the Falls of the Montmorency, and then the great river is divided for twenty-five miles by the Isle of Orleans. It is said that the waters of the Charles and the St. Lawrence do not mix till they meet each other at the foot of this island.

I do not know that I am particularly happy at describing a waterfall, and what little capacity I may have in this way I would wish to keep for Niagara. One thing I can say very positively about Montmorency, and one piece of advice I can give to those who visit the falls. The place from which to see them is not the horrible little wooden temple, which has been built immediately over them on that side which lies nearest to Quebec. The stranger is put down at a gate through which a path leads to this temple, and at which a woman demands from him twenty-five

cents for the privilege of entrance. Let him by all means pay the
twenty-five cents. Why should he attempt to see the falls for nothing,
seeing that this woman has a vested interest in the showing of them? I
declare that if I thought that I should hinder this woman from her
perquisites by what I write, I would leave it unwritten, and let my
readers pursue their course to the temple—to their manifest injury.
But they will pay the twenty-five cents. Then let them cross over the
bridge, eschewing the temple, and wander round on the open field till
they get the view of the falls, and the view of Quebec also, from the
other side. It is worth the twenty-five cents, and the hire of the carriage
also. Immediately over the falls there was a suspension bridge, of
which the supporting, or rather non-supporting, pillars are still to be
seen. But the bridge fell down one day into the river; and, alas, alas!
with the bridge fell down an old woman, and a boy, and a cart,—a cart
and horse,—and all found a watery grave together in the spray. No
attempt has been made since that to renew the suspension bridge; but
the present wooden bridge has been built higher up, in lieu of it.

Strangers naturally visit Quebec in summer or autumn, seeing that
a Canada winter is a season with which a man cannot trifle; but I
imagine that the mid-winter is the best time for seeing the Falls of
Montmorency. The water in its fall is dashed into spray, and that
spray becomes frozen, till a cone of ice is formed immediately under
the cataract, which gradually rises till the temporary glacier reaches
nearly half-way to the level of the higher river. Up this men climb,—
and ladies also, I am told,—and then descend with pleasant rapidity
on sledges of wood, sometimes not without an innocent tumble in the
descent. As we were at Quebec in September, we did not experience
the delights of this pastime.

As I was too early for the ice cone under the Montmorency Falls, so
also was I too late to visit the Saguenay river which runs into the St.
Lawrence, some hundred miles below Quebec. I presume that the
scenery of the Saguenay is the finest in Canada. During the summer
steamers run down the St. Lawrence and up the Saguenay, but I was
too late for them. An offer was made to us through the kindness of Sir
Edmund Head, who was then the Governor-General, of the use of a
steam-tug belonging to a gentleman who carries on a large commercial
enterprise at Chicoutimi, far up the Saguenay; but an acceptance
of this offer would have entailed some delay at Quebec, and as we
were anxious to get into the North Western States before the winter
commenced, we were obliged with great regret to decline the
journey.

I feel bound to say that a stranger regarding Quebec merely as a town, finds very much of which he cannot but complain. The footpaths through the streets are almost entirely of wood, as indeed seems to be general throughout Canada. Wood is of course the cheapest material, and though it may not be altogether good for such a purpose it would not create animadversion if it were kept in tolerable order. But in Quebec the paths are intolerably bad. They are full of holes. The boards are rotten and worn in some places to dirt. The nails have gone, and the broken planks go up and down under the feet, and in the dark they are absolutely dangerous. But if the paths are bad the roadways are worse. The street through the lower town along the quays is, I think, the most disgraceful thoroughfare I ever saw in any town. I believe the whole of it, or at any rate a great portion, has been paved with wood; but the boards have been worked into mud, and the ground under the boards has been worked into holes, till the street is more like the bottom of a filthy ditch than a roadway through one of the most thickly populated parts of a city. Had Quebec in Wolfe's time been as it is now, Wolfe would have stuck in the mud between the river and the rock, before he reached the point which he desired to climb. In the upper town the roads are not so bad as they are below, but still they are very bad. I was told that this arose from disputes among the municipal corporations. Everything in Canada relating to roads, and a very great deal affecting the internal government of the people, is done by these municipalities. It is made a subject of great boast in Canada that the communal authorities do carry on so large a part of the public business, and that they do it generally so well, and at so cheap a rate. I have nothing to say against this, and as a whole believe that the boast is true. I must protest, however, that the streets of the greater cities,—for Montreal is nearly as bad as Quebec,—prove the rule by a very sad exception. The municipalities of which I speak extend, I believe, to all Canada; the two provinces being divided into counties, and the counties subdivided into townships to which, as a matter of course, the municipalities are attached.

From Quebec to Montreal there are two modes of travel. There are the steamers up the St. Lawrence which, as all the world know is, or at any rate hitherto has been, the high road of the Canadas; and there is the Grand Trunk Railway. Passengers choosing the latter go towards Portland as far as Richmond, and there join the main line of the road, passing from Richmond on to Montreal. We learned while at Quebec that it behoved us not to leave the colony till we had seen the lake and mountains of Memphra-Magog, and as we were clearly neglecting our duty with regard to the Saguenay, we felt bound to make such amends as lay in our power, by deviating from our way to the lake above named. In order to do this we were obliged to choose the railway, and to go back beyond Richmond to the station at Sherbrooke. Sherbrooke is a large village on the confines of Canada, and as it is on the railway will no doubt become a large town. It is very prettily situated on the meeting of two rivers, it has three or four different churches, and intends to thrive. It possesses two newspapers, of the prosperity of which I should be inclined to feel less assured. The annual subscription to such a newspaper published twice a week is ten shillings per annum. A sale of a thousand copies is not considered bad. Such a sale would produce 500*l.* a year, and this would, if entirely devoted to that purpose, give a moderate income to a gentleman qualified to conduct a newspaper. But the paper and printing must cost something, and the capital invested should receive its proper remuneration. And then,— such at least is the general idea,—the getting together of news and the framing of intelligence is a costly operation. I can only hope that all this is paid for by the advertisements, for I must trust that the editors do not receive less than the moderate sum above named. At Sherbrooke we are still in Lower Canada. Indeed, as regards distance, we are when there nearly as far removed from Upper Canada as at Quebec. But the race of people here is very different. The French population had made their way down into these townships before the English and American war broke out, but had not done so in great numbers. The country was then very unapproachable, being far to the south of the St. Lawrence, and far also from any great line of internal communication towards the Atlantic. But, nevertheless, many settlers made their way in here from the States; men who preferred to live under British rule, and perhaps doubted the stability of the new order of things. They or their children have remained here since, and as the whole country has been opened up by the railway many others have flocked in. Thus a better class of people than the French hold possession of the larger farms, and are on the whole doing well. I am told that many Americans are now coming here, driven over the borders from Maine, New Hampshire, and Vermont, by fears of the war and the weight of taxation. I do not think that fears of war or the paying of taxes drive many individuals away from home. Men who would be so influenced have not the amount of foresight which would induce them to avoid such evils; or, at any rate, such fears would act slowly. Labourers, however, will go where work is certain, where work is well paid, and where the wages to be earned will give plenty in return. It may be that work will become scarce in the States, as it has done with those poor jewellers at Attleborough, of whom we spoke, and that food will become dear. If this be so, labourers from the States will no doubt find their way into Canada.

From Sherbrooke we went with the mails on a pair-horse waggon to Magog. Cross country mails are not interesting to the generality of readers, but I have a professional liking for them myself. I have spent the best part of my life in looking after and I hope in improving such mails, and I always endeavour to do a stroke of work when I come across them. I learned on this occasion that the conveyance of mails with a pair of horses in Canada costs little more than half what is paid for the same work in England with one horse, and something less than what is paid in Ireland, also for one horse. But in Canada the average pace is only five miles an hour. In Ireland it is seven, and the time is accurately kept, which does not seem to be the case in Canada. In England the pace is eight miles an hour. In Canada and in Ireland these conveyances carry passengers; but in England they are prohibited from doing so. In Canada the vehicles are much better got up than they are in England, and the horses too look better. Taking Ireland as a whole they are more respectable in appearance there than in England. From all which it appears that pace is the article that costs the highest price, and that appearance does not go for much in the bill. In Canada the roads are very bad in comparison with the English or Irish roads; but to make up for this, the price of forage is very low.

I have said that the cross mail conveyances in Canada did not seem to be very closely bound as to time; but they are regulated by clock-work in comparison with some of them in the United States. "Are you going this morning?" I said to a mail-driver in Vermont. "I thought you always started in the evening." "Wa'll; I guess I do. But it rained some last night, so I jist stayed at home." I do not know that I ever felt more shocked in my life, and I could hardly keep my tongue off the man. The mails, however, would have paid no respect to me in Vermont, and I was obliged to walk away crestfallen.

We went with the mails from Sherbrooke to a village called Magog at the outlet of the lake, and from thence by a steamer up the lake to a solitary hotel called the Mountain House, which is built at the foot of the mountain on the shore, and which is surrounded on every side by thick forest. There is no road within two miles of the house. The lake therefore is the only highway, and that is frozen up for four months in the year. When frozen, however, it is still a road, for it is passable for sledges. I have seldom been in a house that seemed so remote from the

world, and so little within reach of doctors, parsons, or butchers.
Bakers in this country are not required, as all persons make their own
bread. But in spite of its position the hotel is well kept, and on the
whole we were more comfortable there than at any other inn in Lower
Canada. The Mountain House is but five miles from the borders of
Vermont, in which State the head of the lake lies. The steamer which
brought us runs on to Newport,—or rather from Newport to Magog
and back again. And Newport is in Vermont.

The one thing to be done at the Mountain House is the ascent of the
mountain called the Owl's Head. The world there offers nothing else of
active enterprise to the traveller, unless fishing be considered an active
enterprise. I am not capable of fishing, therefore we resolved on going
up the Owl's Head. To dine in the middle of the day is absolutely
imperative at these hotels, and thus we were driven to select either the
morning or the afternoon. Evening lights we declared were the best for
all views, and therefore we decided on the afternoon. It is but two
miles; but then, as we were told more than once by those who had
spoken to us on the subject, those two miles are not like other miles. "I
doubt if the lady can do it," one man said to me. I asked if ladies did
not sometimes go up. "Yes; young women do, at times," he said. After
that my wife resolved that she would see the top of the Owl's Head, or
die in the attempt, and so we started. They never think of sending a
guide with one in these places, whereas in Europe a traveller is not
allowed to go a step without one. When I asked for one to show us the
way up Mount Washington, I was told that there were no idle boys
about that place. The path was indicated to us, and off we started with
high hopes.

I have been up many mountains, and have climbed some that were
perhaps somewhat dangerous in their ascent. In climbing the Owl's
Head there is no danger. One is closed in by thick trees the whole way.
But I doubt if I ever went up a steeper ascent. It was very hard work,
but we were not beaten. We reached the top, and there sitting down
thoroughly enjoyed our victory. It was then half-past five o'clock, and
the sun was not yet absolutely sinking. It did not seem to give us any
warning that we should especially require its aid, and as the prospect
below us was very lovely we remained there for a quarter of an hour.
The ascent of the Owl's Head is certainly a thing to do, and I still
think, in spite of our following misfortune, that it is a thing to do late in
the afternoon. The view down upon the lakes and the forests around,
and on the wooded hills below, is wonderfully lovely. I never was on a
mountain which gave me a more perfect command of all the country

round. But as we arose to descend we saw a little cloud coming towards us from over Newport.

The little cloud came on with speed, and we had hardly freed ourselves from the rocks of the summit before we were surrounded by rain. As the rain became thicker, we were surrounded by darkness also, or if not by darkness by so dim a light that it became a task to find our path. I still thought that the daylight had not gone, and that as we descended and so escaped from the cloud we should find light enough to guide us. But it was not so. The rain soon became a matter of indifference, and so also did the mud and briars beneath our feet. Even the steepness of the way was almost forgotten as we endeavoured to thread our path through the forest before it should become impossible to discern the track. A dog had followed us up, and though the beast would not stay with us so as to be our guide, he returned ever and anon and made us aware of his presence by dashing by us. I may confess now that I became much frightened. We were wet through, and a night out in the forest would have been unpleasant to us. At last I did utterly lose the track. It had become quite dark, so dark that we could hardly see each other. We had succeeded in getting down the steepest and worst part of the mountain, but we were still among dense forest-trees, and up to our knees in mud. But the people at the Mountain House were Christians, and men with lanterns were sent hallooing after us through the dark night. When we were thus found we were not many yards from the path, but unfortunately on the wrong side of a stream. Through that we waded and then made our way in safety to the inn. In spite of which misadventure I advise all travellers in Lower Canada to go up the Owl's Head.

On the following day we crossed the lake to Georgeville, and drove round another lake called the Massawhippi back to Sherbrooke. This was all very well, for it showed us a part of the country which is comparatively well tilled, and has been long settled; but the Massawhippi itself is not worth a visit. The route by which we returned occupies a longer time than the other, and is more costly as it must be made in a hired vehicle. The people here are quiet, orderly, and I should say a little slow. It is manifest that a strong feeling against the Northern States has lately sprung up. This is much to be deprecated, but I cannot but say that it is natural. It is not that the Canadians have any special Secession feelings, or that they have entered with peculiar warmth into the questions of American politics; but they have been vexed and acerbated by the braggadocio of the Northern States. They constantly hear that they are to be invaded, and translated into citizens of the Union: that British rule is to be swept off the Continent, and that the star-spangled banner is to be waved over them in pity. The star-spangled banner is in fact a fine flag, and has waved to some purpose; but those who live near it, and not under it, fancy that they hear too much of it. At the present moment the loyalty of both the Canadas to Great Britain is beyond all question. From all that I can hear I doubt whether this feeling in the Provinces was ever so strong, and under such circumstances American abuse of England and American braggadocio is more than usually distasteful. All this abuse and all this braggadocio comes to Canada from the Northern States, and therefore the Southern cause is at the present moment the more popular with them.

I have said that the Canadians hereabouts are somewhat slow. As we were driving back to Sherbrooke it became necessary that we should rest for an hour or so in the middle of the day, and for this purpose we stopped at a village inn. It was a large house, in which there appeared to be three public sitting-rooms of ample size, one of which was occupied as the bar. In this there were congregated some six or seven men, seated in arm-chairs round a stove, and among these I placed myself. No one spoke a word either to me or to any one else. No one smoked, and no one read, nor did they even whittle sticks. I asked a question first of one and then of another, and was answered with monosyllables. So I gave up any hope in that direction, and sat staring at the big stove in the middle of the room, as the others did. Presently another stranger entered, having arrived in a waggon as I had done. He entered the room and sat down, addressing no one, and addressed by no one. After a while, however, he spoke. "Will there be any chance of dinner here?" he said. "I guess there'll be dinner by-and-by," answered the landlord, and then there was silence for another ten minutes, during which the stranger stared at the stove. "Is that dinner any way ready?" he asked again. "I guess it is," said the landlord. And then the stranger went out to see after his dinner himself. When we started at the end of an hour nobody said anything to us. The driver "hitched" on the horses, as they call it, and we started on our way, having been charged nothing for our accommodation. That some profit arose from the horse provender is to be hoped.

On the following day we reached Montreal, which, as I have said before, is the commercial capital of the two Provinces. This question of the capitals is at the present moment a subject of great interest in Canada, but as I shall be driven to say something on the matter when I report myself as being at Ottawa, I will refrain now. There are two special public affairs at the present moment to interest a traveller in Canada. The first I have named, and the second is the Grand Trunk Railway. I have already stated what is the course of this line. It runs from the Western State of Michigan to Portland on the Atlantic in the State of Maine, sweeping the whole length of Canada in its route. It was originally made by three Companies. The Atlantic and St. Lawrence constructed it from Portland to Island Pond on the borders of the States. The St. Lawrence and Atlantic took it from the South Eastern side of the river at Montreal to the same point, viz., Island Pond. And the Grand Trunk Company have made it from Detroit to Montreal, crossing the river there with a stupendous tubular bridge, and have also made the branch connecting the main line with Quebec and Rivière du Loup. This latter company is now incorporated with the St. Lawrence and Atlantic, but has only leased the portion of the line running through the States. This they have done, guaranteeing the shareholders an interest of six per cent. There never was a grander enterprise set on foot. I will not say there never was one more unfortunate, for is there not the Great Eastern, which by the weight and constancy of its failures demands for itself a proud pre-eminence of misfortune? But surely the Grand Trunk comes next to it. I presume it to be quite out of the question that the shareholders should get any interest whatever on their shares for years. The company when I was at Montreal had not paid the interest due to the Atlantic and St. Lawrence Company for the last year, and there was a doubt whether the lease would not be broken. No party that had advanced money to the undertaking was able to recover what had been advanced. I believe that one firm in London had lent nearly a million to the Company and is now willing to accept half the sum so lent in quittance of the whole debt. In 1860 the line could not carry the freight that offered, not having or being able to obtain the necessary rolling stock; and on all sides I heard men discussing whether the line would be kept open for traffic. The Government of Canada advanced to the Company three millions of money, with an understanding that neither interest nor principal should be demanded till all other debts were paid, and all shareholders in receipt of six per cent. interest. But the three millions were clogged with conditions which, though they have been of service to the country, have been so expensive to the Company that it is hardly more solvent with it than it would have been without it. As it is, the whole property seems to be involved in ruin; and yet the line is one of the grandest commercial conceptions that was ever carried out on the face of the globe, and in the process of a few years will do more to make bread cheap in England than any other single enterprise that exists.

I do not know that blame is to be attached to any one. I at least attach no such blame. Probably it might be easy now to show that the road might have been made with sufficient accommodation for ordinary purposes without some of the more costly details. The great tubular bridge on which was expended 1,300,000*l*. might, I should think, have been dispensed with. The Detroit end of the line might have been left for later time. As it stands now, however, it is a wonderful operation carried to a successful issue as far as the public are concerned, and one can only grieve that it should be so absolute a failure to those who have placed their money in it. There are schemes which seem to be too big for men to work out with any ordinary regard to profit and loss. The Great Eastern is one, and this is another. The national advantage arising from such enterprises is immense; but the wonder is that men should be found willing to embark their money where the risk is so great, and the return even hoped for is so small.

While I was in Canada some gentlemen were there from the Lower Provinces—Nova Scotia, that is, and New Brunswick—agitating the subject of another great line of railway from Quebec to Halifax. The project is one in favour of which very much may be said. In a national point of view an Englishman or a Canadian cannot but regret that there should be no winter mode of exit from, or entrance to, Canada, except through the United States. The St. Lawrence is blocked up for four or five months in winter, and the steamers which run to Quebec in the summer run to Portland during the season of ice. There is at present no mode of public conveyance between the Canadas and the Lower Provinces, and an immense district of country on the borders of Lower Canada, through New Brunswick and into Nova Scotia is now absolutely closed against civilization, which by such a railway would be opened up to the light of day. We all know how much the want of such a road was felt when our troops were being forwarded to Canada during the last winter. It was necessary they should reach their destiny without delay; and as the river was closed, and the passing of troops through the States was of course out of the question, that long overland journey across Nova Scotia and New Brunswick became a necessity. It would certainly be a very great thing for British interests if a direct line could be made from such a port as Halifax, a port which is open throughout the whole year, up into the Canadas. If these Colonies belonged to France or to any other despotic Government, the thing would be done. But the Colonies do not belong to any despotic Government.

Such a line would in fact be a continuance of the Grand Trunk; and who that looks at the present state of the finances of the Grand Trunk can think it to be on the cards that private enterprise should come forward with more money,—with more millions? The idea is that England will advance the money, and that the English House of Commons will guarantee the interest, with some counter-guarantee from the Colonies that this interest shall be duly paid. But it would seem that if such Colonial guarantee is to go for anything, the Colonies might raise the money in the money market without the intervention of the British House of Commons.

Montreal is an exceedingly good commercial town, and business there is brisk. It has now 85,000 inhabitants. Having said that of it, I do not know what more there is left to say. Yes; one word there is to say of Sir William Logan the creator of the Geological Museum there and the head of all matters geological throughout the Province. While he was explaining to me with admirable perspicuity the result of investigations into which he had poured his whole heart, I stood by understanding almost nothing, but envying everything. That I understood almost nothing, I know he perceived. That, ever and anon, with all his graciousness became apparent. But I wonder whether he perceived also that I did envy everything. I have listened to geologists by the hour before—have had to listen to them, desirous simply of escape. I have listened and understood absolutely nothing, and have only wished myself away. But I could have listened to Sir William Logan for the whole day, if time allowed. I found even in that hour that some ideas found their way through to me, and I began to fancy that even I could become a geologist at Montreal.

Over and beyond Sir William Logan there is at Montreal for strangers the drive round the mountain, not very exciting; and there is the tubular bridge over the St. Lawrence. This, it must be understood, is not made in one tube, as is that over the Menai Straits, but is divided into, I think, thirteen tubes. To the eye there appear to be twenty-five tubes; but each of the six side tubes is supported by a pier in the middle. A great part of the expense of the bridge was incurred in sinking the shafts for these piers.

V

Upper Canada

OTTAWA is in Upper Canada, but crossing the suspension bridge from Ottawa into Hull the traveller is in Lower Canada. It is therefore exactly in the confines, and has been chosen as the site of the new Government capital very much for this reason. Other reasons have, no doubt, had a share in the decison. At the time when the choice was made Ottawa was not large enough to create the jealousy of the more populous towns. Though not on the main line of railway, it was connected with it by a branch railway, and it is also connected with the St. Lawrence by water communication. And then it stands nobly on a magnificent river, with high overhanging rock, and a natural grandeur of position which has perhaps gone far in recommending it to those whose voice in the matter has been potential. Having the world of Canada from whence to choose the site of a new town, the choosers have certainly chosen well. It is another question whether or no a new town should have been deemed necessary.

Perhaps it may be well to explain the circumstances under which it was thought expedient thus to establish a new Canadian capital. In 1841 when Lord Sydenham was Governor General of the Provinces, the two Canadas, separate till then, were united under one Government. At that time the people of Lower or French Canada, and the people of Upper or English Canada differed much more in their habits and language than they do now. I do not know that the English have become in any way Gallicized, but the French have been very

materially Anglicized. But while this has been in progress, national
jealousy has been at work; and even yet that national jealousy
is not at an end. While the two provinces were divided there were, of
course, two capitals, and two seats of Government. These were at
Quebec for Lower Canada, and at Toronto for Upper Canada, both
which towns are centrically situated as regards the respective
provinces. When the union was effected, it was deemed expedient that
there should be but one capital; and the small town of Kingstown was
selected, which is situated on the lower end of Lake Ontario in the
Upper Province. But Kingstown was found to be inconvenient,
lacking space and accommodation for those who had to follow the
Government, and the Governor removed it and himself to Montreal.
Montreal is in the Lower Province, but is very central to both the
provinces; and it is, moreover, the chief town in Canada. This would
have done very well, but for an unforeseen misfortune.

It will be remembered by most readers that in 1837 took place the
Mackenzie-Papineau rebellion, of which those who were then old
enough to be politicians heard so much in England. I am not going
back to recount the history of the period, otherwise than to say that the
English Canadians at that time, in withstanding and combating the
rebels, did considerable injury to the property of certain French
Canadians, and that when the rebellion had blown over and those in
fault had been pardoned, a question arose whether or no the
Government should make good the losses of those French Canadians
who had been injured. The English Canadians protested that it would
be monstrous that they should be taxed to repair damages suffered by
rebels, and made necessary in the suppression of rebellion. The French
Canadians declared that the rebellion had been only a just assertion of
their rights, that if there had been crime on the part of those who took
up arms that crime had been condoned, and that the damages had not
fallen exclusively or even chiefly on those who had done so. I will give no
opinion on the merits of the question, but simply say that blood ran
very hot when it was discussed. At last the Houses of the Provincial
Parliament, then assembled at Montreal, decreed that the losses
should be made good by the public treasury; and the English mob in
Montreal, when this decree became known, was roused to great wrath
by a decision which seemed to be condemnatory of English loyalty. It
pelted Lord Elgin, the Governor General, with rotten eggs, and
burned down the Parliament House. Hence, there arose, not
unnaturally, a strong feeling of anger on the part of the local
Government against Montreal; and moreover there was no longer a

House in which the Parliament could be held in that town. For these conjoint reasons it was decided to move the seat of Government again, and it was resolved that the Governor and the Parliament should sit alternately at Toronto in Upper Canada, and at Quebec in Lower Canada, remaining four years at each place. They went at first to Toronto for two years only, having agreed that they should be there on this occasion only for the remainder of the term of the then Parliament. After that they were at Quebec for four years; then at Toronto for four; and now are again at Quebec. But this arrangement has been found very inconvenient. In the first place there is a great national expenditure incurred in moving old records, and in keeping double records, in moving the library, and as I have been informed even the pictures. The Government clerks also are called on to move as the Government moves; and though an allowance is made to them from the national purse to cover their loss, the arrangement has nevertheless been felt by them to be a grievance, as may be well understood. The accommodation also for the ministers of the Government, and for members of the two Houses has been insufficient. Hotels, lodgings, and furnished houses could not be provided to the extent required, seeing that they would be left nearly empty for every alternate space of four years. Indeed it needs but little argument to prove that the plan adopted must have been a thoroughly uncomfortable plan, and the wonder is that it should have been adopted. Lower Canada had undertaken to make all her leading citizens wretched, providing Upper Canada would treat hers with equal severity. This has now gone on for some twelve years, and as the system was found to be an unendurable nuisance it has been at last admitted that some steps must be taken towards selecting one capital for the country.

I should here, in justice to the Canadians, state a remark made to me on this matter by one of the present leading politicians of the colony. I cannot think that the migratory scheme was good; but he defended it, asserting that it had done very much to amalgamate the people of the two provinces; that it had brought Lower Canadians into Upper Canada, and Upper Canadians into Lower Canada, teaching English to those who spoke only French before, and making each pleasantly acquainted with the other. I have no doubt that something,—perhaps much,—has been done in this way; but valuable as the result may have been, I cannot think it worth the cost of the means employed. The best answer to the above argument consists in the undoubted fact that a migratory Government would never have been established for such a reason. It was so established because Montreal, the central town, had given offence, and because the jealousy of the provinces against each other would not admit of the Government being placed entirely at Quebec, or entirely at Toronto.

But it was necessary that some step should be taken; and as it was found to be unlikely that any resolution should be reached by the joint provinces themselves, it was loyally and wisely determined to refer the matter to the Queen. That Her Majesty has constitutionally the power to call the Parliament of Canada at any town of Canada which she may select, admits, I conceive, of no doubt. It is, I imagine, within her prerogative to call the Parliament of England where she may please within that realm, though her lieges would be somewhat startled if it were called otherwhere than in London. It was therefore well done to ask Her Majesty to act as arbiter in the matter. But there are not wanting those in Canada who say that in referring the matter to the Queen it was in truth referring it to those by whom very many of the Canadians were least willing to be guided in the matter; to the Governor General namely, and the Colonial Secretary. Many indeed in Canada now declare that the decision simply placed the matter in the hands of the Governor General.

Be that as it may, I do not think that any unbiassed traveller will doubt that the best possible selection has been made, presuming always, as we may presume in the discussion, that Montreal could not be selected. I take for granted that the rejection of Montreal was regarded as a *sine quâ non* in the decision. To me it appears grievous that this should have been so. It is a great thing for any country to have a large, leading, world-known city, and I think that the Government should combine with the commerce of the country in carrying out this object. But commerce can do a great deal more for Government than Government can do for commerce. Government has selected Ottawa as the capital of Canada; but commerce has already made Montreal the capital, and Montreal will be the chief city of Canada, let Government do what it may to foster the other town. The idea of spiting a town because there has been a row in it seems to me to be preposterous. The row was not the work of those who have made Montreal rich and respectable. Montreal is more centrical than Ottawa,—nay, it is as nearly centrical as any town can be. It is easier to get to Montreal from Toronto, than to Ottawa;—and if from Toronto, then from all that distant portion of Upper Canada, back of Toronto. To all Lower Canada Montreal is, as a matter of course, much easier of access than Ottawa. But having said so much in favour of Montreal, I will again admit that, putting aside Montreal, the best possible selection has been made.

When Ottawa was named, no time was lost in setting to work to prepare for the new migration. In 1859 the Parliament was removed to Quebec, with the understanding that it should remain there till the new buildings should be completed. These buildings were absolutely commenced in April 1860, and it was, and I believe still is, expected that they will be completed in 1863. I am now writing in the winter of 1861; and, as is necessary in Canadian winters, the works are suspended. But unfortunately they were suspended in the early part of October,—on the 1st of October,—whereas they might have been continued, as far as the season is concerned, up to the end of November. We reached Ottawa on the 3rd of October, and more than a thousand men had then been just dismissed. All the money in hand had been expended, and the Government,—so it was said,—could give no more money till Parliament should meet again. This was most unfortunate. In the first place the suspension was against the contract as made with the contractors for the building; in the next place there was the delay; and then, worst of all, the question again became agitated whether the colonial legislature were really in earnest with reference to Ottawa. Many men of mark in the colony were still anxious—I believe are still anxious,—to put an end to the Ottawa scheme, and think that there still exists for them a chance of success. And very many men who are not of mark are thus united, and a feeling of doubt on the subject has been created. 225,000*l.* has already been spent on these buildings, and I have no doubt myself that they will be duly completed, and duly used.

We went up to the new town by boat, taking the course of the river Ottawa. We passed St. Ann's, but no one at St. Ann's seemed to know anything of the brothers who were to rest there on their weary oars. At Maxwellstown I could hear nothing of Annie Laurie or of her trysting place on the braes, and the turnpike man at Tara could tell me nothing of the site of the hall, and had never even heard of the harp. When I go down South I shall expect to find that the negro melodies have not yet reached "Old Virginie." This boat conveyance from Montreal to Ottawa is not all that could be wished in convenience, for it is allied too closely with railway travelling. Those who use it leave Montreal by a railway; after nine miles, they are changed into a steamboat. Then they encounter another railway, and at last reach Ottawa in a second steamboat. But the river is seen, and a better idea of the country is obtained than can be had solely from the railway cars. The scenery is by no means grand, nor is it strikingly picturesque; but it is in its way interesting. For a long portion of the river the old primeval forests come down close to the water's edge, and in the fall of the year the brilliant colouring is very lovely. It should not be imagined,—as I think it often is imagined,—that these forests are made up of splendid trees, or that splendid trees are even common. When timber grows on undrained ground, and when it is uncared for, it does not seem to approach nearer to its perfection than wheat and grass do under similar circumstances. Seen from a little distance the colour and effect is good, but the trees themselves have shallow roots and grow up tall, narrow, and shapeless. It necessarily is so with all timber that is not thinned in its growth. When fine forest trees are found, and are left standing alone by any cultivator who may have taste enough to wish for such adornment, they almost invariably die. They are robbed of the sickly shelter by which they have been surrounded; the hot sun strikes the uncovered fibres of the roots, and the poor solitary invalid languishes and at last dies.

As one ascends the river, which by its breadth forms itself into lakes, one is shown Indian villages clustering down upon the bank. Some years ago these Indians were rich, for the price of furs, in which they dealt, was high; but furs have become cheaper, and the beavers with which they used to trade are almost valueless. That a change in the fashion of hats should have assisted to polish these poor fellows off the face of creation must, one may suppose, be very unintelligible to them; but nevertheless it is probably a subject of deep speculation. If the reading world were to take to sermons again and eschew their novels, Messrs. Thackeray, Dickens, and some others would look about them and inquire into the causes of such a change with considerable acuteness. They might not, perhaps, hit the truth, and these Indians are much in that predicament. It is said that very few pure-blooded Indians are now to be found in their villages, but I doubt whether this is not erroneous. The children of the Indians are now fed upon baked bread, and on cooked meat, and are brought up in houses. They are nursed somewhat as the children of the white men are nursed; and these practices no doubt have done much towards altering their appearance. The negroes who have been bred in the States, and whose fathers have been so bred before them, differ both in colour and form from their brothers who have been born and nurtured in Africa.

I said in the last chapter that the city of Ottawa was still to be built; but I must explain, lest I should draw down on my head the wrath of the Ottawaites, that the place already contains a population of 15,000 inhabitants. As, however, it is being prepared for four times that number—for eight times that number let us hope—and as it straggles over a vast extent of ground, it gives one the idea of a city in an active course of preparation. In England we know nothing about unbuilt cities. With us four or five blocks of streets together never assume that ugly, unfledged appearance which belongs to the half-finished carcase of a house, as they do so often on the other side of the Atlantic. Ottawa is preparing for itself broad streets, and grand thoroughfares. The buildings already extend over a length considerably exceeding two miles, and half a dozen hotels have been opened, which, if I were writing a guide-book in a complimentary tone, it would be my duty to describe as first-rate. But the half-dozen first-rate hotels, though open, as yet enjoy but a moderate amount of custom. All this justifies me, I think, in saying that the city has as yet to get itself built. The manner in which this is being done justifies me also in saying that the Ottawaites are going about their task with a worthy zeal.

To me I confess that the nature of the situation has great charms,—regarding it as the site for a town. It is not on a plain, and from the form of the rock overhanging the river, and of the hill that falls from thence down to the water, it has been found impracticable to lay out the place in right-angled parallelograms. A right-angled parallelogramical city, such as are Philadelphia and the new portion of New York, is from its very nature odious to me. I know that much may be said in its favour—that drainage and gas-pipes come easier to such a shape, and that ground can be better economized. Nevertheless I prefer a street that is forced to twist itself about. I enjoy the narrowness of Temple Bar, and the misshapen curvature of Pickett Street. The disreputable dinginess of Holywell Street is dear to me, and I love to thread my way up by the Olympic into Covent Garden. Fifth Avenue in New York is as grand as paint and glass can make it; but I would not live in a palace in Fifth Avenue if the corporation of the city would pay my baker's and butcher's bills.

The town of Ottawa lies between two waterfalls. The upper one, or Rideau Fall, is formed by the confluence of a small river with the larger one; and the lower fall—designated as lower because it is at the foot of the hill, though it is higher up the Ottawa river—is called the Chaudière, from its resemblance to a boiling kettle. This is on the Ottawa river itself. The Rideau fall is divided into two branches, thus forming an island in the middle as is the case at Niagara. It is pretty enough, and worth visiting, even were it further from the town than it is; but by those who have hunted out many cataracts in their travels it will not be considered very remarkable. The Chaudière fall I did think very remarkable. It is of trifling depth, being formed by fractures in the rocky bed of the river; but the waters have so cut the rock as to create beautiful forms in the rush which they make in their descent. Strangers are told to look at these falls from the suspension bridge; and it is well that they should do so. But in so looking at them they obtain but a very small part of their effect. On the Ottawa side of the bridge is a brewery, which brewery is surrounded by a huge timber-yard. This timber-yard I found to be very muddy, and the passing and repassing through it is a work of trouble; but nevertheless let the traveller by all means make his way through the mud, and scramble over the timber, and cross the plank bridges which traverse the streams of the sawmills, and thus take himself to the outer edge of the woodwork over the water. If he will then seat himself, about the hour of sunset, he will see the Chaudière fall aright.

But the glory of Ottawa will be—and, indeed, already is—the set of public buildings which is now being erected on the rock which guards as it were the town from the river. How much of the excellence of these buildings may be due to the taste of Sir Edmund Head, the late Governor, I do not know. That he has greatly interested himself in the subject is well known: and as the style of the different buildings is so much alike as to make one whole, though the designs of different architects were selected, and these different architects employed, I imagine that considerable alterations must have been made in the original drawings. There are three buildings, forming three sides of a quadrangle; but they are not joined, the vacant spaces at the corner being of considerable extent. The fourth side of the quadrangle opens upon one of the principal streets of the town. The centre building is intended for the Houses of Parliament, and the two side buildings for the Government offices. Of the first Messrs. Fuller and Jones are the architects, and of the latter Messrs. Stent and Laver. I did not have the pleasure of meeting any of these gentlemen; but I take upon myself to say that as regards purity of art and manliness of conception their joint work is entitled to the very highest praise. How far the buildings may be well arranged for the required purposes, how far they may be economical in construction, or specially adapted to the severe climate of the country, I cannot say; but I have no hesitation in risking my reputation for judgment in giving my warmest commendation to them as regards beauty of outline and truthful nobility of detail.

I will not attempt to describe them, for I should interest no one in doing so, and should certainly fail in my attempt to make any reader understand me. I know no modern Gothic purer of its kind, or less sullied with fictitious ornamentation. Our own Houses of Parliament are very fine, but it is, I believe, generally felt that the ornamentation is too minute; and, moreover, it may be questioned whether perpendicular Gothic is capable of the highest nobility which architecture can achieve. I do not pretend to say that these Canadian public buildings will reach that highest nobility. They must be finished before any final judgment can be pronounced; but I do feel very certain that that final judgment will be greatly in their favour. The total frontage of the quadrangle, including the side buildings, is 1200 feet; that of the centre building is 475. As I have said before, £225,000 has already been expended, and it is estimated that the total cost, including the arrangement and decoration of the ground behind the building and in the quadrangle, will be half a million.

The buildings front upon what will, I suppose, be the principal street of Ottawa, and they stand upon a rock looking immediately down upon the river. In this way they are blessed with a site peculiarly happy. Indeed I cannot at this moment remember any so much so. The castle of Edinburgh stands very well; but then, like many other castles, it stands on a summit by itself, and can only be approached by a steep ascent. These buildings at Ottawa, though they look down from a grand eminence immediately on the river, are approached from the town without any ascent. The rock, though it falls almost precipitously down to the water, is covered with trees and shrubs, and then the river that runs beneath is rapid, bright, and picturesque in the irregularity of all its lines. The view from the back of the library, up to the Chaudière falls, and to the saw-mills by which they are surrounded, is very lovely. So that I will say again, that I know no site for such a set of buildings so happy as regards both beauty and grandeur. It is intended that the library, of which the walls were only ten feet above the ground when I was there, shall be an octagonal building, in shape and outward character like the chapter-house of a cathedral. This structure will, I presume, be surrounded by gravel walks and green sward. Of the library there is a large model showing all the details of the architecture; and if that model be ultimately followed, this building alone will be worthy of a visit from English tourists. To me it was very wonderful to find such an edifice in the course of erection on the banks of a wild river, almost at the back of Canada. But if ever I visit Canada again it will be to see those buildings when completed.

And now, like all friendly critics, having bestowed my modicum of praise, I must proceed to find fault. I cannot bring myself to

administer my sugar-plum without adding to it some bitter morsel by
way of antidote. The building to the left of the quadrangle as it is
entered is deficient in length, and on that account appears mean to the
eye. The two side buildings are brought up close to the street, so that
each has a frontage immediately on the street. Such being the case they
should be of equal length, or nearly so. Had the centre of one fronted
the centre of the other, a difference of length might have been allowed;
but in this case the side front of the smaller one would not have reached
the street. As it is, the space between the main building and the smaller
wing is disproportionably large, and the very distance at which it
stands will, I fear, give to it that appearance of meanness of which I
have spoken. The clerk of the works, who explained to me with much
courtesy the plan of the buildings, stated that the design of this wing
was capable of elongation, and had been expressly prepared with that
object. If this be so, I trust that the defect will be remedied.

The great trade of Canada is lumbering; and lumbering consists in
cutting down pine trees up in the far distant forests, in hewing or
sawing them into shape for market, and getting them down the rivers
to Quebec, from whence they are exported to Europe, and chiefly to
England. Timber in Canada is called lumber; those engaged in the
trade are called lumberers, and the business itself is called lumbering.
After a lapse of time it must no doubt become monotonous to those
engaged in it, and the name is not engaging; but there is much about it
that is very picturesque. A saw-mill worked by water power is almost
always a pretty object, and stacks of new cut timber are pleasant to the
smell, and group themselves not amiss on the water's edge. If I had the
time, and were a year or two younger, I should love well to go up
lumbering into the woods. The men for this purpose are hired in the
fall of the year, and are sent up hundreds of miles away to the pine
forests in strong gangs. Everything is there found for them. They make
log huts for their shelter, and food of the best and the strongest is taken
up for their diet. But no strong drink of any kind is allowed, nor is any
within reach of the men. There are no publics, no shebeen houses, no
grog-shops. Sobriety is an enforced virtue; and so much is this considered by the masters, and understood by the men, that very little
contraband work is done in the way of taking up spirits to these
settlements. It may be said that the work up in the forests is done with
the assistance of no stronger drink than tea; and it is very hard work.
There cannot be much work that is harder; and it is done amidst the
snows and forests of a Canadian winter. A convict in Bermuda cannot
get through his daily eight hours of light labour without an allowance

of rum; but a Canadian lumberer can manage to do his daily task on tea without milk. These men, however, are by no means teetotallers. When they come back to the towns they break out, and reward themselves for their long enforced moderation. The wages I found to be very various, running from thirteen or fourteen dollars a month to twenty-eight or thirty, according to the nature of the work. The men who cut down the trees receive more than those who hew them when down, and these again more than the under class who make the roads and clear the ground. These money wages, however, are in addition to their diet. The operation requiring the most skill is that of marking the trees for the axe. The largest only are worth cutting; and form and soundness must also be considered.

But if I were about to visit a party of lumberers in the forest, I should not be disposed to pass a whole winter with them. Even of a very good thing one may have too much. I would go up in the spring, when the rafts are being formed in the small tributary streams, and I would come down upon one of them, shooting the rapids of the rivers as soon as the first freshets had left the way open. A freshet in the rivers is the rush of waters occasioned by melting snow and ice. The first freshets take down the winter waters of the nearer lakes and rivers. Then the streams become for a time navigable, and the rafts go down. After that comes the second freshet, occasioned by the melting of far-off snow and ice, up in the great northern lakes which are little known. These rafts are of immense construction, such as those which we have seen on the Rhone and Rhine, and often contain timber to the value of two, three, and four thousand pounds. At the rapids the large rafts are, as it were, unyoked, and divided into small portions, which go down separately. The excitement and motion of such transit must, I should say, be very joyous. I was told that the Prince of Wales desired to go down a rapid on a raft, but that the men in charge would not undertake to say that there was no possible danger. Whereupon those who accompanied the prince requested his Royal Highness to forbear. I fear that in these careful days crowned heads and their heirs must often find themselves in the position of Sancho at the banquet. The sailor prince who came after his brother was allowed to go down a rapid, and got, as I was told, rather a rough bump as he did so.

Ottawa is a great place for these timber rafts. Indeed, it may, I think, be called the head-quarters of timber for the world. Nearly all the best pine wood comes down the Ottawa and its tributaries. The other rivers by which timber is brought down to the St. Lawrence are chiefly the St. Maurice, the Madawaska, and the Saguenay; but the

Ottawa and its tributaries water 75,000 square miles; whereas the other three rivers with their tributaries water only 53,000. The timber from the Ottawa and St. Maurice finds its way down the St. Lawrence to Quebec, where, however, it loses the whole of its picturesque character. The Saguenay and the Madawaska fall into the St. Lawrence below Quebec.

From Ottawa we went by rail to Prescott, which is surely one of the most wretched little places to be found in any country. Immediately opposite to it, on the other side of the St. Lawrence, is the thriving town of Ogdensburgh. But Ogdensburgh is in the United States. Had we been able to learn at Ottawa any facts as to the hours of the river steamers and railways we might have saved time and have avoided Prescott; but this was out of the question. Had I asked the exact hour at which I might reach Calcutta by the quickest route, an accurate reply would not have been more out of the question. I was much struck at Prescott—and indeed all through Canada, though more in the upper than in the lower province—by the sturdy roughness, some would call it insolence, of those of the lower classes of the people with whom I was brought into contact. If the words "lower classes" give offence to any reader, I beg to apologize;—to apologize and to assert that I am one of the last of men to apply such a term in a sense of reproach to those who earn their bread by the labour of their hands. But it is hard to find terms which will be understood; and that term, whether it give offence or no, will be understood. Of course such a complaint as that I now make is very common as made against the States. Men in the States with horned hands and fustian coats are very often most unnecessarily insolent in asserting their independence. What I now mean to say is that precisely the same fault is to be found in Canada. I know well what the men mean when they offend in this manner. And when I think on the subject with deliberation, at my own desk, I can not only excuse, but almost approve them. But when one personally encounters their corduroy braggadocio; when the man to whose services one is entitled answers one with determined insolence; when one is bidden to follow "that young lady," meaning the chambermaid, or desired, with a toss of the head, to wait for the "gentleman who is coming," meaning the boots, the heart is sickened, and the English traveller pines for the civility,—for the servility, if my American friends choose to call it so,—of a well-ordered servant. But the whole scene is easily construed, and turned into English. A man is asked by a stranger some question about his employment, and he replies in a tone which seems to imply anger, insolence, and a dishonest intention to evade the service for which he is paid. Or if there be no question of service or payment, the man's manner will be the same, and the stranger feels that he is slapped in the face and insulted. The translation of it is this. The man questioned, who is aware that as regards coat, hat, boots, and outward cleanliness he is below him by whom he is questioned, unconsciously feels himself called upon to assert his political equality. It is his shibboleth that he is politically equal to the best, that he is independent, and that his labour, though it earn him but a dollar a day by porterage, places him as a citizen on an equal rank with the most wealthy fellow-man that may employ or accost him. But being so inferior in that coat, hat and boots matter, he is forced to assert his equality by some effort. As he improves in externals he will diminish the roughness of his claim. As long as the man makes his claim with any roughness, so long does he acknowledge within himself some feeling of external inferiority. When that has gone,—when the American has polished himself up by education and general well being to a feeling of external equality with gentlemen, he shows, I think, no more of that outward braggadocio of independence than a Frenchman.

But the blow at the moment of the stroke is very galling. I confess that I have occasionally all but broken down beneath it. But when it is thought of afterwards it admits of full excuse. No effort that a man can make is better than a true effort at independence. But this insolence is a false effort, it will be said. It should rather be called a false accompaniment to a life-long true effort. The man probably is not dishonest, does not desire to shirk any service which is due from him,—is not even inclined to insolence. Accept his first declaration of equality for that which it is intended to represent, and the man afterwards will be found obliging and communicative. If occasion offer he will sit down in the room with you, and will talk with you on any subject that he may choose; but having once ascertained that you show no resentment for this assertion of equality, he will do pretty nearly all that he is asked. He will at any rate do as much in that way as an Englishman. I say thus much on this subject now especially, because I was quite as much struck by the feeling in Canada as I was within the States.

From Prescott we went on by the Grand Trunk Railway to Toronto, and stayed there for a few days. Toronto is the capital of the province of Upper Canada, and I presume will in some degree remain so in spite of Ottawa and its pretensions. That is, the law courts will still be held there. I do not know that it will enjoy any other supremacy, unless it be that of trade and population. Some few years ago Toronto was advancing with rapid strides, and was bidding fair to rival Quebec, or even perhaps Montreal. Hamilton, also, another town of Upper Canada, was going a head in the true American style; but then reverses came in trade, and the towns were checked for a while. Toronto, with a neighbouring suburb which is a part of it, as Southwark is of London, contains now over 50,000 inhabitants. The streets are all parallelogramical, and there is not a single curvature to rest the eye. It is built down close upon Lake Ontario; and as it is also on the Grand Trunk Railway it has all the aid which facility of traffic can give it.

The two sights of Toronto are the Osgoode Hall and the University. The Osgoode Hall is to Upper Canada what the Four Courts are to Ireland. The law courts are all held there. Exteriorly little can be said for Osgoode Hall, whereas the exterior of the Four Courts in Dublin is very fine; but as an interior the temple of Themis at Toronto beats hollow that which the goddess owns in Dublin. In Dublin the Courts themselves are shabby, and the space under the dome is not so fine as the exterior seems to promise that it should be. In Toronto the Courts themselves are, I think, the most commodious that I ever saw, and the passages, vestibules, and hall are very handsome. In Upper Canada the common law judges and those in Chancery are divided as they are in England; but it is, as I was told, the opinion of Canadian lawyers that the work may be thrown together. Appeal is allowed in criminal cases; but as far as I could learn such power of appeal is held to be both troublesome and useless. In Lower Canada the old French laws are still administered.

But the University is the glory of Toronto. This is a Gothic building and will take rank after, but next to the buildings at Ottawa. It will be the second piece of noble architecture in Canada, and as far as I know on the American continent. It is, I believe, intended to be purely Norman, though I doubt whether the received types of Norman architecture have not been departed from in many of the windows. Be this as it may the College is a manly, noble structure, free from false decoration, and infinitely creditable to those who projected it. I was informed by the head of the College that it has been open only two years, and here also I fancy that the colony has been much indebted to the taste of the late Governor, Sir Edmund Head.

Toronto as a city is not generally attractive to a traveller. The country around it is flat; and, though it stands on a lake, that lake has no attributes of beauty. Large inland seas such as are these great Northern lakes of America never have such attributes. Picturesque mountains rise from narrow valleys, such as form the beds of lakes in Switzerland, Scotland, and Northern Italy. But from such broad waters as those of Lake Ontario, Lake Erie, and Lake Michigan, the shores shelve very gradually, and have none of the materials of lovely scenery.

The streets in Toronto are framed with wood, or rather planked, as are those of Montreal and Quebec; but they are kept in better order. I should say that the planks are first used at Toronto, then sent down by the lake to Montreal, and when all but rotted out there, are again floated off by the St. Lawrence to be used in the thoroughfares of the old French capital. But if the streets of Toronto are better than those of the other towns, the roads round it are worse. I had the honour of meeting two distinguished members of the Provincial Parliament at dinner some few miles out of town, and, returning back a short while after they had left our host's house, was glad to be of use in picking them up from a ditch into which their carriage had been upset. To me it appeared all but miraculous that any carriage should make its way over that road without such misadventure. I may perhaps be allowed to hope that the discomfiture of those worthy legislators may lead to some improvement in the thoroughfare.

I had on a previous occasion gone down the St. Lawrence, through the thousand isles, and over the rapids in one of those large summer steamboats which ply upon the lake and river. I cannot say that I was much struck by the scenery, and therefore did not encroach upon my time by making the journey again. Such an opinion will be regarded as heresy by many who think much of the thousand islands. I do not believe that they would be expressly noted by any traveller who was not expressly bidden to admire them.

From Toronto we went across to Niagara, re-entering the States at Lewiston in New York.

VI

The Connexion of the Canadas with Great Britain

WHEN the American war began troops were sent out to Canada, and when I was in the Provinces more troops were then expected. The matter was much talked of, as a matter of course, in Canada; and it had been discussed in England before I left. I had seen much said about it in the English papers since, and it also had become the subject of very hot question among the politicians of the northern States. The measure had at that time given more umbrage to the North than anything else done or said by England from the beginning of the war up to that time, except the declaration made by Lord John Russell in the House of Commons as to the neutrality to be preserved by England between the two belligerents. The argument used by the northern States was this. If France collects men and material of war in the neighbourhood of England, England considers herself injured, calls for an explanation, and talks of invasion. Therefore as England is now collecting men and material of war in our neighbourhood, we will consider ourselves injured. It does not suit us to ask for an explanation, because it is not our habit to interfere with other nations. We will not pretend to say that we think we are to be invaded. But as we clearly are injured, we will express our anger at that injury, and when the opportunity shall come will take advantage of having that new grievance.

As we all know, a very large increase of force was sent when we were still in doubt as to the termination of the Trent affair, and imagined that war was imminent. But the sending of that large force did not anger the Americans, as the first despatch of troops to Canada had angered them. Things had so turned out that measures of military precaution were acknowledged by them to be necessary. I cannot, however, but think that Mr. Seward might have spared that offer to send British troops across Maine; and so, also, have all his country-men thought by whom I have heard the matter discussed.

As to any attempt at invasion of Canada by the Americans, or idea of punishing the alleged injuries suffered by the States from Great Britain by the annexation of those provinces, I do not believe that any sane-minded citizens of the States believe in the possibility of such retaliation. Some years since the Americans thought that Canada might shine in the Union firmament as a new star, but that delusion is, I think, over. Such annexation if ever made, must have been made not only against the arms of England but must also have been made in accordance with the wishes of the people so annexed. It was then believed that the Canadians were not averse to such a change, and there may possibly have then been among them the remnant of such a wish. There is certainly no such desire now, not even a remnant of such a desire; and the truth on this matter is, I think, generally acknow-ledged. The feeling in Canada is one of strong aversion to the United States Government, and of predilection for self-government under the English Crown. A fainéant Governor and the prestige of British power is now the political aspiration of the Canadians in general; and I think that this is understood in the States. Moreover the States have a job of work on hand which, as they themselves are well aware, is taxing all their energies. Such being the case I do not think that England needs to fear any invasion of Canada, authorized by the States Government.

This feeling of a grievance on the part of the States was a manifest absurdity. The new reinforcement of the garrisons in Canada did not, when I was in Canada, amount as I believe to more than 2000 men. But had it amounted to 20,000 the States would have had no just ground for complaint. Of all nationalities that in modern days have risen to power, they above all others have shown that they would do what they liked with their own, indifferent to foreign councils, and deaf to foreign remonstrance. "Do you go your way, and let us go ours. We will trouble you with no question, nor do you trouble us." Such has been their national policy, and it has obtained for them great respect. They have resisted the temptation of putting their fingers into the caldron of foreign policy; and foreign politicians, acknowledging their reserve in this respect, have not been offended at the bristles with which their Noli me tangere has been proclaimed. Their intelligence has been appreciated, and their conduct has been respected. But if this has been their line of policy, they must be entirely out of court in raising any question as to the position of British troops on British soil.

"It shows us that you doubt us," an American says, with an air of injured honour—or did say, before that Trent affair. "And it is done to express sympathy with the South. The Southerners understand it, and we understand it also. We know where your hearts are; nay, your very souls. They are among the slave-begotten cotton bales of the rebel South." Then comes the whole of the long argument, in which it seems so easy to an Englishman to prove that England in the whole of this sad matter has been true and loyal to her friend. She could not interfere when the husband and wife would quarrel. She could only grieve, and wish that things might come right and smooth for both parties. But the argument though so easy is never effectual.

It seems to me foolish in an American to quarrel with England for sending soldiers to Canada; but I cannot say that I thought it was well done to send them at the beginning of the war. The English Government did not, I presume, take this step with reference to any possible invasion of Canada by the Government of the States. We are fortifying Portsmouth, and Portland, and Plymouth, because we would fain be safe against the French army acting under a French Emperor. But we sent 2000 troops to Canada, if I understand the matter rightly, to guard our provinces against the filibustering energies of a mass of unemployed American soldiers, when those soldiers should come to be disbanded. When this war shall be over—a war during which not much, if any, under a million of American citizens will have been under arms—it will not be easy for all who survive to return to their old homes and old occupations. Nor does a disbanded soldier always make a good husbandman, notwithstanding the great examples of Cincinnatus and Bird-o'-freedom Sawin. It may be that a considerable amount of filibustering energy will be afloat, and that the then Government of those who neighbour us in Canada will have other matters in hand more important to them than the controlling of these unruly spirits. That, as I take it, was the evil against which we of Great Britain and of Canada desired to guard ourselves.

But I doubt whether 2000 or 10,000 British soldiers would be any effective guard against such inroads, and I doubt more strongly whether any such external guarding will be necessary. If the Canadians were prepared to fraternize with filibusters from the States, neither three nor ten thousand soldiers would avail against such a feeling over a frontier stretching from the State of Maine to the shores of Lake Huron and Lake Erie. If such a feeling did exist, if the Canadians wished the change, in God's name let them go. Is it for their sakes and not for our own that we would have them bound to us? But the Canadians are averse to such a change with a degree of feeling that amounts to national intensity. Their sympathies are with the Southern States, not because they care for cotton, not because they are anti-abolitionists, not because they admire the hearty pluck of those who are endeavouring to work out for themselves a new revolution. They sympathize with the South from strong dislike to the aggression, the braggadocio, and the insolence they have felt upon their own borders. They dislike Mr. Seward's weak and vulgar joke with the Duke of Newcastle. They dislike Mr. Everett's flattering hints to his country-men as to the one nation that is to occupy the whole continent. They dislike the Monroe doctrine. They wonder at the meekness with which England has endured the vauntings of the northern States, and are endued with no such meekness of their own. They would, I believe, be well prepared to meet and give an account of any filibusters who might visit them; and I am not sure that it is wisely done on our part to show any intention of taking the work out of their hands.

But I am led to this opinion in no degree by a feeling that Great Britain ought to grudge the cost of the soldiers. If Canada will be safer with them, in heaven's name let her have them. It has been argued in many places, not only with regard to Canada, but as to all our self-governed colonies, that military service should not be given at British expense and with British men to any colony which has its own representative government, and which levies its own taxes. "While Great Britain absolutely held the reins of government, and did as it pleased with the affairs of its dependencies," such politicians say, "it was just and right that she should pay the bill. As long as her govern-ment of a colony was paternal, so long was it right that the mother country should put herself in the place of a father, and enjoy a father's undoubted prerogative of putting his hand into his breeches pocket to provide for all the wants of his child. But when the adult son set up for himself in business, having received education from the parent, and having had his apprentice fees duly paid, then that son should settle his own bills, and look no longer to the paternal pocket." Such is the law of the world all over, from little birds whose young fly away when fledged, upwards to men and nations. Let the father work for the child while he is a child, but when the child has become a man let him lean no longer on his father's staff.

The argument is, I think, very good; but it proves, not that we are
relieved from the necessity of assisting our colonies with payments
made out of British taxes, but that we are still bound to give such
assistance; and that we shall continue to be so bound as long as we
allow these colonies to adhere to us, or as they allow us to adhere to
them. In fact the young bird is not yet fully fledged. That illustration of
the father and the child is a just one, but in order to make it just it
should be followed throughout. When the son is in fact established on
his own bottom, then the father expects that he will live without
assistance. But when the son does so live he is freed from all paternal
control. The father, while he expects to be obeyed, continues to fill the
paternal office of paymaster,—of paymaster, at any rate, to some
extent. And so, I think, it must be with our colonies. The Canadas at
present are not independent, and have not political power of their own
apart from the political power of Great Britain. England has declared
herself neutral as regards the Northern and Southern States, and by
that neutrality the Canadas are bound; and yet the Canadas were not
consulted in the matter. Should England go to war with France,
Canada must close her ports against French vessels. If England
chooses to send her troops to Canadian barracks, Canada cannot
refuse to accept them. If England should send to Canada an unpopular
Governor, Canada has no power to reject his services. As long as
Canada is a colony, so called, she cannot be independent, and should
not be expected to walk alone. It is exactly the same with the colonies
of Australia, with New Zealand, with the Cape of Good Hope, and
with Jamaica. While England enjoys the prestige of her colonies, while
she boasts that such large and now populous territories are her dependencies, she must and should be content to pay some portion of the bill.
Surely it is absurd on our part to quarrel with Caffre warfare, with
New Zealand fighting, and the rest of it. Such complaints remind one
of an ancient paterfamilias, who insists on having his children and his
grandchildren under the old paternal roof, and then grumbles because
the butcher's bill is high. Those who will keep large households and
bountiful tables should not be afraid of facing the butcher's bill, or
unhappy at the tonnage of the coal. It is a grand thing, that power of
keeping a large table; but it ceases to be grand when the items heaped
upon it cause inward groans and outward moodiness.

Why should the colonies remain true to us as children are true to
their parents, if we grudge them the assistance which is due to a child?
They raise their own taxes, it is said, and administer them. True; and
it is well that the growing son should do something for himself. While

the father does all for him the son's labour belongs to the father. Then comes a middle state in which the son does much for himself, but not all. In that middle state now stand our prosperous colonies. Then comes the time when the son shall stand alone by his own strength; and to that period of manly self-respected strength let us all hope that those colonies are advancing. It is very hard for a mother country to know when such a time has come; and hard also for the child-colony to recognize justly the period of its own maturity. Whether or no such severance may ever take place without a quarrel, without weakness on one side and pride on the other, is a problem in the world's history yet to be solved. The most successful child that ever yet has gone off from a successful parent and taken its own path into the world, is without doubt the nation of the United States. Their present troubles are the result and the proofs of their success. The people that were too great to be dependent on any nation have now spread till they are themselves too great for a single nationality. No one now thinks that that daughter should have remained longer subject to her mother. But the severance was not made in amity, and the shrill notes of the old family quarrel are still sometimes heard across the waters.

From all this the question arises whether that problem may ever be solved with reference to the Canadas. That it will never be their destiny to join themselves to the States of the Union, I feel fully convinced. In the first place it is becoming evident from the present circumstances of the Union,—if it had never been made evident by history before,—that different people with different habits living at long distances from each other cannot well be brought together on equal terms under one Government. That noble ambition of the Americans that all the continent north of the isthmus should be united under one flag, has already been thrown from its saddle. The North and South are virtually separated, and the day will come in which the West also will secede. As population increases and trades arise peculiar to those different climates, the interests of the people will differ, and a new secession will take place beneficial alike to both parties. If this be so, if even there be any tendency this way, it affords the strongest argument against the probability of any future annexation of the Canadas. And then, in the second place, the feeling of Canada is not American, but British. If ever she be separated from Great Britain, she will be separated as the States were separated. She will desire to stand alone, and to enter herself as one among the nations of the earth.

She will desire to stand alone;—alone, that is without dependence either on England or on the States. But she is so circumstanced geographically that she can never stand alone without amalgamation with out other North American provinces. She has an outlet to the sea at the Gulf of St. Lawrence, but it is only a summer outlet. Her winter outlet is by railway through the States, and no other winter outlet is possible for her except through the sister provinces. Before Canada can be nationally great, the line of railway which now runs for some hundred miles below Quebec to Rivière du Loup, must be continued on through New Brunswick and Nova Scotia to the port of Halifax.

When I was in Canada I heard the question discussed of a Federal Government between the provinces of the two Canadas, New Brunswick and Nova Scotia. To these were added, or not added, according to the opinion of those who spoke, the smaller outlying colonies of Newfoundland and Prince Edward's Island. If a scheme for such a Government were projected in Downing Street, all would no doubt be included, and a clean sweep would be made without difficulty. But the project as made in the colonies appears in different guises as it comes either from Canada or from one of the other provinces. The Canadian idea would be that the two Canadas should form two States of such a confederation, and the other provinces a third State. But this slight participation in power would hardly suit the views of New Brunswick and Nova Scotia. In speaking of such a Federal Government as this, I shall of course be understood as meaning a confederation acting in connection with a British Governor, and dependent upon Great Britain as far as the different colonies are now dependent.

I cannot but think that such a confederation might be formed with great advantage to all the colonies and to Great Britain. At present the Canadas are in effect almost more distant from Nova Scotia and New Brunswick than they are from England. The intercourse between them is very slight—so slight that it may almost be said that there is no intercourse. A few men of science or of political importance may from time to time make their way from one colony into the other, but even this is not common. Beyond that they seldom see each other. Though New Brunswick borders, both with Lower Canada and with Nova Scotia, thus making one whole of the three colonies, there is neither railroad nor stage conveyance running from one to the other. And yet their interests should be similar. From geographical position their modes of life must be alike, and a close conjunction between them is essentially necessary to give British North America any political importance in the world. There can be no such conjunction, no amalgamation of interests, until a railway shall have been made joining the Canada Grand Trunk Line with the two outlying colonies. Upper

Canada can feed all England with wheat, and could do so without any aid of railway through the States, if a railway were made from Quebec to Halifax. But then comes the question of the cost. The Canada Grand Trunk is at the present moment at the lowest ebb of commercial misfortune, and with such a fact patent to the world what company will come forward with funds for making four or five hundred miles of railway, through a district of which one half is not yet prepared for population? It would be, I imagine, out of the question that such a speculation should for many years give any fair commercial interest on the money, to be expended. But nevertheless to the colonies,—that is, to the enormous regions of British North America,—such a railroad would be invaluable. Under such circumstances it is for the Home Government and the colonies between them to see how such a measure may be carried out. As a national expenditure to be defrayed in the course of years by the territories interested, the sum of money required would be very small.

But how would this affect England? And how would England be affected by a union of the British North American colonies under one Federal Government? Before this question can be answered, he who prepares to answer it must consider what interest England has in her colonies, and for what purpose she holds them. Does she hold them for profit, or for glory, or for power; or does she hold them in order that she may carry out the duty which has devolved upon her of extending civilization, freedom, and well-being through the new uprising nations of the world? Does she hold them, in fact, for her own benefit, or does she hold them for theirs? I know nothing of the ethics of the Colonial Office, and not much perhaps of those of the House of Commons; but looking at what Great Britain has hitherto done in the way of colonization, I cannot but think that the national ambition looks to the welfare of the colonists, and not to home aggrandisement. That the two may run together is most probable. Indeed there can be no glory to a people so great or so readily recognized by mankind at large as that of spreading civilization from East to West, and from North to South. But the one object should be the prosperity of the colonists; and not profit, nor glory, nor even power to the parent country.

There is no virtue of which more has been said and sung than patriotism, and none which when pure and true has led to finer results. Dulce et decorum est pro patriâ mori. To live for one's country also is a very beautiful and proper thing. But if we examine closely much patriotism, that is so called, we shall find it going hand in hand with a good deal that is selfish, and with not a little that is devilish. It was some fine fury of patriotic feeling which enabled the national poet to put into the mouth of every Englishman that horrible prayer with regard to our enemies, which we sing when we wish to do honour to our sovereign. It did not seem to him that it might be well to pray that their hearts should be softened, and our own hearts softened also. National success was all that a patriotic poet could desire, and therefore in our national hymn have we gone on imploring the Lord to arise and scatter our enemies; to confound their politics, whether they be good or ill; and to expose their knavish tricks,—such knavish tricks being taken for granted. And then with a steady confidence we used to declare how certain we were that we should achieve all that was desirable, not exactly by trusting to our prayer to heaven, but by relying almost exclusively on George the Third or George the Fourth. Now I have always thought that that was rather a poor patriotism. Luckily for us our national conduct has not squared itself with our national anthem. Any patriotism must be poor which desires glory or even profit for a few at the expense of many, even though the few be brothers and the many aliens. As a rule patriotism is a virtue only because man's aptitude for good is so finite, that he cannot see and comprehend a wider humanity. He can hardly bring himself to understand that salvation should be extended to Jew and Gentile alike. The word philanthropy has become odious, and I would fain not use it; but the thing itself is as much higher than patriotism, as heaven is above the earth.

A wish that British North America should ever be severed from England, or that the Australian colonies should ever be so severed, will by many Englishmen be deemed unpatriotic. But I think that such severance is to be wished if it be the case that the colonies standing alone would become more prosperous than they are under British rule. We have before us an example in the United States of the prosperity which has attended such a rupture of old ties. I will not now contest the point with those who say that the present moment of an American civil war is ill chosen for vaunting that prosperity. There stand the cities which the people have built, and their power is attested by the world-wide importance of their present contest. And if the States have so risen since they left their parent's apron-string, why should not British North America rise as high? That the time has as yet come for such rising I do not think; but that it will soon come I do most heartily hope. The making of the railway of which I have spoken, and the amalgama-tion of the provinces would greatly tend to such an event. If, therefore, England desires to keep these colonies in a state of dependency; if it be more essential to her to maintain her own power with regard to them than to increase their influence; if her main object be to keep the colonies and not to improve the colonies, then I should say that an amalgamation of the Canadas with Nova Scotia and New Brunswick should not be regarded with favour by statesmen in Downing Street. But if, as I would fain hope, and do partly believe, such ideas of national power as these are now out of vogue with British statesmen, then I think that such an amalgamation should receive all the support which Downing Street can give it.

The United States severed themselves from Great Britain with a great struggle and after heartburnings and bloodshed. Whether Great Britain will ever allow any colony of hers to depart from out of her nest, to secede and start for herself, without any struggle or heartburnings, with all furtherance for such purpose which an old and powerful country can give to a new nationality then first taking its own place in the world's arena, is a problem yet to be solved. There is, I think, no more beautiful sight than that of a mother, still in all the glory of womanhood, preparing the wedding trousseau for her daughter. The child hitherto has been obedient and submissive. She has been one of a household in which she has held no command. She has sat at table as a child, fitting herself in all things to the behests of others. But the day of her power and her glory, and also of her cares and solicitude is at hand. She is to go forth, and do as she best may in the world under that teaching which her old home has given her. The hour of separation has come; and the mother, smiling through her tears, sends her forth decked with a bounteous hand and furnished with full stores, so that all may be well with her as she enters on her new duties. So is it that England should send forth her daughters. They should not escape from her arms with shrill screams and bleeding wounds, with ill-omened words which live so long, though the speakers of them lie cold in their graves.

But this sending forth of a child-nation to take its own political status in the world has never yet been done by Great Britain. I cannot remember that such has ever been done by any great power with reference to its dependency;—by any power that was powerful enough to keep such dependency within its grasp. But a man thinking on these matters cannot but hope that a time will come when such amicable severance may be effected. Great Britain cannot think that through all coming ages she is to be the mistress of the vast continent of Australia, lying on the other side of the globe's surface; that she is to be the mistress of all South Africa, as civilization shall extend northward;

that the enormous territories of British North America are to be subject for ever to a veto from Downing Street. If the history of past empires does not teach her that this may not be so, at least the history of the United States might so teach her. "But we have learned a lesson from those United States," the patriot will argue who dares to hope that the glory and extent of the British Empire may remain unimpaired *in sæcula sæculorum*. "Since that day we have given political rights to our colonies, and have satisfied the political longings of their inhabitants. We do not tax their tea and stamps, but leave it to them to tax themselves as they may please." True. But in political aspirations the giving of an inch has ever created the desire for an ell. If the Australian colonies, even now,—with their scanty population and still young civilization, chafe against imperial interference, will they submit to it when they feel within their veins all the full blood of political manhood? What is the cry even of the Canadians—of the Canadians who are thoroughly loyal to England? Send us a fainéant Governor, a King Log, who will not presume to interfere with us; a Governor who will spend his money and live like a gentleman and care little or nothing for politics. That is the Canadian *beau idéal* of a Governor. They are to govern themselves; and he who comes to them from England is to sit among them as the silent representative of England's protection. If that be true—and I do not think that any who know the Canadas will deny it—must it not be presumed that they will soon also desire a fainéant minister in Downing Street? Of course they will so desire. Men do not become milder in their aspirations for political power, the more that political power is extended to them. Nor would it be well that they should be so humble in their desires. Nations devoid of political power have never risen high in the world's esteem. Even when they have been commercially successful, commerce has not brought to them the greatness which it has always given when joined with a strong political existence. The Greeks are commercially rich and active; but "Greece" and "Greek" are bye-words now for all that is mean. Cuba is a colony, and putting aside the cities of the States, the Havana is the richest town on the other side of the Atlantic and commercially the greatest; but the political villainy of Cuba, her daily importation of slaves, her breaches of treaty, and the bribery of her all but royal Governor are known to all men. But Canada is not dishonest; Canada is no bye-word for anything evil; Canada eats her own bread in the sweat of her brow, and fears a bad word from no man. True. But why does New York with its suburbs boast a million of inhabitants, while Montreal has 85,000? Why has that babe in years, Chicago,

120,000, while Toronto has not half the number? I do not say that Montreal and Toronto should have gone ahead abreast with New York and Chicago. In such races one must be first, and one last. But I do say that the Canadian towns will have no equal chance, till they are actuated by that feeling of political independence which has created the growth of the towns in the United States.

I do not think that the time has yet come in which Great Britain should desire the Canadians to start for themselves. There is the making of that railroad to be effected, and something done towards the union of those provinces. Canada could no more stand alone without New Brunswick and Nova Scotia, than could those latter colonies without Canada. But I think it would be well to be prepared for such a coming day; and that it would at any rate be well to bring home to ourselves and realize the idea of such secession on the part of our colonies, when the time shall have come at which such secession may be carried out with profit and security to them. Great Britain, should she ever send forth her child alone into the world, must of course guarantee her security. Such guarantees are given by treaties; and in the wording of them it is presumed that such treaties will last for ever. It will be argued that in starting British North America as a political power on its own bottom, we should bind ourself to all the expense of its defence, while we should give up all right to any interference in its concerns; and that from a state of things so unprofitable as this there would be no prospect of deliverance. But such treaties, let them be worded how they will, do not last for ever. For a time, no doubt, Great Britain would be so hampered—if indeed she would feel herself hampered by extending her name and prestige to a country bound to her by ties such as those which would then exist between her and this new nation. Such treaties are not everlasting, nor can they be made to last even for ages. Those who word them seem to think that powers and dynasties will never pass away. But they do pass away, and the balance of power will not keep itself fixed for ever on the same pivot. The time may come—that it may not come soon we will all desire—but the time may come when the name and prestige of what we call British North America will be as serviceable to Great Britain as those of Great Britain are now serviceable to her colonies.

But what shall be the new form of government for the new kingdom? That is a speculation very interesting to a politician; though one which to follow out at great length in these early days would be rather premature. That it should be a kingdom—that the political arrangement should be one of which a crowned hereditary king should form a part, nineteen out of every twenty Englishmen would desire; and, as I fancy, so would also nineteen out of every twenty Canadians. A king for the United States when they first established themselves was impossible. A total rupture from the Old World and all its habits was necessary for them. The name of a king, or monarch, or sovereign had become horrible to their ears. Even to this day they have not learned the difference between arbitrary power retained in the hand of one man, such as that now held by the Emperor over the French, and such hereditary headship in the State as that which belongs to the Crown in Great Britain. And this was necessary, seeing that their division from us was effected by strife, and carried out with war and bitter animosities. In those days also there was a remnant, though but a small remnant, of the power of tyranny left within the scope of the British Crown. That small remnant has been removed; and to me it seems that no form of existing government—no form of government that ever did exist, gives or has given so large a measure of individual freedom to all who live under it as a constitutional monarchy in which the Crown is divested of direct political power.

I will venture then to suggest a king for this new nation; and seeing that we are rich in princes there need be no difficulty in the selection. Would it not be beautiful to see a new nation established under such auspices, and to establish a people to whom their independence had been given,—to whom it had been freely surrendered as soon as they were capable of holding the position assigned to them?

VII

Niagara

Of all the sights on this earth of ours which tourists travel to see,—at least of all those which I have seen,—I am inclined to give the palm to the Falls of Niagara. In the catalogue of such sights I intend to include all buildings, pictures, statues, and wonders of art made by men's hands, and also all beauties of nature prepared by the Creator for the delight of his creatures. This is a long word; but as far as my taste and judgment go, it is justified. I know no other one thing so beautiful, so glorious, and so powerful. I would not by this be understood as saying that a traveller wishing to do the best with his time should first of all places seek Niagara. In visiting Florence he may learn almost all that modern art can teach. At Rome he will be brought to understand the cold hearts, correct eyes, and cruel ambition of the old Latin race. In Switzerland he will surround himself with a flood of grandeur and loveliness, and fill himself, if he be capable of such filling, with a flood of romance. The Tropics will unfold to him all that vegetation in its greatest richness can produce. In Paris he will find the supreme of polish, the *ne plus ultra* of varnish according to the world's capability of varnishing. And in London he will find the supreme of power, the *ne plus ultra* of work according to the world's capability of working. Any one of such journeys may be more valuable to a man,— nay, any one such journey must be more valuable to a man, than a visit to Niagara. At Niagara there is that fall of waters alone. But that fall is more graceful than Giotto's tower, more noble than the Apollo. The peaks of the Alps are not so astounding in their solitude. The valleys of the Blue Mountains in Jamaica are less green. The finished glaze of life in Paris is less invariable; and the full tide of trade round the Bank of England is not so inexorably powerful.

I came across an artist at Niagara who was attempting to draw the spray of the waters. "You have a difficult subject," said I. "All subjects are difficult," he replied, "to a man who desires to do well." "But yours, I fear, is impossible," I said. "You have no right to say so till I have finished my picture," he replied. I acknowledged the justice of his rebuke, regretted that I could not remain till the completion of his work should enable me to revoke my words, and passed on. Then I began to reflect whether I did not intend to try a task as difficult in describing the falls, and whether I felt any of that proud self-confidence which kept him happy at any rate while his task was in hand. I will not say that it is as difficult to describe aright that rush of waters, as it is to paint it well. But I doubt whether it is not quite as difficult to write a description that shall interest the reader, as it is to paint a picture of them that shall be pleasant to the beholder. My friend the artist was at any rate not afraid to make the attempt, and I also will try my hand.

That the waters of Lake Erie have come down in their courses from the broad basins of Lake Michigan, Lake Superior, and Lake Huron; that these waters fall into Lake Ontario by the short and rapid river of Niagara, and that the Falls of Niagara are made by a sudden break in the level of this rapid river, is probably known to all who will read this book. All the waters of these huge northern inland seas run over that breach in the rocky bottom of the stream; and thence it comes that the flow is unceasing in its grandeur, and that no eye can perceive a difference in the weight, or sound, or violence of the fall, whether it be visited in the drought of autumn, amidst the storms of winter, or after the melting of the upper worlds of ice in the days of the early summer. How many cataracts does the habitual tourist visit at which the waters fail him? But at Niagara the waters never fail. There it thunders over its ledge in a volume that never ceases and is never diminished;—as it has done from times previous to the life of man, and as it will do till tens of thousands of years shall see the rocky bed of the river worn away, back to the upper lake.

This stream divides Canada from the States, the western or farthermost bank belonging to the British Crown, and the eastern or nearer bank being in the State of New York. In visiting Niagara it always becomes a question on which side the visitor shall take up his quarters. On the Canada side there is no town, but there is a large hotel, beautifully placed immediately opposite to the falls, and this is generally thought to be the best locality for tourists. In the State of New York is the town called Niagara Falls, and here there are two large hotels, which, as to their immediate site, are not so well placed as that in Canada. I first visited Niagara some three years since. I stayed then at the Clifton House on the Canada side, and have since sworn by that position. But the Clifton House was closed for the season when I was last there, and on that account we went to the Cataract House in the town on the other side. I now think that I should set up my staff on the American side if I went again. My advice on the subject to any party starting for Niagara would depend upon their habits, or on their nationality. I would send Americans to the Canadian side, because they dislike walking; but English people I would locate on the American side, seeing that they are generally accustomed to the frequent use of their own legs. The two sides are not very easily approached, one from the other. Immediately below the falls there is a ferry, which may be traversed at the expense of a shilling; but the labour of getting up and down from the ferry is considerable, and the passage becomes wearisome. There is also a bridge, but it is two miles down the river, making a walk or drive of four miles necessary, and the toll for passing is four shillings or a dollar in a carriage, and one shilling on foot. As the greater variety of prospect can be had on the American side, as the island between the two falls is approachable from the American side and not from the Canadian, and as it is in this island that visitors will best love to linger and learn to measure in their minds the vast triumph of waters before them, I recommend such of my readers as can trust a little,—it need be but a little,—to their own legs, to select their hotel at Niagara Falls town.

It has been said that it matters much from what point the falls are first seen, but to this I demur. It matters, I think, very little, or not at all. Let the visitor first see it all, and learn the whereabouts of every point, so as to understand his own position and that of the waters; and then having done that in the way of business let him proceed to enjoyment. I doubt whether it be not the best to do this with all sight seeing. I am quite sure that it is the way in which acquaintance may be best and most pleasantly made with a new picture.

The falls are, as I have said, made by a sudden breach in the level of the river. All cataracts are, I presume, made by such breaches; but generally the waters do not fall precipitously as they do at Niagara, and never elsewhere, as far as the world yet knows, has a breach so sudden been made in a river carrying in its channel such or any approach to such a body of water. Up above the falls, for more than a mile, the waters leap and burst over rapids, as though conscious of the destiny that awaits them. Here the river is very broad, and comparatively shallow, but from shore to shore it frets itself into little torrents, and begins to assume the majesty of its power. Looking at it even here, in the expanse which forms itself over the greater fall, one feels sure that no strongest swimmer could have a chance of saving himself, if fate had cast him in even among those petty whirlpools. The waters, though so broken in their descent, are deliciously green. This colour as seen early in the morning, or just as the sun has set, is so bright as to give to the place of its chiefest charms.

This will be best seen from the further end of the island,—Goat Island, as it is called, which, as the reader will understand, divides the river immediately above the falls. Indeed the island is a part of that precipitously broken ledge over which the river tumbles; and no doubt in process of time will be worn away and covered with water. The time, however, will be very long. In the meanwhile it is perhaps a mile round, and is covered thickly with timber. At the upper end of the island the waters are divided, and coming down in two courses, each over its own rapids, form two separate falls. The bridge by which the island is entered is a hundred yards or more above the smaller fall. The waters here have been turned by the island, and make their leap into the body of the river below at a right angle with it,—about two hundred yards below the greater fall. Taken alone this smaller cataract would, I imagine, be the heaviest fall of water known, but taken in conjunction with the other it is terribly shorn of its majesty. The waters here are not green as they are at the larger cataract, and though the ledge has been hollowed and bowed by them so as to form a curve, that curve does not deepen itself into a vast abyss as it does at the horseshoe up above. This smaller fall is again divided, and the visitor passing down a flight of steps and over a frail wooden bridge finds himself on a smaller island in the midst of it.

But we will go at once on to the glory, and the thunder, and the majesty, and the wrath of that upper hell of waters. We are still, let the reader remember, on Goat Island, still in the States, and on what is called the American side of the main body of the river. Advancing beyond the path leading down to the lesser fall, we come to that point of the island at which the waters of the main river begin to descend. From hence across to the Canadian side the cataract continues itself in one unabated line. But the line is very far from being direct or straight.

After stretching for some little way from the shore, to a point in the river which is reached by a wooden bridge at the end of which stands a tower upon the rock,—after stretching to this, the line of the ledge bends inwards against the flood,—in, and in, and in, till one is led to think that the depth of that horse-shoe is immeasurable. It has been cut with no stinting hand. A monstrous cantle has been worn back out of the centre of the rock, so that the fury of the waters converges, and the spectator as he gazes into the hollow with wishful eyes fancies that he can hardly trace out the centre of the abyss.

Go down to the end of that wooden bridge, seat yourself on the rail, and there sit till all the outer world is lost to you. There is no grander spot about Niagara than this. The waters are absolutely around you. If you have that power of eye-control which is so necessary to the full enjoyment of scenery you will see nothing but the water. You will certainly hear nothing else; and the sound, I beg you to remember, is not an ear-cracking, agonizing crash and clang of noises; but is melodious, and soft withal, though loud as thunder. It fills your ears, and as it were envelopes them, but at the same time you can speak to your neighbour without an effort. But at this place, and in these moments, the less of speaking I should say the better. There is no grander spot than this. Here, seated on the rail of the bridge, you will not see the whole depth of the fall. In looking at the grandest works of nature, and of art too, I fancy, it is never well to see all. There should be something left to the imagination, and much should be half concealed in mystery. The greatest charm of a mountain range is the wild feeling that there must be strange unknown desolate worlds in those far-off valleys beyond. And so here, at Niagara, that converging rush of waters may fall down, down at once into a hell of rivers for what the eye can see. It is glorious to watch them in their first curve over the rocks. They come green as a bank of emeralds; but with a fitful flying colour, as though conscious that in one moment more they would be dashed into spray and rise into air, pale as driven snow. The vapour rises high into the air, and is gathered there, visible always as a permanent white cloud over the cataract; but the bulk of the spray which fills the lower hollow of that horse-shoe is like a tumult of snow. This you will not fully see from your seat on the rail. The head of it rises ever and anon out of that caldron below, but the caldron itself will be invisible. It is ever so far down,—far as your own imagination can sink it. But your eyes will rest full upon the curve of the waters. The shape you will be looking at is that of a horse-shoe, but of a horse-shoe miraculously deep from toe to heel;—and this depth becomes greater as you sit there. That which at first was only great and beautiful, becomes gigantic and sublime till the mind is at loss to find an epithet for its own use. To realize Niagara you must sit there till you see nothing else than that which you have come to see. You will hear nothing else, and think of nothing else. At length you will be at one with the tumbling river before you. You will find yourself among the waters as though you belonged to them. The cool liquid green will run through your veins, and the voice of the cataract will be the expression of your own heart. You will fall as the bright waters fall, rushing down into your new world with no hesitation and with no dismay; and you will rise again as the spray rises, bright, beautiful, and pure. Then you will flow away in your course to the uncompassed, distant, and eternal ocean.

When this state has been reached and has passed away you may get off your rail and mount the tower. I do not quite approve of that tower, seeing that it has about it a gingerbread air, and reminds one of those well-arranged scenes of romance in which one is told that on the left you turn to the lady's bower, price sixpence; and on the right ascend to the knight's bed, price sixpence more, with a view of the hermit's tomb thrown in. But nevertheless the tower is worth mounting, and no money is charged for the use of it. It is not very high, and there is a balcony at the top on which some half dozen persons may stand at ease. Here the mystery is lost, but the whole fall is seen. It is not even at this spot brought so fully before your eye,—made to show itself in so complete and entire a shape, as it will do when you come to stand near to it on the opposite or Canadian shore. But I think that it shows itself more beautifully. And the form of the cataract is such, that, here in Goat Island, on the American side, no spray will reach you, although you are absolutely over the waters. But on the Canadian side, the road as it approaches the fall is wet and rotten with spray, and you, as you stand close upon the edge, will be wet also. The rainbows as they are seen through the rising cloud—for the sun's rays as seen through these waters show themselves in a bow as they do when seen through rain,—are pretty enough, and are greatly loved. For myself I do not care for this prettiness at Niagara. It is there, but I forget it,—and do not mind how soon it is forgotten.

But we are still on the tower; and here I must declare that though I forgive the tower, I cannot forgive the horrid obelisk which has latterly been built opposite to it, on the Canadian side, up above the fall; built apparently,—for I did not go to it,—with some camera obscura intention for which the projector deserves to be put in Coventry by all good Christian men and women. At such a place as Niagara tasteless buildings, run up in wrong places with a view to money making, are perhaps necessary evils. It may be that they are not evils at all;—that they give more pleasure than pain, seeing that they tend to the enjoyment of the multitude. But there are edifices of this description which cry aloud to the gods by the force of their own ugliness and malposition. As to such it may be said that there should somewhere exist a power capable of crushing them in their birth. This new obelisk or picture-building at Niagara is one of such.

And now we will cross the water, and with this object will return by the bridge out of Goat Island on the main land of the American side. But as we do so let me say that one of the great charms of Niagara consists in this,—that over and above that one great object of wonder and beauty, there is so much little loveliness;—loveliness especially of water I mean. There are little rivulets running here and there over little falls, with pendent boughs above them, and stones shining under their shallow depths. As the visitor stands and looks through the trees the rapids glitter before him, and then hide themselves behind islands. They glitter and sparkle in far distances under the bright foliage till the remembrance is lost, and one knows not which way they run. And then the river below, with its whirlpool;—but we shall come to that by-and-by, and to the mad voyage which was made down the rapids by that mad captain who ran the gauntlet of the waters at the risk of his own life, with fifty to one against him, in order that he might save another man's property from the Sheriff.

The readiest way across to Canada is by the ferry; and on the American side this is very pleasantly done. You go into a little house, pay 20 cents, take a seat on a wooden car of wonderful shape, and on the touch of a spring find yourself travelling down an inclined plane of terrible declivity and at a very fast rate. You catch a glance of the river below you, and recognize the fact that if the rope by which you are held should break, you would go down at a very fast rate indeed,—and find your final resting place in the river. As I have gone down some dozen times and have come to no such grief, I will not presume that you will be less lucky. Below there is a boat generally ready. If it be not there, the place is not chosen amiss for a rest of ten minutes, for the lesser fall is close at hand, and the larger one is in full view. Looking at the rapidity of the river you will think that the passage must be dangerous and difficult. But no accidents ever happen, and the lad who takes you over seems to do it with sufficient ease. The walk up the hill on the other side is another thing. It is very steep, and for those who have not good locomotive power of their own, will be found to be disagreeable.

In the full season, however, carriages are generally waiting there. In so short a distance I have always been ashamed to trust to other legs than my own, but I have observed that Americans are always dragged up. I have seen single young men of from eighteen to twenty-five, from whose outward appearance no story of idle luxurious life can be read, carried about alone in carriages over distances which would be counted as nothing by any healthy English lady of fifty. None but the old and invalids should require the assistance of carriages in seeing Niagara, but the trade in carriages is to all appearance the most brisk trade there.

Having mounted the hill on the Canada side you will walk on towards the falls. As I have said before, you will from this side look directly into the full circle of the upper cataract, while you will have before you at your left hand the whole expanse of the lesser fall. For those who desire to see all at a glance, who wish to comprise the whole with their eyes, and to leave nothing to be guessed, nothing to be surmised, this, no doubt, is the best point of view.

You will be covered with spray as you walk up to the ledge of rocks, but I do not think that the spray will hurt you. If a man gets wet through going to his daily work, cold, catarrh, cough, and all their attendant evils may be expected; but these maladies usually spare the tourist. Change of air, plenty of air, excellence of air, and increased exercise make these things powerless. I should therefore bid you disregard the spray. If, however, you are yourself of a different opinion, you may hire a suit of oil-cloth clothes, for, I believe, a quarter of a dollar. They are nasty of course, and have this further disadvantage, that you become much more wet having them on than you would be without them.

Here, on this side, you walk on to the very edge of the cataract, and, if your tread be steady and your legs firm, you dip your foot into the water exactly at the spot where the thin outside margin of the current reaches the rocky edge and jumps to join the mass of the fall. The bed of white foam beneath is certainly seen better here than elsewhere, and the green curve of the water is as bright here as when seen from the wooden rail across. But nevertheless I say again that that wooden rail is the one point from whence Niagara may be best seen aright.

Close to the cataract, exactly at the spot from whence in former days the Table Rock used to project from the land over the boiling caldron below, there is now a shaft down which you will descend to the level of the river, and pass between the rock and the torrent. This Table Rock broke away from the cliff and fell, as up the whole course of the river the seceding rocks have split and fallen from time to time through countless years, and will continue to do till the bed of the upper lake is reached. You will descend this shaft, taking to yourself or not taking to yourself a suit of oil-clothes as you may think best. I have gone with and without the suit, and again recommend that they be left behind. I am inclined to think that the ordinary payment should be made for their use, as otherwise it will appear to those whose trade it is to prepare them that you are injuring them in their vested rights.

Some three years since I visited Niagara on my way back to England from Bermuda, and in a volume of travels which I then published I endeavoured to explain the impression made upon me by this passage between the rock and the waterfall. An author should not quote himself; but as I feel myself bound, in writing a chapter specially about Niagara, to give some account of this strange position, I will venture to repeat my own words.

In the spot to which I allude the visitor stands on a broad safe path, made of shingles, between the rock over which the water rushes and the rushing water. He will go in so far that the spray rising back from the bed of the torrent does not incommode him. With this exception, the further he can go in the better; but circumstances will clearly show him the spot to which he should advance. Unless the water be driven in by a very strong wind, five yards make the difference between a comparatively dry coat and an absolutely wet one. And then let him stand with his back to the entrance, thus hiding the last glimmer of the expiring day. So standing he will look up among the falling waters, or down into the deep misty pit, from which they reascend in almost as palpable a bulk. The rock will be at his right hand, high and hard, and dark and straight, like the wall of some huge cavern, such as children enter in their dreams. For the first five minutes he will be looking but at the waters of a cataract,—at the waters, indeed, of such a cataract as we know no other, and at their interior curves which elsewhere we cannot see. But by-and-by all this will change. He will no longer be on a shingly path beneath a waterfall; but that feeling of a cavern wall will grow upon him, of a cavern deep, below roaring seas, in which the waves are there, though they do not enter in upon him; or rather not the waves, but the very bowels of the ocean. He will feel as though the floods surrounded him, coming and going with their wild sounds, and he will hardly recognize that though among them he is not in them. And they, as they fall with a continual roar, not hurting the ear, but musical withal, will seem to move as the vast ocean waters may perhaps move in their internal currents. He will lose the sense of one continued descent, and think that they are passing round him in their appointed courses. The broken spray that rises from the depth below, rises so strongly, so palpably, so rapidly, that the motion in every direction will seem equal. And, as he looks on, strange colours will show themselves through the mist; the shades of grey will become green or blue, with ever and anon a flash of white; and then, when some gust of wind blows in with greater violence, the sea-girt cavern will become all dark and black. Oh, my friend, let there be no one there to speak to thee then; no, not even a brother. As you stand there speak only to the waters.

Two miles below the falls the river is crossed by a suspension bridge of marvellous construction. It affords two thoroughfares, one above the other. The lower road is for carriages and horses, and the upper one bears a railway belonging to the Great Western Canada line. The view from hence both up and down the river is very beautiful, for the bridge is built immediately over the first of a series of rapids. One mile below the bridge these rapids end in a broad basin called the whirlpool, and, issuing out of this, the current turns to the right through a narrow channel overhung by cliffs and trees, and then makes its way down to Lake Ontario with comparative tranquillity.

But I will beg you to take notice of those rapids from the bridge and to ask yourself what chance of life would remain to any ship, craft, or boat required by destiny to undergo navigation beneath the bridge and down into that whirlpool. Heretofore all men would have said that no chance of life could remain to so ill-starred a bark. The navigation, however, has been effected. But men used to the river still say that the chances would be fifty to one against any vessel which should attempt to repeat the experiment.

The story of that wondrous voyage was as follows. A small steamer called the Maid of the Mist was built upon the river, between the falls and the rapids, and was used for taking adventurous tourists up amidst the spray, as near to the cataract as was possible. The Maid of the Mist plied in this way for a year or two, and was, I believe, much patronized during the season. But in the early part of last summer an evil time had come. Either the Maid got into debt, or her owner had embarked in other and less profitable speculations. At any rate he became subject to the law, and tidings reached him that the Sheriff would seize the Maid. On most occasions the Sheriff is bound to keep such intentions secret, seeing that property is moveable, and that an insolvent debtor will not always await the officers of justice. But with the poor Maid there was no need of such secrecy. There was but a mile or so of water on which she could ply, and she was forbidden by the nature of her properties to make any way upon land. The Sheriff's prey therefore was easy and the poor Maid was doomed.

In any country in the world but America such would have been the case, but an American would steam down Phlegethon to save his property from the Sheriff; he would steam down Phlegethon or get some one else to do it for him. Whether or no in this case the captain of the boat was the proprietor, or whether, as I was told, he was paid for the job, I do not know; but he determined to run the rapids, and he procured two others to accompany him in the risk. He got up his steam, and took the Maid up amidst the spray according to his custom. Then suddenly turning on his course, he with one of his companions fixed himself at the wheel, while the other remained at his engine. I wish I could look into the mind of that man and understand what his thoughts were at that moment; what were his thoughts and what his beliefs. As to one of the men I was told that he was carried down, not knowing what he was about to do, but I am inclined to believe that all the three were joined together in the attempt.

I was told by a man who saw the boat pass under the bridge, that she made one long leap down as she came thither, that her funnel was at once knocked flat on the deck by the force of the blow, that the waters covered her from stem to stern, and that then she rose again and skimmed into the whirlpool a mile below. When there she rode with comparative ease upon the waters, and took the sharp turn round into the river below without a struggle. The feat was done, and the Maid was rescued from the Sheriff. It is said that she was sold below at the mouth of the river, and carried from thence over Lake Ontario and down the St. Lawrence to Quebec.

VIII

North and West

FROM Niagara we determined to proceed north-west; as far to the north-west as we could go with any reasonable hope of finding American citizens in a state of political civilization, and perhaps guided also in some measure by our hopes as to hotel accommodation. Looking to these two matters we resolved to get across to the Mississippi, and to go up that river as far as the town of St. Paul and the falls of St. Anthony, which are some twelve miles above the town; then to descend the river as far as the States of Iowa on the west, and Illinois on the east; and to return eastwards through Chicago and the large cities on the southern shores of Lake Erie, from whence we would go across to Albany, the capital of New York State, and down the Hudson to New York, the capital of the Western world. For such a journey, in which scenery was one great object, we were rather late, as we did not leave Niagara till the 10th of October; but though the winters are extremely cold through all this portion of the American continent—15, 20, and even 25 degrees below zero being an ordinary state of the atmosphere in latitudes equal to those of Florence, Nice, and Turin—nevertheless the autumns are mild, the noon day being always warm, and the colours of the foliage are then in all their glory. I was also very anxious to ascertain, if it might be in my power to do so, with what spirit or true feeling as to the matter, the work of recruiting for the now enormous army of the States was going on in those remote regions. That men should be on fire in Boston and New York, in

Philadelphia, and along the borders of secession, I could understand. I could understand also that they should be on fire throughout the cotton, sugar, and rice plantations of the South. But I could hardly understand that this political fervour should have communicated itself to the far-off farmers who had thinly spread themselves over the enormous wheat-growing districts of the North-West. St. Paul, the capital of Minnesota, is 900 miles directly north of St. Louis, the most northern point to which slavery extends in the Western States of the Union, and the farming lands of Minnesota stretch away again for some hundreds of miles north and west of St. Paul. Could it be that those scanty and far-off pioneers of agriculture, those frontier farmers who are nearly one half German and nearly the other half Irish, would desert their clearings and ruin their chances of progress in the world for distant wars of which the causes must, as I thought, be to them unintelligible? I had been told that distance had but lent enchantment to the view, and that the war was even more popular in the remote and newly settled States than in those which have been longer known as great political bodies. So I resolved that I would go and see.

It may be as well to explain here that that great political Union hitherto called the United States of America may be more properly divided into three than into two distinct interests. In England we have long heard of North and South as pitted against each other, and we have always understood that the southern politicans or democrats have prevailed over the northern politicians or republicans, because they were assisted in their views by northern men of mark who have held southern principles;—that is, by northern men who have been willing to obtain political power by joining themselves to the southern party. That as far as I can understand has been the general idea in England, and in a broad way it has been true. But as years have advanced and as the States have extended themselves westward, a third large party has been formed, which sometimes rejoices to call itself The Great West; and though at the present time the West and the North are joined together against the South, the interests of the North and the West are not, I think, more closely interwoven than are those of the West and South; and when the final settlement of this question shall be made, there will doubtless be great difficulty in satisfying the different aspirations and feelings of two great free soil populations. The North, I think, will ultimately perceive that it will gain much by the secession of the South; but it will be very difficult to make the West believe that secession will suit its views.

I will attempt in a rough way to divide the States, as they seem to divide themselves, into these three parties. As to the majority of them there is no difficulty in locating them; but this cannot be done with absolute certainty as to some few that lie on the borders.

New England consists of six States, of which all of course belong to the North. They are Maine, New Hampshire, Vermont, Massachusetts, Rhode Island, and Connecticut; the six States which should be most dear to England, and in which the political success of the United States as a nation is to my eyes the most apparent. But even in them there was till quite of late a strong section so opposed to the republican party as to give a material aid to the South. This, I think, was particularly so in New Hampshire, from whence President Pierce came. He had been one of the senators from New Hampshire; and yet to him as President, is affixed the disgrace, whether truly affixed or not I do not say, of having first used his power in secretly organizing those arrangements which led to secession and assisted at its birth. In Massachusetts also itself there was a strong democratic party, of which Massachusetts now seems to be somewhat ashamed. Then, to make up the North, must be added the two great States of New York and Pennsylvania, and the small State of New Jersey. The West will not agree even to this absolutely, seeing that they claim all territory west of the Alleghenies, and that a portion of Pennsylvania, and some part also of New York lie westward of that range; but in endeavouring to make these divisions ordinarily intelligible I may say that the North consists of the nine States above named. But the North will also claim Maryland and Delaware, and the eastern half of Virginia. The North will claim them though they are attached to the South by joint participation in the great social institution of slavery, for Maryland, Delaware, and Virginia are slave States;—and I think that the North will ultimately make good its claim. Maryland and Delaware lie, as it were, behind the capital, and Eastern Virginia is close upon the capital. And these regions are not tropical in their climate or influences. They are and have been slave States; but will probably rid themselves of that taint and become a portion of the free North.

The southern or slave States, properly so called, are easily defined. They are Texas, Louisiana, Arkansas, Mississippi, Alabama, Florida, Georgia, South Carolina, and North Carolina. The South will also claim Tennessee, Kentucky, Missouri, Virginia, Delaware, and Maryland, and will endeavour to prove its right to the claim by the fact of the social institution being the law of the land in those States. Of Delaware, Maryland, and Eastern Virginia, I have already spoken. Western Virginia is, I think, so little tainted with slavery, that, as she stands even at present, she properly belongs to the West. As I now write the struggle is going on in Kentucky and Missouri. In Missouri the slave population is barely more than a tenth of the whole, while in South Carolina and Mississippi it is more than half. And, therefore, I venture to count Missouri among the western States, although slavery is still the law of the land within its borders. It is surrounded on three sides by free States of the West, and its soil, let us hope, must become free. Kentucky I must leave as doubtful, though I am inclined to believe that slavery will be abolished there also. Kentucky at any rate will never throw in its lot with the southern States. As to Tennessee, it seceded heart and soul, and I fear that it must be accounted as southern, although the northern army has now, in May 1862, possessed itself of the greater part of the State.

To the great West remains an enormous territory, of which, however, the population is as yet but scanty; though perhaps no portion of the world has increased so fast in population as have these western States. The list is as follows: Ohio, Indiana, Illinois, Michigan, Wisconsin, Minnesota, Iowa, Kansas,—to which I would add Missouri, and probably the western half of Virginia. We have then to account for the two already admitted States on the Pacific, California and Oregon, and also for the unadmitted Territories, Dacotah, Nebraska, Washington, Utah, New Mexico, Colorado, and Nevada. I should be refining too much for my present very general purpose, if I were to attempt to marshal these huge but thinly populated regions in either rank. Of California and Oregon it may probably be said that it is their ambition to form themselves into a separate division;—a division which may be called the further West.

I know that all statistical statements are tedious, and I believe that but few readers believe them. I will, however, venture to give the populations of these States in the order I have named them, seeing that power in America depends almost entirely on population. The census of 1860 gave the following results:—

In the North.

Maine	..	..	..	..	..	619,000
New Hampshire	..	..	..	..	..	326,872
Vermont	..	..	..	..	..	325,827
Massachusetts	..	..	..	..	..	1,231,494
Rhode Island	..	..	..	..	..	174,621
Connecticut	..	..	..	..	..	460,670
New York	..	..	..	..	..	3,851,563
Pennsylvania	..	..	..	..	..	2,916,018
New Jersey	..	..	..	..	..	676,034
Total						10,582,099

In the South—the population of which must be divided into free and slave.

				FREE	SLAVE	TOTAL
Texas	..	..	..	415,999	184,956	600,955
Louisiana	..	..	..	354,245	312,186	666,431
Arkansas	..	..	..	331,710	109,065	440,775
Mississippi	..	..	..	407,051	479,607	886,658
Alabama	..	..	..	520,444	435,473	955,917
Florida	..	..	..	81,885	63,809	145,694
Georgia	..	..	..	615,366	467,461	1,082,827
South Carolina	..	..	..	308,186	407,185	715,371
North Carolina	..	..	..	679,965	328,377	1,008,342
Tennessee	..	..	..	859,578	287,112	1,146,690
Total				4,574,429	3,075,231	7,649,660

In the West.

Ohio	..	..	..	..	..	2,377,917
Indiana	..	..	..	..	..	1,350,802
Illinois	..	..	..	..	..	1,691,238
Michigan	..	..	..	..	..	754,291
Wisconsin	..	..	..	..	..	763,485
Minnesota	..	..	..	..	..	172,796
Iowa	..	..	..	..	..	682,002
Kansas	..	..	..	..	..	143,645
Missouri	..	..	..	..	..	1,204,214*
Total						9,140,390

* Of which number, in Missouri, 115,619 are slaves.

In the doubtful States.

				FREE	SLAVE	TOTAL
Maryland ..	..	..	..	646,183	85,382	731,565
Delaware ..	..	..	..	110,548	1,805	112,353
Virginia ..	..	..	..	1,097,373	495,826	1,593,199
Kentucky ..	..	..	..	920,077	225,490	1,145,567
Total				2,774,181	808,503	3,582,684

To these must be added to make up the population of the United States, as it stood in 1860.

The separate district of Columbia, in which is included Washington, the seat of the Federal Government .				..	..	75,321
California	..	..	..	..	..	384,770
Oregon	..	..	..	..	..	52,566
The Territories of	..	..	..	..	..	
Dacotah	..	..	..	..	..	4,839
Nebraska	..	..	..	..	..	28,892
Washington	..	..	..	..	..	11,624
Utah	..	..	..	..	..	49,000
New Mexico	..	..	..	..	..	93,024
Colorado	..	..	..	..	..	34,197
Nevada	..	..	..	..	..	6,857
Total						741,090

And thus the total population may be given as follows:—

North	..	..	..	..	..	10,582,099
South	..	..	..	..	..	7,649,660
West	..	..	..	..	..	9,140,390
Doubtful	..	..	..	..	..	3,582,684
Outlying States and Territories		..	..	..		741,090
Total						31,695,923

Each of the three interests would consider itself wronged by the division above made, but the South would probably be the loudest in asserting its grievance. The South claims all the slave States, and would point to secession in Virginia to justify such claim,—and would point also to Maryland and Baltimore, declaring that secession would be as strong there as at New Orleans, if secession were practicable. Maryland and Baltimore lie behind Washington, and are under the heels of the northern troops, so that secession is not practicable; but, the South would say that they have seceded in heart. In this the South would have some show of reason for its assertion; but, nevertheless, I shall best convey a true idea of the position of these States by classing them as doubtful. When secession shall have been accomplished,—if ever it be accomplished,—it will hardly be possible that they should adhere to the South.

It will be seen by the above tables that the population of the West is nearly equal to that of the North, and that therefore western power is almost as great as northern. It is almost as great already, and as population in the West increases faster than it does in the North, the two will soon be equalized. They are already sufficiently on a par to enable them to fight on equal terms, and they will be prepared for fighting—political fighting, if no other—as soon as they have established their supremacy over a common enemy.

Whilst I am on the subject of population, I should explain—though the point is not one which concerns the present argument—that the numbers given, as they regard the South, include both the whites and blacks, the free men and the slaves. The political power of the South is of course in the hands of the white race only, and the total white population should therefore be taken as the number indicating the southern power. The political power of the South, however, as contrasted with that of the North, has, since the commencement of the Union, been much increased by the slave population. The slaves have been taken into account in determining the number of representatives which should be sent to Congress by each State. That number depends on the population, but it was decided in 1787, that in counting up the number of representatives to which each State should be held to be entitled, five slaves should represent three white men. A southern population, therefore, of five thousand free men and five thousand slaves would claim as many representatives as a northern population of eight thousand free men, although the voting would be confined to the free population. This has ever since been the law of the United States.

The western power is nearly equal to that of the North, and this fact, somewhat exaggerated in terms, is a frequent boast in the mouths of western men. "We ran Fremont for President," they say, "and had it not been for northern men with southern principles, we should have put him in the White House instead of the traitor Buchanan. If that had been done, there would have been no secession." How things might have gone had Fremont been elected in lieu of Buchanan, I will not pretend to say; but the nature of the argument shows the difference that exists between northern and western feeling. At the time that I was in the West, General Fremont was the great topic of public interest. Every newspaper was discussing his conduct, his ability as a soldier, his energy, and his fate. At that time General Maclellan was in command at Washington on the Potomac, it being understood that he held his power directly under the President,—free from the exercise of control on the part of the veteran General Scott, though at that time General Scott had not actually resigned his position as head of the army. And General Fremont, who some five years before had been "run" for President by the Western States, held another command of nearly equal independence in Missouri. He had been put over General Lyon in the western command, and directly after this General Lyon had fallen in battle at Springfield, in the first action in which the opposing armies were engaged in the West. General Fremont at once proceeded to carry matters with a very high hand. On the 30th of August, 1861, he issued a proclamation by which he declared martial law at St. Louis, the city at which he held his head quarters, and indeed throughout the State of Missouri generally. In this proclamation he declared his intention of exercising a severity beyond that ever threatened, as I believe, in modern warfare. He defines the region presumed to be held by his army of occupation, drawing his lines across the State, and then declares "that, all persons who shall be taken with arms in their hands within those lines shall be tried by Court Martial, and if found guilty will be shot." He then goes on to say that he will confiscate all the property of persons in the State who shall have taken up arms against the Union, or who shall have taken part with the enemies of the Union, and *that he will make free all slaves belonging to such persons.* This proclamation was not approved at Washington, and was modified by the order of the President. It was understood also that he issued orders for military expenditure, which were not recognized at Washington, and men began to understand that the army in the West was gradually assuming that irresponsible military position, which in disturbed countries and in times of civil war has so frequently resulted in a military dictatorship. Then there arose a clamour for the removal of General Fremont. A semi-official account of his proceedings, which had reached Washington from an officer under his command, was made public; and also the correspondence which took place on the subject between the President and General Fremont's wife. The officer in question was thereupon placed under arrest, but immediately released by orders from Washington. He then made official complaint of his General, sending forward a list of charges in which Fremont was accused of rashness, incompetency, want of fidelity of the interests of the Government, and disobedience to orders from head quarters. After a while the Secretary of War himself proceeded from Washington to the quarters of General Fremont at St. Louis, and remained there for a day or two, making or pretending to make inquiry into the matter. But when he returned he left the General still in command. During the whole month of October the papers were occupied in declaring in the morning that General Fremont had been recalled from his command, and in the evening that he was to remain. In the mean time they who befriended his cause, and this included the whole West, were hoping from day to day that he would settle the matter for himself and silence his accusers, by some great military success. General Price held the command opposed to him, and men said that Fremont would sweep General Price and his army down the valley of the Mississippi into the sea. But General Price would not be so swept, and it began to appear that a guerilla warfare would prevail; that Genereal Price, if driven southwards, would reappear behind the backs of his pursuers, and that General Fremont would not accomplish all that was expected of him with that rapidity for which his friends had given him credit. So the newspapers still went on waging the war, and every morning General Fremont was recalled, and every evening they who had recalled him were shown up as having known nothing of the matter.

"Never mind; he is a pioneer man, and will do a'most anything he puts his hand to," his friends in the West still said. "He understands the frontier." Understanding the frontier is a great thing in Western America, across which the vanguard of civilization continues to march on in advance from year to year. "And it's he that is bound to sweep slavery from off the face of this Continent. He's the man, and he's about the only man." I am not qualified to write the life of General Fremont, and can at present only make this slight reference to the details of his romantic career. That it has been full of romance, and that the man himself is indued with a singular energy and a high romantic idea of what may be done by power and will, there is no doubt. Five times he has crossed the continent of North America from Missouri to Oregon and California, enduring great hardships in the service of advancing civilization and knowledge. That he has considerable talent, immense energy, and strong self-confidence, I believe. He is a frontier man; one of those who care nothing for danger, and who would dare anything with the hope of accomplishing a great career. But I have never heard that he has shown any practical knowledge of high military matters. It may be doubted whether a man of this stamp is well fitted to hold the command of a nation's army for great national purposes. May it not even be presumed that a man of this class is of all men the least fitted for such a work? The officer required should be a man with two specialities—a speciality for military tactics, and a speciality for national duty. The army in the West was far removed from head quarters in Washington, and it was peculiarly desirable that the General commanding it should be one possessing a strong idea of obedience to the control of his own Government. Those frontier capabilities, that self-dependent energy for which his friends gave Fremont,—and probably justly gave him,—such unlimited credit are exactly the qualities which are most dangerous in such a position.

I have endeavoured to explain the circumstances of the Western command in Missouri, as they existed at the time when I was in the North-Western States, in order that the double action of the North and West may be understood. I, of course, was not in the secret of any official persons, but I could not but feel sure that the Government in Washington would have been glad to have removed Fremont at once from the command, had they not feared that by doing so they would have created a schism, as it were, in their own camp, and have done much to break up the integrity or oneness of northern loyalty. The western people almost to a man desired abolition. The States there were sending out their tens of thousands of young men into the army with a prodigality as to their only source of wealth which they hardly recognized themselves, because this to them was a fight against slavery. The western population has been increased to a wonderful degree by a German infusion;—so much so that the western towns appear to have been peopled with Germans. I found regiments of volunteers consisting wholly of Germans. And the Germans are all abolitionists. To all the men of the West the name of Fremont is dear. He is their hero, and their Hercules. He is to cleanse the stables of the southern king, and turn the waters of emancipation through the foul stalls of slavery. And, therefore, though the Cabinet in Washington would have been glad for many reasons to have removed Fremont in October last, it was at first scared from committing itself to so strong a measure. At last, however, the charges made against him were too fully substantiated to allow of their being set on one side, and early in November 1861, he was superseded. I shall be obliged to allude again to General Fremont's career as I go on with my narrative.

At this time the North was looking for a victory on the Potomac; but they were no longer looking for it with that impatience which in the summer had led to the disgrace at Bull's Run. They had recognized the fact that their troops must be equipped, drilled, and instructed; and they had also recognized the perhaps greater fact, that their enemies were neither weak, cowardly, nor badly officered. I have always thought that the tone and manner with which the North bore the defeat at Bull's Run was creditable to it. It was never denied, never explained away, never set down as trifling. "We have been whipped!" was what all Northerners said,—"We've got an almighty whipping, and here we are." I have heard many Englishmen complain of this, saying that the matter was taken almost as a joke,—that no disgrace was felt, and the licking was owned by a people who ought never to have allowed that they had been licked. To all this, however, I demur. Their only chance of speedy success consisted in their seeing and recognizing the truth. Had they confessed the whipping and then sat down with their hands in their pockets,—had they done as second-rate boys at school will do, declare that they had been licked, and then feel that all the trouble is over,—they would indeed have been open to reproach. The older mother across the water would in such case have disowned her son. But they did the very reverse of this. "I have been whipped," Jonathan said, and he immediately went into training under a new system for another fight.

And so all through September and October the great armies on the Potomac rested comparatively in quiet, the northern forces drawing to themselves immense levies. The general confidence in Maclellan was then very great, and the cautious measures by which he endeavoured to bring his vast untrained body of men under discipline were such as did at that time recommend themselves to most military critics. Early in September the northern party obtained a considerable advantage by taking the fort at Cape Hatteras, in North Carolina, situated on one of those long banks which lie along the shores of the Southern States; but towards the end of October they experienced a considerable reverse in an attack which was made on the Secessionists by General Stone, and in which Colonel Baker was killed. Colonel Baker had been senator for Oregon, and was well known as an orator. Taking all things together, however, nothing material had been done up to the end of October; and at that time northern men were waiting—not perhaps impatiently, considering the great hopes, and perhaps great fears which filled their hearts, but with eager expectation for some event of which they might talk with pride.

The man to whom they had trusted all their hopes was young for so great a command. I think that at this time (October 1861) General Maclellan was not yet thirty-five. He had served early in life in the Mexican war, having come originally from Pennsylvania, and having

been educated at the military college at West Point. During our war
with Russia he was sent to the Crimèa by his own Government in
conjunction with two other officers of the United States army, that
they might learn all that was to be learned there as to military tactics,
and report especially as to the manner in which fortifications were
made and attacked. I have been informed that a very able report was
sent in by them to the Government, on their return, and that this was
drawn up by Maclellan. But in America a man is not only a soldier or
always a soldier; nor is he always a clergyman if once a clergyman. He
takes a spell at anything suitable that may be going. And in this way
Maclellan was for some years engaged on the Central Illinois Railway,
and was for a considerable time the head manager of that concern. We
all know with what suddenness he rose to the highest command in the
army immediately after the defeat at Bull's Run.

I have endeavoured to describe what were the feelings of the West in
the autumn of 1861 with regard to the war. The excitement and
eagerness there were very great, and they were perhaps as great in the
North. But in the North the matter seemed to me to be regarded from a
different point of view. As a rule, the men of the North are not
abolitionists. It is quite certain that they were not so before secession
began. They hate slavery as we in England hate it; but they are aware,
as also are we, that the disposition of four million of black men and
women forms a question which cannot be solved by the chivalry of any
modern Orlando. The property invested in these four million slaves
forms the entire wealth of the South. If they could be wafted by a
philanthropic breeze back to the shores of Africa,—a breeze of which
the philanthropy would certainly not be appreciated by those so
wafted,—the South would be a wilderness. The subject is one as full of
difficulty as any with which politicians of these days are tormented.
The Northerners fully appreciate this, and as a rule are not abolitionists in the western sense of the word. To them the war is recommended
by precisely those feelings which animated us when we fought for our
colonies,—when we strove to put down American independence.
Secession is rebellion against the Government: and is all the more
bitter to the North because that rebellion broke out at the first moment
of northern ascendancy. "We submitted," the North says, "to southern Presidents, and southern statesmen, and southern councils, because we obeyed the vote of the people. But as to you—the voice of the
people is nothing in your estimation! At the first moment in which the
popular vote places at Washington a President with northern feelings,
you rebel. We submitted in your days; and by heaven, you shall

submit in ours! We submitted loyally; through love of the law and the Constitution. You have disregarded the law, and thrown over the Constitution. But you shall be made to submit, as a child is made to submit to its governor."

It must also be remembered that on commercial questions the North and the West are divided. The Morrill tariff is as odious to the West as it is to the South. The South and West are both agricultural productive regions, desirous of sending cotton and corn to foreign countries and of receiving back foreign manufactures on the best terms. But the North is a manufacturing country. A poor manufacturing country as regards excellence of manufacture—and therefore the more anxious to foster its own growth by protective laws. The Morrill tariff is very injurious to the West, and is odious there. I might add that its folly has already been so far recognized even in the North, as to make it very generally odious there also.

So much I have said endeavouring to make it understood how far the North and West were united in feeling against the South in the autumn of 1861, and how far there existed between them a diversity of interests.

IX

From Niagara to the Mississippi

FROM Niagara we went by the Canada Great Western Railway to Detroit, the big city of Michigan. It is an American institution that the States should have a commercial capital, or what I call their big city, as well as a political capital, which may as a rule be called the State's central city. The object in choosing the political capital is average nearness of approach from the various confines of the State; but commerce submits to no such Procrustean laws in selecting her capitals, and consequently she has placed Detroit on the borders of Michigan, on the shore of the neck of water which joins Lake Huron to Lake Erie through which all the trade must flow which comes down from Lakes Michigan, Superior, and Huron, on its way to the eastern States and to Europe. We had thought of going from Buffalo across Lake Erie to Detroit; but we found that the better class of steamers had been taken off the waters for the winter. And we also found that navigation among these lakes is a mistake whenever the necessary journey can be taken by railway. Their waters are by no means smooth; and then there is nothing to be seen. I do not know whether others may have a feeling, almost instinctive, that lake navigation must be pleasant,—that lakes must of necessity be beautiful. I have such a feeling; but not now so strongly as formerly. Such an idea should be kept for use in Europe, and never brought over to America with other travelling gear. The lakes in America are cold, cumbrous, uncouth, and uninteresting; intended by nature for the conveyance of cereal produce, but not for the comfort of travelling men and women. So we gave up our plan of traversing the lake, and passing back into Canada by the suspension bridge at Niagara, we reached the Detroit river at Windsor by the Great Western line, and passed thence by the ferry into the city of Detroit.

In making this journey at night we introduced ourselves to the thoroughly American institution of sleeping-cars;—that is, of cars in which beds are made up for travellers. The traveller may have a whole bed, or half a bed, or no bed at all as he pleases, paying a dollar or half a dollar extra should he choose the partial or full fruition of a couch. I confess I have always taken a delight in seeing these beds made up, and consider that the operations of the change are generally as well executed as the manœuvres of any pantomime in Drury Lane. The work is usually done by negroes or coloured men; and the domestic negroes of America are always light-handed and adroit. The nature of an American car is no doubt known to all men. It looks as far removed from all bedroom accommodation, as the baker's barrow does from the steam-engine into which it is to be converted by harlequin's wand. But the negro goes to work much more quietly than the harlequin, and for every four seats in the railway car he builds up four beds, almost as quickly as the hero of the pantomime goes through his performance. The great glory of the Americans is in their wondrous contrivances,— in their patent remedies for the usually troublous operations of life. In their huge hotels all the bell-ropes of each house ring on one bell only, but a patent indicator discloses a number, and the whereabouts of the ringer is shown. One fire heats every room, passage, hall, and cupboard,—and does it so effectually that the inhabitants are all but stifled. Soda-water bottles open themselves without any trouble of wire or strings. Men and women go up and down stairs without motive power of their own. Hot and cold water are laid on to all the chambers;—though it sometimes happens that the water from both taps is boiling, and that when once turned on it cannot be turned off again by any human energy. Everything is done by a new and wonderful patent contrivance; and of all their wonderful contrivances that of their railroad beds is by no means the least. For every four seats the negro builds up four beds,—that is, four half-beds or ac-commodation for four persons. Two are supposed to be below on the level of the ordinary four seats, and two up above on shelves which are let down from the roof. Mattresses slip out from one nook and pillows from another. Blankets are added, and the bed is ready. Any over particular individual—an islander, for instance, who hugs his chains—will generally prefer to pay the dollar for the double accommodation. Looking at the bed in the light of a bed,—taking as it were an abstract view of it,—or comparing it with some other bed or beds with which the occupant may have acquaintance, I cannot say that it is in all respects perfect. But distances are long in America; and he who declines to travel by night will lose very much time. He who does so travel will find the railway bed a great relief. I must confess that the feeling of dirt on the following morning is rather oppressive.

From Windsor on the Canada side we passed over to Detroit in the State of Michigan by a steam ferry. But ferries in England and ferries in America are very different. Here on this Detroit ferry, some hundred of passengers who were going forward from the other side without delay, at once sat down to breakfast. I may as well explain the way in which disposition is made of one's luggage as one takes these long journeys. The traveller when he starts has his baggage checked. He abandons his trunk—generally a box studded with nails, as long as a coffin and as high as a linen chest,—and in return for this he receives an iron ticket with a number on it. As he approaches the end of his first instalment of travel, and while the engine is still working its hardest, a man comes up to him, bearing with him suspended on a circular bar an infinite variety of other checks. The traveller confides to this man his wishes; and if he be going further without delay, surrenders his check and receives a counter-check in return. Then while the train is still in motion, the new destiny of the trunk is imparted to it. But another man, with another set of checks, also comes the way, walking leisurely through the train as he performs his work. This is the minister of the hotel-omnibus institution. His business is with those who do not travel beyond the next terminus. To him, if such be your intention, you make your confidence, giving up your tallies and taking other tallies, by way of receipt; and your luggage is afterwards found by you in the hall of your hotel. There is undoubtedly very much of comfort in this; and the mind of the traveller is lost in amazement as he thinks of the futile efforts with which he would struggle to regain his luggage were there no such arrangement. Enormous piles of boxes are disclosed on the platform at all the larger stations, the numbers of which are roared forth with quick voice by some two or three railway denizens at once. A modest English voyager with six or seven small packages, would stand no chance of getting anything if he were left to his own devices. As it is I am bound to say that the thing is well done. I have had my desk with all my money in it lost for a day, and my black leather bag was on one occasion sent back over the line. They, however, were recovered; and on the whole I feel grateful to the check system of the American railways. And then, too, one never hears of extra luggage. Of weight they are quite regardless. On two or three occasions an overwrought official has muttered between his teeth that ten packages were a great many, and that some of those "light fixings" might have been made up into one. And when I came to understand that the number of every check was entered in a book, and re-entered at every change, I did whisper to my wife that she ought to do without a bonnet-box. The ten, however, went on, and were always duly protected. I must add, however, that articles requiring tender treatment will sometimes reappear a little the worse from the hardships of their journey.

I have not much to say of Detroit; not much, that is, beyond what I have to say of all the North. It is a large well-built half-finished city, lying on a convenient water way, and spreading itself out with promises of a wide and still wider prosperity. It has about it perhaps as little of intrinsic interest as any of those large western towns which I visited. It is not so pleasant as Milwaukee, nor so picturesque as St. Paul, nor so grand as Chicago, nor so civilized as Cleveland, nor so busy as Buffalo. Indeed Detroit is neither pleasant nor picturesque at all. I will not say that it is uncivilized, but it has a harsh, crude, unprepossessing appearance. It has some 70,000 inhabitants, and good accommodation for shipping. It was doing an enormous business before the war began, and when these troublous times are over will no doubt again go ahead. I do not, however, think it well to recommend any Englishman to make a special visit to Detroit, who may be wholly uncommercial in his views and travel in search of that which is either beautiful or interesting.

From Detroit we continued our course westward across the State of Michigan through a country that was absolutely wild till the railway pierced it. Very much of it is still absolutely wild. For miles upon miles the road passes the untouched forest, showing that even in Michigan the great work of civilization has hardly more than been commenced. As one thinks of the all but countless population which is before long to be fed from these regions, of the cities which will grow here, and of the amount of government which in due time will be required, one can hardly fail to feel that the division of the United States into separate nationalities is merely a part of the ordained work of creation, as arranged for the well-being of mankind. The States already boast of thirty millions of inhabitants,—not of unnoticed and unnoticeable beings, requiring little, knowing little, and doing little, such as are the

Eastern hordes which may be counted by tens of millions; but of men
and women who talk loudly and are ambitious, who eat beef, who read
and write, and understand the dignity of manhood. But these thirty
millions are as nothing to the crowds which will grow sleek and talk
loudly, and become aggressive on these wheat and meat producing
levels. The country is as yet but touched by the pioneering hand of
population. In the old countries agriculture, following on the heels of
pastoral patriarchal life, preceded the birth of cities. But in this young
world the cities have come first. The new Jasons, blessed with the
experience of the old world adventurers, have gone forth in search of
their golden fleeces armed with all that the science and skill of the East
had as yet produced, and in settling up their new Colchis have begun
by the erection of first-class hotels and the fabrication of railroads. Let
the old world bid them God speed in their work. Only it would be well
if they could be brought to acknowledge from whence they have
learned all that they know.

Our route lay right across the State to a place called Grand Haven
on Lake Michigan, from whence we were to take boat for Milwaukee, a
town in Wisconsin on the opposite or western shore of the lake.
Michigan is sometimes called the Peninsular State from the fact that
the main part of its territory is surrounded by Lakes Michigan and
Huron, by the little Lake St. Clair, and by Lake Erie. It juts out to the
northward from the main land of Indiana and Ohio, and is circumna-
vigable on the east, north, and west. These particulars refer, however,
to a part of the State only, for a portion of it lies on the other side of
Lake Michigan, between that and Lake Superior. I doubt whether any
large inland territory in the world is blessed with such facilities of
water carriage.

On arriving at Grand Haven we found that there had been a storm
on the lake, and that the passengers from the trains of the preceding
day were still remaining there, waiting to be carried over to Milwaukee. The water, however,—or the sea as they all call it,—was still
very high, and the captain declared his intention of remaining there
that night. Whereupon all our fellow-travellers huddled themselves
into the great lake steam-boat, and proceeded to carry on life there as
though they were quite at home. The men took themselves to the
bar-room and smoked cigars and talked about the war with their feet
upon the counter, and the women got themselves into rocking-chairs
in the saloon and sat there listless and silent, but not more listless and
silent than they usually are in the big drawing-rooms of the big hotels.
There was supper there, precisely at six o'clock, beefsteaks, and tea,

and apple jam, and hot cakes, and light fixings, to all which luxuries an American deems himself entitled, let him have to seek his meal where he may. And I was soon informed with considerable energy, that let the boat be kept there as long as it might by stress of weather, the beefsteaks and apple jam, light fixings and heavy fixings, must be supplied at the cost of the owners of the ship. "Your first supper you pay for," my informant told me, "because you eat that on your own account. What you consume after that comes of their doing, because they don't start; and if it's three meals a day for a week, it's their look out." It occurred to me that under such circumstances a captain would be very apt to sail either in foul weather or in fair.

It was a bright moonlight night, moonlight such as we rarely have in England, and I started off by myself for a walk, that I might see of what nature were the environs of Grand Haven. A more melancholy place I never beheld. The town of Grand Haven itself is placed on the opposite side of a creek, and was to be reached by a ferry. On our side, to which the railway came and from which the boat was to sail, there was nothing to be seen but sandhills which stretched away for miles along the shore of the lake. There were great sand mountains, and sand valleys, on the surface of which were scattered the debris of dead trees, scattered logs white with age, and boughs half buried beneath the sand. Grand Haven itself is but a poor place, not having succeeded in catching much of the commerce which comes across the lake from Wisconsin, and which takes itself on eastwards by the railway. Altogether it is a dreary place, such as might break a man's heart, should he find that inexorable fate required him there to pitch his tent.

On my return I went down into the bar-room of the steamer, put my feet upon the counter, lit my cigar, and struck into the debate then proceeding on the subject of the war. I was getting West, and General Fremont was the hero of the hour. "He's a frontier man, and that's what we want. I guess he'll about go through. Yes, sir." "As for relieving General Fre-mont,"—with the accent always strongly on the "mont,"—"I guess you may as well talk of relieving the whole West. They won't meddle with Fre-mont. They are beginning to know in Washington what stuff he's made of." "Why, sir; there are 50,000 men in these States who will follow Fre-mont, who would not stir a foot after any other man." From which, and the like of it in many other places, I began to understand how difficult was the task which the statesmen in Washington had in hand.

I received no pecuniary advantage whatever from that law as to the steam-boat meals which my new friend had revealed to me. For my one supper of course I paid, looking forward to any amount of subsequent gratuitous provisions. But in the course of the night the ship sailed, and we found ourselves at Milwaukee in time for breakfast on the following morning.

Milwaukee is a pleasant town, a very pleasant town, containing 45,000 inhabitants. How many of my readers can boast that they know anything of Milwaukee, or even have heard of it? To me its name was unknown until I saw it on huge railway placards stuck up in the smoking-rooms and lounging halls of all American hotels. It is the big town of Wisconsin, whereas Madison is the capital. It stands immediately on the western shore of Lake Michigan, and is very pleasant. Why it should be so, and why Detroit should be the contrary, I can hardly tell; only I think that the same verdict would be given by any English tourist. It must be always borne in mind that 10,000 or 40,000 inhabitants in an American town, and especially in any new western town, is a number which means much more than would be implied by any similar number as to an old town in Europe. Such a population in America consumes double the amount of beef which it would in England, wears double the amount of clothes, and demands double as much of the comforts of life. If a census could be taken of the watches it would be found, I take it, that the American population possessed among them nearly double as many as would the English; and I fear also that it would be found that many more of the Americans were readers and writers by habit. In any large town in England it is probable that a higher excellence of education would be found than in Milwaukee, and also a style of life into which more of refinement and more of luxury had found its way. But the general level of these things, of material and intellectual well being—of beef, that is, and book learning—is no doubt infinitely higher in a new American than in an old European town. Such an animal as a beggar is as much unknown as a mastodon. Men out of work and in want are almost unknown. I do not say that there are none of the hardships of life,—and to them I will come by-and-by; but want is not known as a hardship in these towns, nor is that dense ignorance in which so large a proportion of our town populations is still steeped. And then the town of 40,000 inhabitants is spread over a surface which would suffice in England for a city of four times the size. Our towns in England,—and the towns, indeed, of Europe generally,—have been built as they have been wanted. No aspiring ambition as to hundreds of thousands of people warmed the bosoms of their first founders. Two or three dozen men required habitations in the same locality, and clustered them together closely.

Many such have failed and died out of the world's notice. Others have thriven, and houses have been packed on to houses till London and Manchester, Dublin and Glasgow have been produced. Poor men have built, or have had built for them, wretched lanes; and rich men have erected grand palaces. From the nature of their beginnings such has, of necessity, been the manner of their creation. But in America, and especially in western America, there has been no such necessity and there is no such result. The founders of cities have had the experience of the world before them. They have known of sanitary laws as they began. That sewerage, and water, and gas, and good air would be needed for a thriving community has been to them as much a matter of fact as are the well understood combinations between timber and nails, and bricks and mortar. They have known that water carriage is almost a necessity for commercial success, and have chosen their sites accordingly. Broad streets cost as little, while land by the foot is not as yet of value to be regarded, as those which are narrow; and therefore the sites of towns have been prepared with noble avenues, and imposing streets. A city at its commencement is laid out with an intention that it shall be populous. The houses are not all built at once, but there are the places allocated for them. The streets are not made, but there are the spaces. Many an abortive attempt at municipal greatness has so been made and then all but abandoned. There are wretched villages with huge straggling parallel ways which will never grow into towns. They are the failures,—failures in which the pioneers of civilization, frontier men as they call themselves, have lost their tens of thousands of dollars. But when the success comes; when the happy hit has been made, and the ways of commerce have been truly foreseen with a cunning eye, then a great and prosperous city springs up, ready made, as it were, from the earth. Such a town is Milwaukee, now containing 45,000 inhabitants, but with room apparently for double that number; with room for four times that number, were men packed as closely there as they are with us.

In the principal business streets of all these towns one sees vast buildings. They are usually called blocks, and are often so denominated in large letters on their front, as Portland Block, Devereux Block, Buel's Block. Such a block may face to two, three, or even four streets, and, as I presume, has generally been a matter of one special speculation. It may be divided into separate houses, or kept for a single purpose, such as that of an hotel, or grouped into shops below, and into various sets of chambers above. I have had occasion in various towns to mount the stairs within these blocks, and have generally found some portion of them vacant;—have sometimes found the greater portion of them vacant. Men build on an enormous scale, three times, ten times as much as is wanted. The only measure of size is an increase on what men have built before. Monroe P. Jones, the speculator, is very probably ruined, and then begins the world again, nothing daunted. But Jones's block remains, and gives to the city in its aggregate a certain amount of wealth. Or the block becomes at once of service and finds tenants. In which case Jones probably sells it and immediately builds two others twice as big. That Monroe P. Jones will encounter ruin is almost a matter of course; but then he is none the worse for being ruined. It hardly makes him unhappy. He is greedy of dollars with a terrible covetousness; but he is greedy in order that he may speculate more widely. He would sooner have built Jones's tenth block with a prospect of completing a twentieth, than settle himself down at rest for life as the owner of a Chatsworth or a Woburn. As for his children he has no desire of leaving them money. Let the girls marry. And for the boys,—for them it will be good to begin as he begun. If they cannot build blocks for themselves, let them earn their bread in the blocks of other men. So Monroe P. Jones, with his million of dollars accomplished, advances on to a new frontier, goes to work again on a new city, and loses it all. As an individual I differ very much from Monroe P. Jones. The first block accomplished, with an adequate rent accruing to me as the builder, I fancy that I should never try a second. But Jones is undoubtedly the man for the West. It is that love of money to come, joined to a strong disregard for money made, which constitutes the vigorous frontier mind, the true pioneering organization. Monroe P. Jones would be a great man to all posterity, if only he had a poet to sing of his valour.

It may be imagined how large in proportion to its inhabitants will be a town which spreads itself in this way. There are great houses left untenanted, and great gaps left unfilled. But if the place be successful,—if it promises success, it will be seen at once that there is life all through it. Omnibuses, or street cars working on rails run hither and thither. The shops that have been opened are well filled. The great hotels are thronged. The quays are crowded with vessels, and a general feeling of progress pervades the place. It is easy to perceive whether or no an American town is going ahead. The days of my visit to Milwaukee were days of civil war and national trouble, but in spite of civil war and national trouble Milwaukee looked healthy.

I have said that there was but little poverty,—little to be seen of real want in these thriving towns, but that they who laboured in them had

nevertheless their own hardships. This is so. I would not have any man
believe that he can take himself to the western States of America,—to
those States of which I am now speaking,—Michigan, Wisconsin,
Minnesota, Iowa, or Illinois, and there by industry escape the ills to
which flesh is heir. The labouring Irish in these towns eat meat seven
days a week, but I have met many a labouring Irishman among them
who has wished himself back in his old cabin. Industry is a good thing,
and there is no bread so sweet as that which is eaten in the sweat of a
man's brow; but labour carried to excess wearies the mind as well as
body, and the sweat that is ever running makes the bread bitter. There
is, I think, no task-master over free labour so exacting as an American.
He knows nothing of hours, and seems to have that idea of a man
which a lady always has of a horse. He thinks that he will go for ever. I
wish those masons in London who strike for nine hours' work with ten
hours' pay could be driven to the labour market of western America
for a spell. And moreover, which astonished me, I have seen men
driven and hurried,—as it were forced forward at their work, in a
manner which to an English workman would be intolerable. This surprised me much, as it was at variance with our,—or perhaps I should
say with my,—preconceived ideas as to American freedom. I had
fancied that an American citizen would not submit to be driven;—that
the spirit of the country if not the spirit of the individual would have
made it impossible. I thought that the shoe would have pinched quite
on the other foot. But I found that such driving did exist; and American masters in the West with whom I had an opportunity of discussing the subject all admitted it. "Those men 'll never half move unless
they're driven," a foreman said to me once as we stood together over
some twenty men who were at their work. "They kinder look for it, and
don't well know how to get along when they miss it." It was not his
business at this moment to drive;—nor was he driving. He was standing at some little distance from the scene with me, and speculating on
the sight before him. I thought the men were working at their best; but
their movements did not satisfy his practised eye, and he saw at a
glance that there was no one immediately over them.

But there is worse even than this. Wages in these regions are what
we should call high. An agricultural labourer will earn perhaps fifteen
dollars a month and his board; and a town labourer will earn a dollar a
day. A dollar may be taken as representing four shillings, though it is
in fact more. Food in these parts is much cheaper than in England, and
therefore the wages must be considered as very good. In making,
however, a just calculation it must be borne in mind that clothing is

dearer than in England and that much more of it is necessary. The wages nevertheless are high, and will enable the labourer to save money,—if only he can get them paid. The complaint that wages are held back and not even ultimately paid is very common. There is no fixed rule for satisfying all such claims once a week; and thus debts to labourers are contracted and when contracted are ignored. With us there is a feeling that it is pitiful, mean almost beyond expression, to wrong a labourer of his hire. We have men who go in debt to tradesmen perhaps without a thought of paying them;—but when we speak of such a one who has descended into the lowest mire of insolvency, we say that he has not paid his washerwoman. Out there in the West the washerwoman is as fair game as the tailor, the domestic servant as the wine merchant. If a male be honest he will not willingly take either goods or labour without payment; and it may be hard to prove that he who takes the latter is more dishonest than he who takes the former; but with us there is a prejudice in favour of one's washerwoman by which the western mind is not weakened. "They certainly have to be smart to get it," a gentleman said to me whom I taxed on the subject. "You see on the frontier a man is bound to be smart. If he ain't smart he'd better go back East;—perhaps as far as Europe. He'll do there." I had got my answer, and my friend had turned the question. But the fact was admitted by him as it had been by many others.

Why this should be so, is a question, to answer which thoroughly would require a volume in itself. As to the driving, why should men submit to it, seeing that labour is abundant, and that in all newly settled countries the labourer is the true hero of the age? In answer to this is to be alleged the fact that hired labour is chiefly done by fresh comers, by Irish and Germans, who have not as yet among them any combination sufficient to protect them from such usage. The men over them are new as masters,—masters who are rough themselves, who themselves have been roughly driven, and who have not learned to be gracious to those below them. It is a part of their contract that very hard work shall be exacted; and the driving resolves itself into this,—that the master looking after his own interest is constantly accusing his labourer of a breach of his part of the contract. The men no doubt do become used to it, and slacken probably in their endeavours when the tongue of the master or foreman is not heard. But as to that matter of non-payment of wages, the men must live; and here as elsewhere the master who omits to pay once, will hardly find labourers in future. The matter would remedy itself elsewhere, and does it not do so here? This

of course is so, and it is not to be understood that labour as a rule is
defrauded of its hire. But the relation of the master and the man admits
of such fraud here much more frequently than in England. In England
the labourer who did not get his wages on the Saturday could not go on
for the next week. To him under such circumstances the world would
be coming to an end. But in the western States, the labourer does not
live so completely from hand to mouth. He is rarely paid by the week,
is accustomed to give some credit, and till hard pressed by bad
circumstances generally has something by him. They do save money,
and are thus fattened up to a state which admits of victimization. I
cannot owe money to the little village cobbler who mends my shoes,
because he demands and receives his payment when his job is done.
But to my friend in Regent Street I extend my custom on a different
system; and when I make my start for continental life, I have with him
a matter of unsettled business to a considerable extent. The American
labourer is in the condition of the Regent Street boot-maker;—
excepting in this respect, that he gives his credit under compulsion.
"But does not the law set him right? Is there no law against debtors?"
The laws against debtors are plain enough as they are written down,
but seem to be anything but plain when called into action. They are
perfectly understood, and operations are carried on with the express
purpose of evading them. If you proceed against a man, you find that
his property is in the hands of some one else. You work in fact for Jones
who lives in the next street to you; but when you quarrel with Jones
about your wages, you find that according to law you have been
working for Smith in another State. In all countries such dodges are
probably practicable. But men will or will not have recourse to such
dodges according to the light in which they are regarded by the
community. In the Western States such dodges do not appear to
be regarded as disgraceful. "It behoves a frontier man to be smart,
sir."

Honesty is the best policy. That is a doctrine which has been widely
preached, and which has recommended itself to many minds as being
one of absolute truth. It is not very ennobling in its sentiment, seeing
that it advocates a special virtue, not on the ground that that virtue is in
itself a thing beautiful, but on account of the immediate reward which
will be its consequence. Smith is enjoined not to cheat Jones, because
he will, in the long run, make more money by dealing with Jones on the
square. This is not teaching of the highest order; but it is teaching well
adapted to human circumstances, and has obtained for itself a wide
credit. One is driven, however, to doubt whether even this teaching is

not too high for the frontier man. Is it possible that a frontier man should be scrupulous and at the same time successful? Hitherto those who have allowed scruples to stand in their way have not succeeded; and they who have succeeded and made for themselves great names,—who have been the pioneers of civilization,—have not allowed ideas of exact honesty to stand in their way. From General Jason down to General Fremont there have been men of great aspirations but of slight scruples. They have been ambitious of power and desirous of progress, but somewhat regardless how power and progress shall be attained. Clive and Warren Hastings were great frontier men, but we cannot imagine that they had ever realized the doctrine that honesty is the best policy. Cortez, and even Columbus, the prince of frontier men, are in the same category. The names of such heroes is legion. But with none of them has absolute honesty been a favourite virtue. "It behoves a frontier man to be smart, sir." Such, in that or other language, has been the prevailing idea. Such is the prevailing idea. And one feels driven to ask oneself whether such must not be the prevailing idea with those who leave the world and its rules behind them, and go forth with the resolve that the world and its rules shall follow them.

Of filibustering, annexation, and polishing savages off the face of creation there has been a great deal, and who can deny that humanity has been the gainer? It seems to those who look widely back over history, that all such works have been carried on in obedience to God's laws. When Jacob by Rebecca's aid cheated his elder brother he was very smart; but we cannot but suppose that a better race was by this smartness put in possession of the patriarchal sceptre. Esau was polished off, and readers of Scripture wonder why heaven with its thunder did not open over the heads of Rebecca and her son. But Jacob with all his fraud was the chosen one. Perhaps the day may come when scrupulous honesty may be the best policy even on the frontier. I can only say that hitherto that day seems to be as distant as ever. I do not pretend to solve the problem, but simply record my opinion that under circumstances as they still exist I should not willingly select a frontier life for my children.

I have said that all great frontier men have been unscrupulous. There is, however, an exception in history which may perhaps serve to prove the rule. The Puritans who colonized New England were frontier men, and were, I think, in general scrupulously honest. They had their faults. They were stern, austere men, tyrannical at the backbone when power came in their way,—as are all pioneers;—hard upon vices for which they who made the laws had themselves no minds; but they were not dishonest.

At Milwaukee I went up to see the Wisconsin volunteers, who were then encamped on open ground in the close vicinity of the town. Of Wisconsin I had heard before,—and have heard the same opinion repeated since,—that it was more backward in its volunteering than its neighbour States in the West. Wisconsin has 760,000 inhabitants, and its tenth thousand of volunteers was not then made up; whereas Indiana with less than double its number had already sent out thirty-six thousand. Iowa, with a hundred thousand less of inhabitants, had then made up fifteen thousand. But nevertheless to me it seemed that Wisconsin was quite alive to its presumed duty in that respect. Wisconsin with its three quarters of a million of people is as large as England. Every acre of it may be made productive, but as yet it is not half cleared. Of such a country its young men are its heart's blood. Ten thousand men fit to bear arms carried away from such a land to the horrors of civil war is a sight as full of sadness as any on which the eye can rest. Ah me, when will they return, and with what altered hopes! It is, I fear, easier to turn the sickle into the sword, than to recast the sword back again into the sickle!

We found a completed regiment at Wisconsin consisting entirely of Germans. A thousand Germans had been collected in that State and brought together in one regiment, and I was informed by an officer on the ground that there are many Germans in sundry other of the Wisconsin regiments. It may be well to mention here that the number of Germans through all these western States is very great. Their number and well-being were to me astonishing. That they form a great portion of the population of New York, making the German quarter of that city the third largest German town in the world, I have long known; but I had no previous idea of their expansion westward. In Detroit nearly every third shop bore a German name, and the same remark was to be made at Milwaukee;—and on all hands I heard praises of their morals, of their thrift, and of their new patriotism. I was continually told how far they exceeded the Irish settlers. To me in all parts of the world an Irishman is dear. When handled tenderly he becomes a creature most loveable. But with all my judgment in the Irishman's favour, and with my prejudices leaning the same way, I feel myself bound to state what I heard and what I saw as to the Germans.

But this regiment of Germans, and another not completed regiment, called from the State generally, were as yet without arms, accoutrements, or clothing. There was the raw material of the regiment, but there was nothing else. Winter was coming on,—winter in which the mercury is commonly 20 degrees below zero,—and the men were in tents with no provision against the cold. These tents held each two men, and were just large enough for two to lie. The canvas of which they were made seemed to me to be thin, but was I think always double. At this camp there was a house in which the men took their meals, but I visited other camps in which there was no such accommodation. I saw the German regiment called to its supper by tuck of drum, and the men marched in gallantly, armed each with a knife and spoon. I managed to make my way in at the door after them, and can testify to the excellence of the provisions of which their supper consisted. A poor diet never enters into any combination of circumstances contemplated by an American. Let him be where he will, animal food is, with him, the first necessary of life, and he is always provided accordingly. As to those Wisconsin men whom I saw, it was probable that they might be marched off, down south to Washington, or to the doubtful glories of the western campaign under Fremont before the winter commenced. The same might have been said of any special regiment. But taking the whole mass of men who were collected under canvas at the end of the autumn of 1861, and who were so collected without arms or military clothing, and without protection from the weather, it did seem that the task taken in hand by the commissariat of the northern army was one not devoid of difficulty.

The view from Milwaukee over Lake Michigan is very pleasing. One looks upon a vast expanse of water to which the eye finds no bounds, and therefore there are none of the common attributes of lake beauty; but the colour of the lake is bright, and within a walk of the city the traveller comes to the bluffs or low round-topped hills from which he can look down upon the shores. These bluffs form the beauty of Wisconsin and Minnesota, and relieve the eye after the flat level of Michigan. Round Detroit there is no rising ground, and therefore, perhaps, it is that Detroit is uninteresting.

I have said that those who are called on to labour in these States have their own hardships, and I have endeavoured to explain what are the sufferings to which the town labourer is subject. To escape from this is the labourer's great ambition, and his mode of doing so consists almost universally in the purchase of land. He saves up money in order that he may buy a section of an allotment, and thus become his own master. All his savings are made with a view to his independence. Seated on his own land he will have to work probably harder than ever, but he will work for himself. No taskmaster can then stand over him and wound his pride with harsh words. He will be his own master; will eat the food which he himself has grown, and live in the cabin which his own hands have built. This is the object of his life; and to secure this position he is content to work late and early and to undergo the indignities of previous servitude. The Government price for land is about five shillings an acre—one dollar and a quarter—and the settler may get it for this price if he be contented to take it not only untouched as regards clearing, but also far removed from any completed road. The traffic in these lands has been the great speculating business of western men. Five or six years ago, when the rage for such purchases was at its height, land was becoming a scarce article in the market! Individuals or companies bought it up with the object of reselling it at a profit; and many no doubt did make money. Railway companies were, in fact, companies combined for the purchase of land. They purchased land, looking to increase the value of it five-fold by the opening of a railroad. It may easily be understood that a railway, which could not be in itself remunerative, might in this way become a lucrative speculation. No settler could dare to place himself absolutely at a distance from any thoroughfare. At first the margins of nature's highways, the navigable rivers and lakes, were cleared. But as the railway system grew and expanded itself, it became manifest that lands might be rendered quickly available which were not so circumstanced by nature. A company which had purchased an enormous territory from the United States Government at five shillings an acre might well repay itself all the cost of a railway through that territory, even though the receipts of the railway should do no more than maintain the current expenses. It is in this way that the thousands of miles of American railroads have been opened; and here again must be seen the immense advantages which the States as a new country have enjoyed. With us the purchase of valuable land for railways, together with the legal expenses which those compulsory purchases entailed, have been so great that with all our traffic railways are not remunerative. But in the States the railways have created the value of the land. The States have been able to begin at the right end, and to arrange that the districts which are benefited shall themselves pay for the benefit they receive.

The Government price of land is 125 cents, or about five shillings an acre; and even this need not be paid at once if the settler purchase directly from the Government. He must begin by making certain improvements on the selected land,—clearing and cultivating some small portion, building a hut, and probably sinking a well. When this has been done,—when he has thus given a pledge of his intentions by depositing on the land the value of a certain amount of labour, he cannot be removed. He cannot be removed for a term of years, and then if he pays the price of the land it becomes his own with an indefeasible title. Many such settlements are made on the purchase of warrants for land. Soldiers returning from the Mexican wars were donated with warrants for land,—the amount being 160 acres, or the quarter of a section. The localities of such lands were not specified, but the privilege granted was that of occupying any quarter-section not hitherto tenanted. It will of course be understood that lands favourably situated would be tenanted. Those contiguous to railways were of course so occupied, seeing that the lines were not made till the lands were in the hands of the companies. It may therefore be understood of what nature would be the traffic in these warrants. The owner of a single warrant might find it of no value to him. To go back utterly into the woods, away from river or road, and there to commence with 160 acres of forest, or even of prairie, would be a hopeless task even to an American settler. Some mode of transport for his produce must be found before his produce would be of value,—before indeed he could find the means of living. But a company buying up a large aggregate of such warrants would possess the means of making such allotments valuable and of reselling them at greatly increased prices.

The primary settler, therefore,—who, however, will not usually have been the primary owner,—goes to work upon his land amidst all the wildness of nature. He levels and burns the first trees, and raises his first crop of corn amidst stumps still standing four or five feet above the soil; but he does not do so till some mode of conveyance has been found for him. So much I have said hoping to explain the mode in which the frontier speculator paves the way for the frontier agriculturist. But the permanent farmer very generally comes on the land as the third owner. The first settler is a rough fellow, and seems to be so wedded to his rough life that he leaves his land after his first wild work is done, and goes again further off to some untouched allotment. He finds that he can sell his improvements at a profitable rate and takes the price. He is a preparer of farms rather than a farmer. He has no love for the soil which his hand has first turned. He regards it merely as an investment; and when things about him are beginning to wear an aspect of comfort,—when his property has become valuable, he sells it, packs up his wife and little ones, and goes again into the woods. The western American has no love for his own soil, or his own house. The matter with him is simply one of dollars. To keep a farm which he could sell at an advantage from any feeling of affection,—from what we should call an association of ideas,—would be to him as ridiculous as the keeping of a family pig would be in an English farmer's establishment. The pig is a part of the farmer's stock in trade, and must go the way of all pigs. And so is it with house and land in the life of the frontier man in the western States.

But yet this man has his romance, his high poetic feeling, and above all his manly dignity. Visit him, and you will find him without coat or waistcoat, unshorn, in ragged blue trousers and old flannel shirt, too often bearing on his lantern jaws the signs of ague and sickness; but he will stand upright before you and speak to you with all the ease of a lettered gentleman in his own library. All the odious incivility of the republican servant has been banished. He is his own master, standing on his own threshold, and finds no need to assert his equality by rudeness. He is delighted to see you, and bids you sit down on his battered bench without dreaming of any such apology as an English cottier offers to a Lady Bountiful when she calls. He has worked out his independence, and shows it in every easy movement of his body. He tells you of it unconsciously in every tone of his voice. You will always find in his cabin some newspaper, some book, some token of advance in education. When he questions you about the old country he astonishes you by the extent of his knowledge. I defy you not to feel that he is superior to the race from whence he has sprung in England or in Ireland. To me I confess that the manliness of such a man is very charming. He is dirty and perhaps squalid. His children are sick and he is without comforts. His wife is pale, and you think you see shortness of life written in the faces of all the family. But over and above it all there is an independence which sits gracefully on their shoulders, and teaches you at the first glance that the man has a right to assume himself to be your equal. It is for this position that the labourer works, bearing hard words and the indignity of tyranny,—suffering also too often the dishonest ill-usage which his superior power enables the master to inflict.

"I have lived very rough," I heard a poor woman say, whose husband had ill-used and deserted her. "I have known what it is to be hungry and cold, and to work hard till my bones have ached. I only wish that I might have the same chance again. If I could have ten acres cleared two miles away from any living being, I could be happy with my children. I find a kind of comfort when I am at work from daybreak to sundown, and know that it is all my own." I believe that life in the backwoods has an allurement to those who have been used to it, that dwellers in cities can hardly comprehend.

From Milwaukee we went across Wisconsin and reached the Mississippi at La Crosse. From hence, according to agreement, we were to start by steamer at once up the river. But we were delayed again, as had happened to us before on Lake Michigan at Grand Haven.

X

The Upper Mississippi

IT had been promised to us that we should start from La Crosse by
the river steamer immediately on our arrival there; but on reaching
La Crosse we found that the vessel destined to take us up the river had
not yet come down. She was bringing a regiment from Minnesota, and
under such circumstances some pardon might be extended to
irregularities. This plea was made by one of the boat clerks in a very
humble tone, and was fully accepted by us. The wonder was that at
such a period all means of public conveyance were not put absolutely
out of gear. One might surmise that when regiments were constantly
being moved for the purposes of civil war, when the whole North had
but the one object of collecting together a sufficient number of men to
crush the South, ordinary travelling for ordinary purposes would be
difficult, slow, and subject to sudden stoppages. Such, however, was
not the case either in the northern or western States. The trains ran
much as usual, and those connected with the boats and railways were
just as anxious as ever to secure passengers. The boat clerk at La
Crosse apologized amply for the delay, and we sat ourselves down with
patience to await the arrival of the second Minnesota regiment on its
way to Washington.

During the four hours that we were kept waiting we were harboured
on board a small steamer, and at about eleven the terribly harsh
whistle that is made by the Mississippi boats informed us that the
regiment was arriving. It came up to the quay in two steamers, 750

being brought in that which was to take us back, and 250 in a smaller one. The moon was very bright, and great flaming torches were lit on the vessel's side, so that all the operations of the men were visible. The two steamers had run close up, thrusting us away from the quay in their passage, but doing it so gently that we did not even feel the motion. These large boats—and their size may be understood from the fact that one of them had just brought down 750 men,—are moved so easily and so gently that they come gliding in among each other without hesitation and without pause. On English waters we do not willingly run ships against each other; and when we do so unwillingly, they bump and crush and crash upon each other, and timbers fly while men are swearing. But here there was neither crashing nor swearing, and the boats noiselessly pressed against each other as though they were cased in muslin and crinoline.

I got out upon the quay and stood close by the plank, watching each man as he left the vessel and walked across towards the railway. Those whom I had previously seen in tents were not equipped, but these men were in uniform and each bore his musket. Taking them all together they were as fine a set of men as I ever saw collected. No man could doubt on seeing them that they bore on their countenances the signs of higher breeding and better education than would be seen in a thousand men enlisted in England. I do not mean to argue from this that Americans are better than English. I do not mean to argue here that they are even better educated. My assertion goes to show that the men generally were taken from a higher level in the community than that which fills our own ranks. It was a matter of regret to me, here and on many subsequent occasions, to see men bound for three years to serve as common soldiers, who were so manifestly fitted for a better and more useful life. To me it is always a source of sorrow to see a man enlisted. I feel that the individual recruit is doing badly with himself— carrying himself and the strength and intelligence which belongs to him to a bad market. I know that there must be soldiers; but as to every separate soldier I regret that he should be one of them. And the higher is the class from which such soldiers are drawn, the greater the intelligence of the men so to be employed, the deeper with me is that feeling of regret. But this strikes one much less in an old country than in a country that is new. In the old countries population is thick, and food sometimes scarce. Men can be spared, and any employment may be serviceable, even though that employment be in itself so unproductive as that of fighting battles or preparing for them. But in the western States of America every arm that can guide a plough is of incalculable value. Minnesota was admitted as a State about three years before this time, and its whole population is not much above 150,000. Of this number perhaps 40,000 may be working men. And now this infant State with its huge territory and scanty population is called upon to send its heart's blood out to the war.

And it has sent its heart's best blood. Forth they came—fine, stalwart, well-grown fellows, looking to my eye as though they had as yet but faintly recognized the necessary severity of military discipline. To them hitherto the war had seemed to be an arena on which each might do something for his country, which that country would recognize. To themselves as yet—and to me also—they were a band of heroes, to be reduced by the compressing power of military discipline to the lower level, but more necessary position of a regiment of soldiers. Ah me! how terrible to them has been the breaking up of that delusion! When a poor yokel in England is enlisted with a shilling and a promise of unlimited beer and glory, one pities and if possible would save him. But with him the mode of life to which he goes may not be so much inferior to that he leaves. It may be that for him soldiering is the best trade possible in his circumstances. It may keep him from the hen-roosts, and perhaps from his neighbours' pantries; and discipline may be good for him. Population is thick with us, and there are many whom it may be well to collect and make available under the strictest surveillance. But of these men whom I saw entering on their career upon the banks of the Mississippi, many were fathers of families, many were owners of lands, many were educated men capable of high aspirations,—all were serviceable members of their State. There were probably there not three or four of whom it would be well that the State should be rid. As soldiers fit, or capable of being made fit for the duties they had undertaken, I could find but one fault with them. Their average age was too high. There were men among them with grizzled beards, and many who had counted thirty, thirty-five, and forty years. They had, I believe, devoted themselves with a true spirit of patriotism. No doubt each had some ulterior hope as to himself,—as has every mortal patriot. Regulus when he returned hopeless to Carthage, trusted that some Horace would tell his story. Each of these men from Minnesota looked probably forward to his reward; but the reward desired was of a high class.

The first great misery to be endured by these regiments will be the military lesson of obedience which they must learn before they can be of any service. It always seemed to me when I came near them that they had not as yet recognized the necessary austerity of an officer's duty. Their idea of a captain was the stage idea of a leader of dramatic banditti, a man to be followed and obeyed as a leader, but to be obeyed with that free and easy obedience which is accorded to the reigning chief of the forty thieves. "Wa'll Captain," I have heard a private say to his officer, as he sat on one seat in a railway-car with his feet upon the back of another. And the captain has looked as though he did not like it. The captain did not like it, but the poor private was being fast carried to that destiny which he would like still less. From the first I have had faith in the northern army; but from the first I have felt that the suffering to be endured by these free and independent volunteers would be very great. A man to be available as a private soldier must be compressed and belted in till he be a machine.

As soon as the men had left the vessel we walked over the side of it and took possession. "I am afraid your cabin won't be ready for a quarter of an hour," said the clerk. "Such a body of men as that will leave some dirt after them." I assured him of course that our expectations under such circumstances were very limited, and that I was fully aware that the boat and the boat's company were taken up with matters of greater moment than the carriage of ordinary passengers. But to this he demurred altogether. "The regiments were very little to them, but occasioned much trouble. Everything, however, should be square in fifteen minutes." At the expiration of the time named the key of our state-room was given to us, and we found the appurtenances as clean as though no soldier had ever put his foot upon the vessel.

From La Crosse to St. Paul, the distance up the river is something over 200 miles, and from St. Paul down to Dubuque, in Iowa, to which we went on our return, the distance is 450 miles. We were therefore for a considerable time on board these boats; more so than such a journey may generally make necessary, as we were delayed at first by the soldiers, and afterwards by accidents, such as the breaking of a paddle-wheel, and other causes to which navigation on the Upper Mississippi seems to be liable. On the whole we slept on board four nights, and lived on board as many days. I cannot say that the life was comfortable, though I do not know that it could be made more so by any care on the part of the boat-owners. My first complaint would be against the great heat of the cabins. The Americans as a rule live in an atmosphere which is almost unbearable by an Englishman. To this cause, I am convinced, is to be attributed their thin faces, their pale skins, their unenergetic temperament—unenergetic as regards physical motion,—and their early old age. The winters are long and cold in America, and mechanical ingenuity is far extended. These two facts together have created a system of stoves, hot-air pipes, steam chambers, and heating apparatus, so extensive that from autumn till the end of spring all inhabited rooms are filled with the atmosphere of a hot oven. An Englishman fancies that he is to be baked, and for a while finds it almost impossible to exist in the air prepared for him. How the heat is engendered on board the river steamers I do not know, but it is engendered to so great a degree that the sitting-cabins are unendurable. The patient is therefore driven out at all hours into the outside balconies of the boat, or on to the top roof,—for it is a roof rather than a deck,—and there as he passes through the air at the rate of twenty miles an hour, finds himself chilled to the very bones. That is my first complaint. But as the boats are made for Americans, and as Americans like hot air, I do not put it forward with any idea that a change ought to be effected. My second complaint is equally unreasonable, and is quite as incapable of a remedy as the first. Nine-tenths of the travellers carry children with them. They are not tourists engaged on pleasure excursions, but men and women intent on the business of life. They are moving up and down, looking for fortune, and in search of new homes. Of course they carry with them all their household gods. Do not let any critic say that I grudge these young travellers their right to locomotion. Neither their right to locomotion is grudged by me, nor any of those privileges which are accorded in America to the rising generation. The habits of their country and the choice of their parents give to them full dominion over all hours and over all places, and it would ill become a foreigner to make such habits and such choice a ground of serious complaint. But nevertheless the uncontrolled energies of twenty children round one's legs do not convey comfort or happiness, when the passing events are producing noise and storm rather than peace and sunshine. I must protest that American babies are an unhappy race. They eat and drink just as they please; they are never punished; they are never banished, snubbed, and kept in the background as children are kept with us; and yet they are wretched and uncomfortable. My heart has bled for them as I have heard them squalling by the hour together in agonies of discontent and dyspepsia. Can it be, I wonder, that children are happier when they are made to obey orders and are sent to bed at six o'clock, than when allowed to regulate their own conduct; that bread and milk is more favourable to laughter and soft childish ways than beef-steaks and pickles three times a day; that an occasional whipping, even, will conduce to rosy cheeks? It is an idea which I should never dare to broach to an American mother; but I must confess that after my travels on the western continent my opinions have a tendency in that direction. Beef-steaks and pickles certainly produce smart little men and women. Let that be taken for granted. But rosy laughter and winning childish ways are, I fancy, the produce of bread and milk. But there was a third reason why travelling on these boats was not as pleasant as I had expected. I could not get my fellow-travellers to talk to me. It must be understood that our fellow-travellers were not generally of that class which we Englishmen, in our pride, designate as gentlemen and ladies. They were people, as I have said, in search of new homes and new fortunes. But I protest that as such they would have been in those parts much more agreeable as companions to me than any gentlemen or any ladies, if only they would have talked to me. I do not accuse them of any incivility. If addressed, they answered me. If application was made by me for any special information, trouble was taken to give it me. But I found no aptitude, no wish for conversation; nay, even a disinclination to converse. In the western States I do not think that I was ever addressed first by an American sitting next to me at table. Indeed I never held any conversation at a public table in the West. I have sat in the same room with men for hours, and have not had a word spoken to me. I have done my very best to break through this ice, and have always failed. A western American man is not a talking man. He will sit for hours over a stove with his cigar in his mouth, and his hat over his eyes, chewing the cud of reflection. A dozen will sit together in the same way, and there shall not be a dozen words spoken between them in an hour. With the women one's chance of conversation is still worse. It seemed as though the cares of the world had been too much for them, and that all talking excepting as to business,—demands for instance on the servants for pickles for their children,—had gone by the board. They were generally hard, dry, and melancholy. I am speaking of course of aged females,—from five and twenty perhaps to thirty, who had long since given up the amusements and levities of life. I very soon abandoned any attempt at drawing a word from these ancient mothers of families; but not the less did I ponder in my mind over the circumstances of their lives. Had things gone with them so sadly, was the struggle for independence so hard, that all the softness of existence had been trodden out of them? In the cities too it was much the same. It seemed to me that a future mother of a family in those parts had left all laughter behind her when she put out her finger for the wedding ring.

For these reasons I must say that life on board these steam-boats was not as pleasant as I had hoped to find it, but for our discomfort in this respect we found great atonement in the scenery through which we passed. I protest that of all the river scenery that I know, that of the Upper Mississippi is by far the finest and the most continued. One thinks of course of the Rhine; but, according to my idea of beauty, the Rhine is nothing to the Upper Mississippi. For miles upon miles, for hundreds of miles, the course of the river runs through low hills, which are there called bluffs. These bluffs rise in every imaginable form, looking sometimes like large straggling unwieldy castles, and then throwing themselves into sloping lawns which stretch back away from the river till the eye is lost in their twists and turnings. Landscape beauty, as I take it, consists mainly in four attributes: in water, in broken land, in scattered timber,—timber scattered as opposed to continuous forest timber,—and in the accident of colour. In all these particulars the banks of the Upper Mississippi can hardly be beaten. There are no high mountains; but high mountains themselves are grand rather than beautiful. There are no high mountains, but there is a succession of hills which group themselves for ever without monotony. It is perhaps the ever-variegated forms of these bluffs which chiefly constitute the wonderful loveliness of this river. The idea constantly occurs that some point on every hillside would form the most charming site ever yet chosen for a noble residence. I have passed up and down rivers clothed to the edge with continuous forest. This at first is grand enough, but the eye and feeling soon become weary. Here the trees are scattered so that the eye passes through them, and ever and again a long lawn sweeps back into the country, and up the steep side of a hill, making the traveller long to stay there and linger through the oaks, and climb the bluffs, and lie about on the bold but easy summits. The boat, however, steams quickly up against the current, and the happy valleys are left behind, one quickly after another. The river is very various in its breadth, and is constantly divided by islands. It is never so broad that the beauty of the banks is lost in the distance or injured by it. It is rapid, but has not the beautifully bright colour of some European rivers,—of the Rhine for instance, and the Rhone. But what is wanting in the colour of the water is more than compensated by the wonderful hues and lustre of the shores. We visited the river in October, and I must presume that they who seek it solely for the sake of scenery should go there in that month. It was not only that the foliage of the trees was bright with every imaginable colour, but that the grass was bronzed, and that the rocks were golden.

And this beauty did not last only for a while and then cease. On the Rhine there are lovely spots and special morsels of scenery with which the traveller becomes duly enraptured. But on the Upper Mississippi there are no special morsels. The position of the sun in the heavens will, as it always does, make much difference in the degree of beauty. The hour before and the half-hour after sunset are always the loveliest for such scenes. But of the shores themselves one may declare that they are lovely throughout those 400 miles which run immediately south from St. Paul.

About half-way between La Crosse and St. Paul we came upon Lake Pepin, and continued our course up the lake for perhaps fifty or sixty miles. This expanse of water is narrow for a lake, and by those who know the lower courses of great rivers, would hardly be dignified by that name. But, nevertheless, the breadth here lessens the beauty. There are the same bluffs, the same scattered woodlands, and the same colours. But they are either at a distance, or else they are to be seen on one side only. The more that I see of the beauty of scenery, and the more I consider its elements, the stronger becomes my conviction that size has but little to do with it, and rather detracts from it than adds to it. Distance gives one of its greatest charms, but it does so by concealing rather than displaying an expanse of surface. The beauty of distance arises from the romance,—the feeling of mystery which it creates. It is like the beauty of woman which allures the more the more that it is veiled. But open, uncovered land and water, mountains which simply rise to great heights with long unbroken slopes, wide expanses of lake, and forests which are monotonous in their continued thickness, are never lovely to me. A landscape should always be partly veiled, and display only half its charms.

To my taste the finest stretch of the river was that immediately above Lake Pepin; but then, at this point, we had all the glory of the setting sun. It was like fairy land, so bright were the golden hues, so fantastic were the shapes of the hills, so broken and twisted the course of the waters! But the noisy steamer went groaning up the narrow passages with almost unabated speed, and left the fairy land behind all too quickly. Then the bell would ring for tea, and the children with the beef-steaks, the pickled onions, and the light fixings would all come over again. The care-laden mothers would tuck the bibs under the chins of their tyrant children, and some embryo senator of four years old would listen with concentrated attention, while the negro servant recapitulated to him the delicacies of the supper-table, in order that he might make his choice with due consideration. "Beef-steak," the embryo four-year-old senator would lisp, "and stewed potato, and buttered toast, and corn cake, and coffee,—and—and—and—; mother, mind you get me the pickles."

St. Paul enjoys the double privilege of being the commercial and political capital of Minnesota. The same is the case with Boston in Massachusetts, but I do not remember another instance in which it is so. It is built on the eastern bank of the Mississippi, though the bulk of the State lies to the west of the river. It is noticeable as the spot up to which the river is navigable. Immediately above St. Paul there are narrow rapids up which no boat can pass. North of this, continuous navigation does not go; but from St. Paul down to New Orleans, and the Gulf of Mexico, it is uninterrupted. The distance to St. Louis in Missouri, a town built below the confluence of the three rivers, Mississippi, Missouri, and Illinois, is 900 miles; and then the navigable waters down to the gulf wash a southern country of still greater extent. No river on the face of the globe forms a highway for the produce of so wide an extent of agricultural land. The Mississippi with its tributaries carried to market, before the war, the produce of Wisconsin, Minnesota, Iowa, Illinois, Indiana, Ohio, Kentucky, Tennessee, Missouri, Kansas, Arkansas, Mississippi, and Louisiana. This country is larger than England, Ireland, Scotland, Holland, Belgium, France, Germany and Spain together, and is undoubtedly composed of much more fertile land. The States named comprise the great centre valley of the continent, and are the farming lands and garden grounds of the western world. He who has not seen corn on the ground in Illinois or Minnesota, does not know to what extent the fertility of land may go, or how great may be the weight of cereal crops. And for all this the Mississippi was the high road to market. When the crop of 1861 was garnered this high road was stopped by the war. What suffering this entailed on the South, I will not here stop to say, but on the West the effect was terrible. Corn was in such plenty, Indian corn that is or maize, that it was not worth the farmer's while to prepare it for market. When I was in Illinois the second quality of Indian corn when shelled was not worth more than from eight to ten cents a bushel. But the shelling and preparation are laborious, and in some instances it was found better to burn it for fuel than to sell it. Respecting the export of corn from the West, I must say a further word or two in the next chapter; but it seemed to be indispensable that I should point out here how great to the United States is the need of the Mississippi. Nor is it for corn and wheat only that its waters are needed. Timber, lead, iron, coal, pork, all find, or should find, their exit to the world at large by this road. There are towns on it, and on its tributaries, already holding more than one hundred and fifty thousand inhabitants. The number of Cincinnati exceeds that, as also does the number of St. Louis. Under these circumstances it is not wonderful that the States should wish to keep in their own hands the navigation of this river.

It is not wonderful. But it will not, I think, be admitted by the politicians of the world, that the navigation of the Mississippi need be closed against the West, even though the southern States should succeed in raising themselves to the power and dignity of a separate nationality. If the waters of the Danube be not open to Austria, it is through the fault of Austria. That the subject will be one of trouble no man can doubt; and of course it would be well for the North to avoid that, or any other trouble. In the meantime the importance of this right of way must be admitted; and it must be admitted also that whatever may be the ultimate resolve of the North, it will be very difficult to reconcile the West to a divided dominion of the Mississippi.

St. Paul contains about fourteen thousand inhabitants, and, like all other American towns, is spread over a surface of ground adapted to the accommodation of a very extended population. As it is belted on one side by the river, and on the other by the bluffs which accompany the course of the river, the site is pretty, and almost romantic. Here also we found a great hotel,—a huge square building, such as we in England might perhaps place near to a railway terminus, in such a city as Glasgow or Manchester; but on which no living Englishman would expend his money in a town even five times as big again as St. Paul. Everything was sufficiently good, and much more than sufficiently plentiful. The whole thing went on exactly as hotels do down in Massachusetts, or the State of New York. Look at the map, and see where St. Paul is. Its distance from all known civilization,—all civilization that has succeeded in obtaining acquaintance with the world at large, is very great. Even American travellers do not go up there in great numbers, excepting those who intend to settle there. A stray sportsman or two, American or English, as the case may be, makes his way into Minnesota for the sake of shooting, and pushes on up through St. Paul to the Red River. Some few adventurous spirits visit the Indian settlements, and pass over into the unsettled regions of Dacotah and Washington territory. But there is no throng of travelling. Nevertheless, an hotel has been built there capable of holding three hundred guests, and other hotels exist in the neighbourhood, one of which is even larger than that at St. Paul. Who can come to them, and create even a hope that such an enterprise may be remunerative? In America it is seldom more than hope, for one always hears that such enterprises fail.

When I was there the war was in hand, and it was hardly to be expected that any hotel should succeed. The landlord told me that he held it at the present time for a very low rent, and that he could just manage to keep it open without loss. The war which hindered people from travelling, and in that way injured the innkeepers, also hindered people from house-keeping, and reduced them to the necessity of boarding out,—by which the innkeepers were, of course, benefited. At St. Paul I found that the majority of the guests were inhabitants of the town, boarding at the hotel, and thus dispensing with the cares of a separate establishment. I do not know what was charged for such accommodation at St. Paul, but I have come across large houses at which a single man could get all that he required for a dollar a day. Now Americans are great consumers, especially at hotels, and all that a man requires includes three hot meals with a choice from about two dozen dishes at each.

From St. Paul there are two waterfalls to be seen, which we, of course, visited. We crossed the river at Fort Snelling, a rickety, ill-conditioned building, standing at the confluence of the Minnesota and Mississippi rivers, built there to repress the Indians. It is, I take it, very necessary, especially at the present moment, as the Indians seem to require repressing. They have learned that the attention of the federal government has been called to the war, and have become bold in consequence. When I was at St. Paul I heard of a party of Englishmen who had been robbed of everything they possessed, and was informed that the farmers in the distant parts of the State were by no means secure. The Indians are more to be pitied than the farmers. They are turning against enemies who will neither forgive nor forget any injuries done. When the war is over they will be improved, and polished, and annexed, till no Indian will hold an acre of land in Minnesota. At present Fort Snelling is the nucleus of a recruiting camp. On the point between the bluffs of the two rivers there is a plain, immediately in front of the fort, and there we saw the newly-joined Minnesota recruits going through their first military exercises. They were in detachments of twenties, and were rude enough at their goose step. The matter which struck me most in looking at them was the difference of condition which I observed in the men. There were the country lads, fresh from the farms, such as we see following the recruiting sergeant through English towns; but there were also men in

black coats and black trousers, with thin boots, and trimmed
beards,—beards which had been trimmed till very lately; and some of
them with beards which showed that they were no longer young. It
was inexpressibly melancholy to see such men as these twisting and
turning about at the corporal's word, each handling some stick in his
hand in lieu of weapon. Of course they were more awkward than the
boys, even though they were twice more assiduous in their efforts. Of
course they were sad, and wretched. I saw men there that were very
wretched,—all but heart-broken, if one might judge from their faces.
They should not have been there handling sticks, and moving their
unaccustomed legs in cramped paces. They were as razors, for which
no better purpose could be found than the cutting of blocks. When
such attempts are made the block is not cut, but the razor is spoilt.
Most unfit for the commencement of a soldier's life were some
that I saw there, but I do not doubt that they had been attracted to
the work by the one idea of doing something for their country in its
trouble.

From Fort Snelling we went on to the Falls of Minnehaha. Minnehaha, laughing water. Such I believe is the interpretation. The name in
this case is more imposing than the fall. It is a pretty little cascade, and
might do for a picnic in fine weather, but it is not a waterfall of which a
man can make much when found so far away from home. Going on
from Minnehaha we came to Minneapolis, at which place there is a
fine suspension bridge across the river, just above the falls of St.
Anthony and leading to the town of that name. Till I got there I could
hardly believe that in these days there should be a living village called
Minneapolis by living men. I presume I should describe it as a town,
for it has a municipality, and a post-office, and, of course, a large hotel.
The interest of the place however is in the saw-mills. On the opposite
side of the water, at St. Anthony, is another very large hotel,—and also
a smaller one. The smaller one may be about the size of the first-class
hotels at Cheltenham or Leamington. They were both closed, and
there seemed to be but little prospect that either would be opened till
the war should be over. The saw-mills, however, were at full work, and
to my eyes were extremely picturesque. I had been told that the beauty
of the falls had been destroyed by the mills. Indeed all who had spoken
to me about St. Anthony had said so. But I did not agree with them.
Here, as at Ottawa, the charm in fact consists, not in an uninterrupted
shoot of water, but in a succession of rapids over a bed of broken rocks.
Among these rocks logs of loose timber are caught, which have escaped
from their proper courses, and here they lie, heaped up in some places,

and constructing themselves into bridges in others, till the freshets of the spring carry them off. The timber is generally brought down in logs to St. Anthony, is sawn there, and then sent down the Mississippi in large rafts. These rafts on other rivers are I think generally made of unsawn timber. Such logs as have escaped in the manner above described are recognized on their passage down the river by their marks, and are made up separately, the original owners receiving the value,—or not receiving it as the case may be. "There is quite a trade going on with the loose lumber," my informant told me. And from his tone I was led to suppose that he regarded the trade as sufficiently lucrative if not peculiarly honest.

There is very much in the mode of life adopted by the settlers in these regions which creates admiration. The people are all intelligent. They are energetic and speculative, conceiving grand ideas, and carrying them out almost with the rapidity of magic. A suspension bridge half a mile long is erected, while in England we should be fastening together a few planks for a foot passage. Progress, mental as well as material, is the demand of the people generally. Everybody understands everything, and everybody intends sooner or later to do everything. All this is very grand;—but then there is a terrible draw-back. One hears on every side of intelligence, but one hears also on every side of dishonesty. Talk to whom you will, of whom you will, and you will hear some tale of successful or unsuccessful swindling. It seems to be the recognized rule of commerce in the Far West that men shall go into the world's markets prepared to cheat and to be cheated. It may be said that as long as this is acknowledged and understood on all sides, no harm will be done. It is equally fair for all. When I was a child there used to be certain games at which it was agreed in beginning either that there should be cheating or that there should not. It may be said that out there in the western States, men agree to play the cheating game; and that the cheating game has more of interest in it than the other. Unfortunately, however, they who agree to play this game on a large scale, do not keep outsiders altogether out of the playground. Indeed outsiders become very welcome to them;—and then it is not pleasant to hear the tone in which such outsiders speak of the peculiarities of the sport to which they have been introduced. When a beginner in trade finds himself furnished with a barrel of wooden nutmegs, the joke is not so good to him as to the experienced merchant who supplies him. This dealing in wooden nutmegs, this selling of things which do not exist, and buying of goods for which no price is ever to be given, is an institution which is much honoured in the West. We call it swindling;—and so do they. But it seemed to me that in the western States the word hardly seemed to leave the same impress on the mind that it does elsewhere.

On our return down the river we passed La Crosse, at which we had embarked, and went down as far as Dubuque in Iowa. On our way down we came to grief and broke one of our paddle-wheels to pieces. We had no special accident. We struck against nothing above or below water. But the wheel went to pieces, and we lay-to on the river side for the greater part of a day while the necessary repairs were being made. Delay in travelling is usually an annoyance, because it causes the unsettlement of a settled purpose. But the loss of the day did us no harm, and our accident had happened at a very pretty spot. I climbed up to the top of the nearest bluff, and walked back till I came to the open country, and also went up and down the river banks, visiting the cabins of two settlers who live there by supplying wood to the river steamers. One of these was close to the spot at which we were lying; and yet though most of our passengers came on shore, I was the only one who spoke to the inmates of the cabin. These people must live there almost in desolation from one year's end to another. Once in a fortnight or so they go up to a market town in their small boats, but beyond that they can have little intercourse with their fellow-creatures. Nevertheless none of these dwellers by the river side came out to speak to the men and women who were lounging about from eleven in the morning till four in the afternoon; nor did one of the passengers except myself knock at the door or enter the cabin, or exchange a word with those who lived there.

I spoke to the master of the house, whom I met outside, and he at once asked me to come in and sit down. I found his father there and his mother, his wife, his brother, and two young children. The wife, who was cooking, was a very pretty, pale, young woman, who, however, could have circulated round her stove more conveniently had her crinoline been of less dimensions. She bade me welcome very prettily, and went on with her cooking, talking the while, as though she were in the habit of entertaining guests in that way daily. The old woman sat in a corner knitting—as old women always do. The old man lounged with a grandchild on his knee, and the master of the house threw himself on the floor while the other child crawled over him. There was no stiffness or uneasiness in their manners, nor was there anything approaching to that republican roughness which so often operates upon a poor, well-intending Englishman like a slap on the cheek. I sat there for about an hour, and when I had discussed with them English politics and the bearing of English politics upon the American war, they told me of their own affairs. Food was very plenty, but life was very hard. Take the year through each man could not earn above half a dollar a day by cutting wood. This, however, they owned, did not take up all their time. Working on favourable wood on favourable days they could each earn two dollars a day; but these favourable circumstances did not come together very often. They did not deal with the boats themselves, and the profits were eaten up by the middleman. He, the middleman, had a good thing of it, because he could cheat the captains of the boats in the measurement of the wood. The chopper was obliged to supply a genuine cord of logs,—true measure. But the man who took it off in the barge to the steamer could so pack it that fifteen true cords would make twenty-two false cords. "It cuts up into a fine trade, you see, sir," said the young man, as he stroked back the little girl's hair from her forehead. "But the captains of course must find it out," said I. This he acknowledged, but argued that the captains on this account insisted on buying the wood so much cheaper, and that the loss all came upon the chopper. I tried to teach him that the remedy lay in his own hands, and the three men listened to me quite patiently while I explained to them how they should carry on their own trade. But the young father had the last word. "I guess we don't get above the fifty cents a day any way." He knew at least where the shoe pinched him. He was a handsome, manly, noble-looking fellow, tall and thin, with black hair and bright eyes. But he had the hollow look about his jaws, and so had his wife, and so had his brother. They all owned to fever and ague. They had a touch of it most years, and sometimes pretty sharply. "It was a coarse place to live in," the old woman said, "but there was no one to meddle with them, and she guessed that it suited." They had books and newspapers, tidy delf, and clean glass upon their shelves, and undoubtedly provisions in plenty. Whether fever and ague yearly, and cords of wood stretched from fifteen to twenty-two are more than a set-off for these good things, I will leave every one to decide according to his own taste.

   In another cabin I found women and children only, and one of the children was in the last stage of illness. But nevertheless the woman of the house seemed glad to see me, and talked cheerfully as long as I would remain. She inquired what had happened to the vessel, but it had never occurred to her to go out and see. Her cabin was neat and well furnished, and there also I saw newspapers and Harper's everlasting magazine. She said it was a coarse, desolate place for living, but that she could raise almost anything in her garden.

I could not then understand, nor can I now understand, why none of the numerous passengers out of the boat should have entered those cabins except myself; and why the inmates of the cabins should not have come out to speak to any one. Had they been surly, morose people, made silent by the specialties of their life, it would have been explicable; but they were delighted to talk and to listen. The fact, I take it, is, that the people are all harsh to each other. They do not care to go out of their way to speak to any one unless something is to be gained. They say that two Englishmen meeting in the desert would not speak unless they were introduced. The further I travel, the less true do I find this of Englishmen, and the more true of other people.

XI

Ceres Americana

WE stopped at the Julien House, Dubuque. Dubuque is a city in Iowa on the western shore of the Mississippi, and as the names both of the town and of the hotel sounded French in my ears, I asked for an explanation. I was then told that Julien Dubuque, a Canadian Frenchman, had been buried on one of the bluffs of the river within the precincts of the present town, that he had been the first white settler in Iowa, and had been the only man who had ever prevailed upon the Indians to work. Among them he had become a great "Medicine," and seems for a while to have had absolute power over them. He died I think in 1800, and was buried on one of the hills over the river: "He was a bold bad man," my informant told me, "and committed every sin under heaven. But he made the Indians work."

Lead mines are the glory of Dubuque, and very large sums of money have been made from them. I was taken out to see one of them, and to go down it; but we found, not altogether to my sorrow, that the works had been stopped on account of the water. No effort has been made in any of these mines to subdue the water, nor has steam been applied to the working of them. The lodes have been so rich with lead that the speculators have been content to take out the metal that was easily reached, and to go off in search of fresh ground when disturbed by water. "And are wages here paid pretty punctually?" I asked. "Well; a man has to be smart, you know." And then my friend went on to acknowledge that it would be better for the country if smartness were not so essential.

Iowa has a population of 674,000 souls, and in October 1861 had already mustered eighteen regiments of 1000 men each. Such a population would give probably 170,000 men capable of bearing arms, and therefore the number of soldiers sent had already amounted to more than a decimation of the available strength of the State. When we were at Dubuque nothing was talked of but the army. It seemed that mines, coal-pits, and corn-fields, were all of no account in comparison with the war. How many regiments could be squeezed out of the State, was the one question which filled all minds; and the general desire was that such regiments should be sent to the western army, to swell the triumph which was still expected for General Fremont, and to assist in sweeping slavery out into the Gulf of Mexico. The patriotism of the West has been quite as keen as that of the North, and has produced results as memorable; but it has sprung from a different source, and been conducted and animated by a different sentiment. National greatness and support of the law have been the ideas of the North; national greatness and abolition of slavery have been those of the West. How they are to agree as to terms when between them they have crushed the South,—that is the difficulty.

At Dubuque in Iowa, I ate the best apple that I ever encountered. I make that statement with the purpose of doing justice to the Americans on a matter which is to them one of considerable importance. Americans as a rule do not believe in English apples. They declare that there are none, and receive accounts of Devonshire cyder with manifest incredulity. "But at any rate there are no apples in England equal to ours." That is an assertion to which an Englishman is called upon to give an absolute assent; and I hereby give it. Apples so excellent as some which were given to us at Dubuque, I have never eaten in England. There is a great jealousy respecting all the fruits of the earth. "Your peaches are fine to look at," was said to me, "but they have no flavour." This was the assertion of a lady, and I made no answer. My idea had been that American peaches had no flavour; that French peaches had none; that those of Italy had none; that little as there might be of which England could boast with truth, she might at any rate boast of her peaches without fear of contradiction. Indeed my idea had been that good peaches were to be got in England only. I am beginning to doubt whether my belief on the matter has not been the product of insular ignorance, and idolatrous self-worship. It may be that a peach should be a combination of an apple and a turnip. "My

great objection to your country, sir," said another, "is that you have
got no vegetables." Had he told me that we had got no seaboard, or no
coals, he would not have surprised me more. No vegetables in England! I could not restrain myself altogether, and replied by a confes-
sion "that we 'raised' no squash." Squash is the pulp of the pumpkin,
and is much used in the States, both as a vegetable and for pies. No
vegetables in England! Did my surprise arise from the insular ignorance and idolatrous self-worship of a Britisher, or was my American
friend labouring under a delusion? Is Covent Garden well supplied
with vegetables, or is it not? Do we cultivate our kitchen gardens with
success, or am I under a delusion on that subject? Do I dream, or is it
true that out of my own little patches at home I have enough for all
domestic purposes of peas, beans, brocoli, cauliflower, celery, beet-
root, onions, carrots, parsnips, turnips, seakale, asparagus, french
beans, artichokes, vegetable marrow, cucumber, tomatoes, endive,
lettuce, as well as herbs of many kinds, cabbages, throughout the year,
and potatoes? No vegetables! Had the gentleman told me that England
did not suit him because we had nothing but vegetables, I should have
been less surprised.

From Dubuque, on the western shore of the river, we passed over to
Dunleath in Illinois, and went on from thence by railway to Dixon. I
was induced to visit this not very flourishing town by a desire to see the
rolling prairie of Illinois, and to learn by eyesight something of the
crops of corn or Indian maize which are produced upon the land. Had
that gentleman told me that we knew nothing of producing corn in
England he would have been nearer the mark; for of corn in the
profusion in which it is grown here we do not know much. Better land
than the prairies of Illinois for cereal crops the world's surface probably cannot show. And here there has been no necessity for the long
previous labour of banishing the forest. Enormous prairies stretch
across the State, into which the plough can be put at once. The earth is
rich with the vegetation of thousands of years, and the farmer's return
is given to him without delay. The land bursts with its own produce,
and the plenty is such that it creates wasteful carelessness in the
gathering of the crop. It is not worth a man's while to handle less than
large quantities. Up in Minnesota I had been grieved by the loose
manner in which wheat was treated. I have seen bags of it upset, and
left upon the ground. The labour of collecting it was more than it was
worth. There wheat is the chief crop, and as the lands become cleared
and cultivation spreads itself, the amount coming down the Missis-
ippi will be increased almost to infinity. The price of wheat in Europe

will soon depend, not upon the value of the wheat in the country which grows it, but on the power and cheapness of the modes which may exist for transporting it. I have not been able to obtain the exact prices with reference to the carriage of wheat from St. Paul, the capital of Minnesota, to Liverpool, but I have done so as regards Indian corn from the State of Illinois. The following statement will show what proportion the value of the article at the place of its growth bears to the cost of the carriage; and it shows also how enormous an effect on the price of corn in England would follow any serious decrease in the cost of carriage.

A bushel of Indian corn at Bloomington in Illinois cost in October, 1861	10 cents
Freight to Chicago	10 ,,
Storeage	2 ,,
Freight from Chicago to Buffalo	22 ,,
Elevating, and canal freight to New York	19 ,,
Transfer in New York and insurance	3 ,,
Ocean freight	23 ,,
Cost of a bushel of Indian corn at Liverpool	89 cents.

Thus corn which in Liverpool costs 3s. 10d., has been sold by the farmer who produced it for 5d.! It is probable that no great reduction can be expected in the cost of ocean transit; but it will be seen by the above figures that out of the Liverpool price of 3s. 10d. or 89 cents, considerably more than half is paid for carriage across the United States. All or nearly all this transit is by water, and there can, I think, be no doubt but that a few years will see it reduced by fifty per cent. In October last the Mississippi was closed, the railways had not rolling stock sufficient for their work, the crops of the two last years had been excessive, and there existed the necessity of sending out the corn before the internal navigation had been closed by frost. The parties who had the transit in their hands put their heads together and were able to demand any prices that they pleased. It will be seen that the cost of carrying a bushel of corn from Chicago to Buffalo, by the lakes, was within one cent of the cost of bringing it from New York to Liverpool. These temporary causes for high prices of transit will cease, a more perfect system of competition between the railways and the water transit will be organized, and the result must necessarily be both an increase of price to the producer and a decrease of price to the consumer. It certainly seems that the produce of cereal crops in the valleys of the Mississippi and its tributaries, increases at a faster rate than population increases. Wheat and corn are sown by the thousand acres in a piece. I heard of one farmer who had 10,000 acres of corn.

Thirty years ago grain and flour were sent westward out of the State of
New York to supply the wants of those who had emigrated into the
prairies, and now we find that it will be the destiny of those prairies to
feed the universe. Chicago is the main point of exportation north-
westward from Illinois, and at the present time sends out from its
granaries more cereal produce than any other town in the world. The
bulk of this passes, in the shape of grain or flour, from Chicago to
Buffalo, which latter place is as it were a gateway leading from the
lakes or big waters to the canals or small waters. I give below the
amount of grain and flour in bushels received into Buffalo for transit in
the month of October during four consecutive years.

October, 1858..	..	..	..	.. 4,429,055 bushels.
,, 1859..	..	..	..	.. 5,523,448 ,,
,, 1860..	..	..	..	.. 6,500,864 ,,
,, 1861..	..	..	..	..12,483,797 ,,

In 1860, from the opening to the close of navigation, 30,837,632
bushels of grain and flour passed through Buffalo. In 1861 the amount
received up to the 31st of October, was 51,969,142 bushels. As the
navigation would be closed during the month of November, the above
figures may be taken as representing not quite the whole amount
transported for the year. It may be presumed the 52,000,000 of
bushels, as quoted above, will swell itself to 60,000,000. I confess that
to my own mind statistical amounts do not bring home any enduring
idea. Fifty million bushels of corn and flour simply seems to mean a
great deal. It is a powerful form of superlative, and soon vanishes
away, as do other superlatives in this age of strong words. I was at
Chicago and at Buffalo in October 1861. I went down to the granaries,
and climbed up into the elevators. I saw the wheat running in rivers
from one vessel into another, and from the railroad vans up into the
huge bins on the top stories of the warehouses;—for these rivers of food
run up hill as easily as they do down. I saw the corn measured by the
forty bushel measure with as much ease as we measure an ounce of
cheese, and with greater rapidity. I ascertained that the work went on,
week day and Sunday, day and night incessantly; rivers of wheat and
rivers of maize ever running. I saw the men bathed in corn as they
distributed it in its flow. I saw bins by the score laden with wheat, in
each of which bins there was space for a comfortable residence. I
breathed the flour, and drank the flour, and felt myself to be enveloped
in a world of breadstuff. And then I believed, understood, and brought
it home to myself as a fact, that here in the corn lands of Michigan, and
amidst the bluffs of Wisconsin, and on the high table plains of

Minnesota, and the prairies of Illinois, had God prepared the food for the increasing millions of the Eastern world, as also for the coming millions of the Western.

I do not find many minds constituted like my own, and therefore I venture to publish the above figures. I believe them to be true in the main, and they will show, if credited, that the increase during the last four years has gone on with more than fabulous rapidity. For myself I own that those figures would have done nothing unless I had visited the spot myself. A man cannot, perhaps, count up the results of such a work by a quick glance of his eye, nor communicate with precision to another the conviction which his own short experience has made so strong within himself;—but to himself seeing is believing. To me it was so at Chicago and at Buffalo. I began then to know what it was for a country to overflow with milk and honey, to burst with its own fruits, and be smothered by its own riches. From St. Paul down the Mississippi by the shores of Wisconsin and Iowa,—by the ports on Lake Pepin,—by La Crosse, from which one railway runs eastward,—by Prairie du Chien the terminus of a second,—by Dunleath, Fulton, and Rock Island from whence three other lines run eastward, all through that wonderful State of Illinois—the farmers' glory,—along the ports of the great lakes,—through Michigan, Indiana, Ohio, and further Pennsylvania, up to Buffalo, the great gate of the western Ceres, the loud cry was this—"How shall we rid ourselves of our corn and wheat?" The result has been the passage of 60,000,000 bushels of breadstuffs through that gate in one year! Let those who are susceptible of statistics ponder that. For them who are not I can only give this advice:—Let them go to Buffalo next October, and look for themselves.

In regarding the above figures and the increase shown between the years 1860 and 1861, it must of course be borne in mind that during the latter autumn no corn or wheat was carried into the southern States, and that none was exported from New Orleans or the mouth of the Mississippi. The States of Mississippi, Alabama, and Louisiana have for some time past received much of their supplies from the north-western lands, and the cutting off of this current of consumption has tended to swell the amount of grain which has been forced into the narrow channel of Buffalo. There has been no southern exit allowed, and the southern appetite has been deprived of its food. But taking this item for all that it is worth,—or taking it, as it generally will be taken, for much more than it can be worth,—the result left will be materially the same. The grand markets to which the western States look and have looked are those of New England, New York, and Europe. Already corn and wheat are not the common crops of New England. Boston, and Hartford, and Lowell are fed from the great western States. The State of New York, which, thirty years ago, was famous chiefly for its cereal produce, is now fed from these States. New York city would be starved if it depended on its own State; and it will soon be as true that England would be starved if it depended on itself. It was but the other day that we were talking of free trade in corn as a thing desirable, but as yet doubtful;—but the other day that Lord Derby who may be Prime Minister tomorrow, and Mr. Disraeli who may be Chancellor of the Exchequer tomorrow, were stoutly of opinion that the corn laws might be and should be maintained;—but the other day that the same opinion was held with confidence by Sir Robert Peel, who, however, when the day for the change came, was not ashamed to become the instrument used by the people for their repeal. Events in these days march so quickly that they leave men behind, and our dear old Protectionists at home will have grown sleek upon American flour before they have realized the fact that they are no longer fed from their own furrows.

I have given figures merely as regards the trade of Buffalo; but it must not be presumed that Buffalo is the only outlet from the great corn lands of northern America. In the first place no grain of the produce of Canada finds its way to Buffalo. Its exit is by the St. Lawrence, or by the Grand Trunk Railway, as I have stated when speaking of Canada. And then there is the passage for large vessels from the Upper Lakes, Lake Michigan, Lake Huron, and Lake Erie, through the Welland Canal, into Lake Ontario, and out by the St. Lawrence. There is also the direct communication from Lake Erie, by the New York and Erie railway to New York. I have more especially alluded to the trade of Buffalo, because I have been enabled to obtain a reliable return of the quantity of grain and flour which passes through that town, and because Buffalo and Chicago are the two spots which are becoming most famous in the cereal history of the western States.

Everybody has a map of North America. A reference to such a map will show the peculiar position of Chicago. It is at the south or head of Lake Michigan, and to it converge railways from Wisconsin, Iowa, Illinois, and Indiana. At Chicago is found the nearest water carriage which can be obtained for the produce of a large portion of these States. From Chicago there is direct water conveyance round through the lakes to Buffalo at the foot of Lake Erie. At Milwaukee, higher up on the lake, certain lines of railway come in, joining the lake to the

Upper Mississippi, and to the wheat-lands of Minnesota. Thence the passage is round by Detroit which is the port for the produce of the greatest part of Michigan, and still it all goes on towards Buffalo. Then on Lake Erie there are the ports of Toledo, Cleveland, and Erie. At the bottom of Lake Erie, there is this city of corn, at which the grain and flour is transhipped into the canal boats and into the railway cars for New York; and there is also the Welland Canal, through which large vessels pass from the upper lakes, without transhipment of their cargo.

I have said above that corn—meaning maize or Indian corn—was to be bought at Bloomington in Illinois for 10 cents or fivepence a bushel. I found this also to be the case at Dixon—and also that corn of inferior quality might be bought for fourpence; but I found also that it was not worth the farmers' while to shell it and sell it at such prices. I was assured that farmers were burning their Indian corn in some places, finding it more available to them as fuel, than it was for the market. The labour of detaching a bushel of corn from the hulls or cobs is considerable, as is also the task of carrying it to market. I have known potatoes in Ireland so cheap that they would not pay for digging and carrying away for purposes of sale. There was then a glut of potatoes in Ireland; and in the same way there was in the autumn of 1861 a glut of corn in the western States. The best qualities would fetch a price, though still a low price; but corn that was not of the best quality was all but worthless. It did for fuel, and was burnt. The fact was that the produce had re-created itself quicker than mankind had multiplied. The ingenuity of man had not worked quick enough for its disposal. The earth had given forth her increase so abundantly that the lap of created humanity could not stretch itself to hold it. At Dixon in 1861 corn cost fourpence a bushel. In Ireland in 1848, it was sold for a penny a pound, a pound being accounted sufficient to sustain life for a day,—and we all felt that at that price food was brought into the country cheaper than it had ever been brought before.

Dixon is not a town of much apparent prosperity. It is one of those places at which great beginnings have been made, but as to which the deities presiding over new towns have not been propitious. Much of it has been burnt down, and more of it has never been built up. It had a straggling, ill-conditioned, uncommercial aspect, very different from the look of Detroit, Milwaukee, or St. Paul. There was, however, a great hotel there, as usual, and a grand bridge over the Rock River, a tributary of the Mississippi which runs by or through the town. I found that life might be maintained on very cheap terms at Dixon. To me as a passing traveller the charges at the hotel were, I take it, the same as elsewhere. But I learned from an inmate there that he with his wife and horse were fed and cared for, and attended for two dollars or 8s. 4d. a day. This included a private sitting-room, coals, light, and all the wants of life—as my informant told me—except tobacco and whiskey. Feeding at such a house means a succession of promiscuous hot meals as often as the digestion of the patient can face them. Now I do not know any locality where a man can keep himself and his wife, with all material comforts, and the luxury of a horse and carriage, on cheaper terms than that. Whether or no it might be worth a man's while to live at all at such a place as Dixon is altogether another question.

We went there because it is surrounded by the prairie, and out into the prairie we had ourselves driven. We found some difficulty in getting away from the corn, though we had selected this spot as one at which the open rolling prairie was specially attainable. As long as I could see a corn-field or a tree I was not satisfied. Nor indeed was I satisfied at last. To have been thoroughly on the prairie and in the prairie I should have been a day's journey from tilled land. But I doubt whether that could now be done in the State of Illinois. I got out into various patches and brought away specimens of corn;—ears bearing sixteen rows of grain, with forty grains in each row; each ear bearing a meal for a hungry man.

At last we did find ourselves on the prairie, amidst the waving grass, with the land rolling on before us in a succession of gentle sweeps, never rising so as to impede the view, or apparently changing in its general level,—but yet without the monotony of flatness. We were on the prairie, but still I felt no satisfaction. It was private property— divided among the holders and pastured over by private cattle. Salisbury plain is as wild, and Dartmoor almost wilder. Deer they told me were to be had within reach of Dixon; but for the buffalo one has to go much further afield than Illinois. The farmer may rejoice in Illinois, but the hunter and the trapper must cross the big rivers and pass away into the western territories before he can find lands wild enough for his purposes. My visit to the corn-fields of Illinois was in its way successful; but I felt as I turned my face eastward towards Chicago that I had no right to boast that I had as yet made acquaintance with a prairie.

All minds were turned to the war, at Dixon as elsewhere. In Illinois the men boasted that as regards the war, they were the leading State of the Union. But the same boast was made in Indiana, and also in Massachusetts; and probably in half the States of the North and West. They, the Illinoisians, call their country the war nest of the West. The population of the State is 1,700,000, and it had undertaken to furnish sixty volunteer regiments of 1000 men each. And let it be borne in mind that these regiments, when furnished, are really full,—absolutely containing the thousand men when they are sent away from the parent States. The number of souls above named will give 420,000 working men, and if out of these 60,000 are sent to the war, the State, which is almost purely agricultural, will have given more than one man in eight. When I was in Illinois, over forty regiments had already been sent—forty-six if I remember rightly,—and there existed no doubt whatever as to the remaining number. From the next State of Indiana, with a population of 1,350,000, giving something less than 350,000 working men, thirty-six regiments had been sent. I fear that I am mentioning these numbers usque ad nauseam; but I wish to impress upon English readers the magnitude of the effort made by the States in mustering and equipping an army within six or seven months of the first acknowledgment that such an army would be necessary. The Americans have complained bitterly of the want of English sympathy, and I think they have been weak in making that complaint. But I would not wish that they should hereafter have the power of complaining of a want of English justice. There can be no doubt that a genuine feeling of patriotism was aroused throughout North and West, and that men rushed into the ranks actuated by that feeling—men for whom war and army life, a camp and fifteen dollars a month, would not of themselves have had any attraction. It came to that, that young men were ashamed not to go into the army. This feeling of course produced coercion, and the movement was in that way tyrannical. There is nothing more tyrannical than a strong popular feeling among a democratic people. During the period of enlistment this tyranny was very strong. But the existence of such a tyranny proves the passion and patriotism of the people. It got the better of the love of money, of the love of children, and of the love of progress. Wives who with their bairns were absolutely dependent on their husbands' labours, would wish their husbands to be at the war. Not to conduce, in some special way, towards the war,—to have neither father there, nor brother, nor son,—not to have lectured, or preached, or written for the war,—to have made no sacrifice for the war, to have had no special and individual interest in the war, was disgraceful. One sees at a glance the tyranny of all this in such a country as the States. One can understand how quickly adverse stories would spread themselves as to the opinion of any man who chose to remain tranquil at such a time. One shudders at the absolute absence of true liberty which such a passion throughout a democratic country must engender. But he who has observed all this must acknowledge that that passion did exist. Dollars, children, progress, education, and political rivalry all gave way to the one strong national desire for the thrashing and crushing of those who had rebelled against the authority of the Stars and Stripes.

When we were at Dixon they were getting up the Dement regiment. The attempt at the time did not seem to be prosperous, and the few men who had been collected had about them a forlorn, ill-conditioned look. But then, as I was told, Dixon had already been decimated and re-decimated by former recruiting colonels. Colonel Dement, from whom the regiment was to be named, and whose military career was only now about to commence, had come late into the field. I did not afterwards ascertain what had been his success, but I hardly doubt that he did ultimately scrape together his thousand men. "Why don't you go?" I said to a burly Irishman who was driving me. "I'm not a sound man, yer honour," said the Irishman. "I'm deficient in me liver." Taking the Irishmen, however, throughout the Union, they had not been found deficient in any of the necessaries for a career of war. I do not think that any men have done better than the Irish in the American army.

From Dixon we went to Chicago. Chicago is in many respects the most remarkable city among all the remarkable cities of the Union. Its growth has been the fastest and its success the most assured. Twenty-five years ago there was no Chicago, and now it contains 120,000 inhabitants. Cincinnati on the Ohio, and St. Louis at the junction of the Missouri and Mississippi, are larger towns; but they have not grown large so quickly nor do they now promise so excessive a development of commerce. Chicago may be called the metropolis of American corn—the favourite city haunt of the American Ceres. The goddess seats herself there amidst the dust of her full barns, and proclaims herself a goddess ruling over things political and philosophical as well as agricultural. Not furrows only are in her thoughts, but free trade also, and brotherly love. And within her own bosom there is a boast that even yet she will be stronger than Mars. In Chicago there are great streets, and rows of houses fit to be the residences of a new Corn Exchange nobility. They look out on the wide lake which is now the highway for breadstuffs, and the merchant, as he shaves at his window, sees his rapid ventures as they pass away, one after the other, towards the East.

I went over one great grain store in Chicago possessed by gentlemen of the name of Sturgess and Buckenham. It was a world in itself,—and the dustiest of all the worlds. It contained, when I was there, half a million bushels of wheat—or a very great many, as I might say in other language. But it was not as a storehouse that this great building was so remarkable, but as a channel or a river course for the flooding freshets of corn. It is so built that both railway vans and vessels come immediately under its claws, as I may call the great trunks of the elevators. Out of the railway vans the corn and wheat is clawed up into the building, and down similar trunks it is at once again poured out into the vessels. I shall be at Buffalo in a page or two, and then I will endeavour to explain more minutely how this is done. At Chicago the corn is bought and does change hands, and much of it, therefore, is stored there for some space of time,—shorter or longer as the case may be. When I was at Chicago, the only limit to the rapidity of its transit was set by the amount of boat accommodation. There were not bottoms enough to take the corn away from Chicago, nor indeed on the railway was there a sufficiency of rolling stock or locomotive power to bring it into Chicago. As I said before, the country was bursting with its own produce and smothered in its own fruits.

At Chicago the hotel was bigger than other hotels, and grander. There were pipes without end for cold water which ran hot, and for hot water which would not run at all. The post-office also was grander and bigger than other post-offices;—though the postmaster confessed to me that that matter of the delivery of letters was one which could not be compassed. Just at that moment it was being done as a private speculation; but it did not pay, and would be discontinued. The theatre too was large, handsome, and convenient; but on the night of my attendance it seemed to lack an audience. A good comic actor it did not lack, and I never laughed more heartily in my life. There was something wrong too just at that time—I could not make out what— in the constitution of Illinois, and the present moment had been selected for voting a new constitution. To us in England such a necessity would be considered a matter of importance, but it did not seem to be much thought of here. "Some slight alteration probably," I suggested. "No," said my informant—one of the judges of their courts—"it is to be a thorough radical change of the whole constitution. They are voting the delegates to-day." I went to see them vote the delegates; but unfortunately got into a wrong place—by invitation—and was turned out, not without some slight tumult. I trust that the new constitution was carried through successfully.

From these little details it may perhaps be understood how a town like Chicago goes on and prospers, in spite of all the drawbacks which are incident to newness. Men in those regions do not mind failures, and when they have failed, instantly begin again. They make their plans on a large scale, and they who come after them fill up what has been wanting at first. Those taps of hot and cold water will be made to run by the next owner of the hotel, if not by the present owner. In another ten years the letters, I do not doubt, will all be delivered. Long before that time the theatre will probably be full. The new constitution is no doubt already at work; and if found deficient, another will succeed to it without any trouble to the State or any talk on the subject through the Union. Chicago was intended as a town of export for corn, and, therefore, the corn stores have received the first attention. When I was there, they were in perfect working order.

From Chicago we went on to Cleveland, a town in the State of Ohio on Lake Erie, again travelling by the sleeping cars. I found that these cars were universally mentioned with great horror and disgust by Americans of the upper class. They always declared that they would not travel in them on any account. Noise and dirt were the two objections. They are very noisy, but to us belonged the happy power of sleeping down noise. I invariably slept all through the night, and knew nothing about the noise. They are also very dirty,—extremely dirty,—dirty so as to cause much annoyance. But then they are not quite so dirty as the day cars. If dirt is to be a bar against travelling in America, men and women must stay at home. For myself I don't much care for dirt, having a strong reliance on soap and water and scrubbing brushes. No one regards poisons who carries antidotes in which he has perfect faith.

Cleveland is another pleasant town,—pleasant as Milwaukee and Portland. The streets are handsome, and are shaded by grand avenues of trees. One of these streets is over a mile in length, and throughout the whole of it, there are trees on each side—not little paltry trees as are to be seen on the boulevards of Paris, but spreading elms,—the beautiful American elm which not only spreads, but droops also, and makes more of its foliage than any other tree extant. And there is a square in Cleveland, well sized, as large as Russell Square I should say, with open paths across it, and containing one or two handsome buildings. I cannot but think that all men and women in London would be great gainers if the iron rails of the squares were thrown down, and the grassy enclosures thrown open to the public. Of course the edges of the turf would be worn, and the paths would not keep their exact shapes. But the prison look would be banished, and the sombre sadness of the squares would be relieved.

I was particularly struck by the size and comfort of the houses at Cleveland. All down that street of which I have spoken, they do not stand continuously together, but are detached and separate; houses which in England would require some fifteen or eighteen hundred a year for their maintenance. In the States, however, men commonly expend upon house rent a much greater proportion of their income than they do in England. With us it is, I believe, thought that a man should certainly not apportion more than a seventh of his spending income to his house rent,—some say not more than a tenth. But in many cities of the States a man is thought to live well within bounds if he so expends a fourth. There can be no doubt as to Americans living in better houses than Englishmen,—making the comparison of course between men of equal incomes. But the Englishman has many more incidental expenses than the American. He spends more on wine, on entertainments, on horses, and on amusements. He has a more numerous establishment, and keeps up the adjuncts and outskirts of his residence with a more finished neatness.

These houses in Cleveland were very good,—as indeed they are in most northern towns; but some of them have been erected with an amount of bad taste that is almost incredible. It is not uncommon to see in front of a square brick house a wooden quasi-Greek portico, with a pediment and Ionic columns, equally high with the house itself. Wooden columns with Greek capitals attached to the doorways, and wooden pediments over the windows, are very frequent. As a rule these are attached to houses which, without such ornamentation, would be simple, unpretentious, square, roomy residences. An Ionic or Corinthian capital stuck on to a log of wood called a column, and then fixed promiscuously to the outside of an ordinary house, is to my eye the vilest of architectural pretences. Little turrets are better than this; or even brown battlements made of mortar. Except in America I do not remember to have seen these vicious bits of white timber,—timber painted white,—plastered on to the fronts and sides of red-brick houses.

Again we went on by rail,—to Buffalo. I have travelled some thousands of miles by railway in the States, taking long journeys by night and longer journeys by day; but I do not remember that while doing so I ever made acquaintance with an American. To an American lady in a railway car I should no more think of speaking than I should to an unknown female in the next pew to me at a London church. It is hard to understand from whence come the laws which govern societies in this respect; but there are different laws in different societies, which soon obtain recognition for themselves. American ladies are much given to talking, and are generally free from all *mauvaise honte.* They are collected in manner, well instructed, and resolved to have their share of the social advantages of the world. In this phase of life they come out more strongly than English women. But on a railway journey, be it ever so long, they are never seen speaking to a stranger. English women, however, on English railways are generally willing to converse. They will do so if they be on a journey; but will not open their mouths if they be simply passing backwards and forwards between their homes and some neighbouring town. We soon learn the rules on these subjects;—but who make the rules? If you cross the Atlantic with an American lady you invariably fall in love with her before the journey is over. Travel with the same woman in a railway car for twelve hours, and you will have written her down in your own mind in quite other language than that of love.

And now for Buffalo, and the elevators. I trust I have made it understood that corn comes into Buffalo, not only from Chicago, of which I have spoken specially, but from all the ports round the lakes; Racine, Milwaukee, Grandhaven, Port Sarnia, Detroit, Toledo, Cleveland, and many others. At these ports the produce is generally bought and sold; but at Buffalo it is merely passed through a gateway. It is taken from vessels of a size fitted for the lakes, and placed in other vessels fitted for the canal. This is the Erie Canal, which connects the lakes with the Hudson River and with New York. The produce which passes through the Welland Canal—the canal which connects Lake Erie and the upper lakes with Lake Ontario and the St. Lawrence—is not transhipped, seeing that the Welland Canal, which is less than thirty miles in length, gives a passage to vessels of 500 tons. As I have before said, 60,000,000 bushels of breadstuff were thus pushed through Buffalo in the open months of the year 1861. These open months run from the middle of April to the middle of November; but the busy period is that of the last two months,—the time that is which intervenes between the full ripening of the corn and the coming of the ice.

An elevator is as ugly a monster as has been yet produced. In uncouthness of form it outdoes those obsolete old brutes who used to roam about the semi-aqueous world, and live a most uncomfortable life with their great hungering stomachs and huge unsatisfied maws. The elevator itself consists of a big moveable trunk,—moveable as is that of an elephant, but not pliable, and less graceful even than an elephant's. This is attached to a huge granary or barn; but in order to give altitude within the barn for the necessary moving up and down of this trunk,—seeing that it cannot be curled gracefully to its purposes as the elephant's is curled,—there is an awkward box erected on the roof of the barn, giving some twenty feet of additional height, up into which the elevator can be thrust. It will be understood, then, that this big moveable trunk, the head of which, when it is at rest, is thrust up into the box on the roof, is made to slant down in an oblique direction from the building to the river. For the elevator is an amphibious institution, and flourishes only on the banks of navigable waters. When its head is ensconced within its box, and the beast of prey is thus nearly hidden within the building, the unsuspicious vessel is brought up within reach of the creature's trunk, and down it comes, like a mosquito's proboscis, right through the deck, in at the open aperture of the hole, and so into the very vitals and bowels of the ship. When there, it goes to work upon its food with a greed and an avidity that is disgusting to a beholder of any taste or imagination. And now I must explain the anatomical arrangement by which the elevator still devours and continues to devour, till the corn within its reach has all been swallowed, masticated, and digested. Its long trunk, as seen slanting down from out of the building across the wharf and into the ship, is a mere wooden pipe; but this pipe is divided within. It has two departments; and as the grain-bearing troughs pass up the one on a pliable band, they pass empty down the other. The system therefore is that of an ordinary dredging machine; only that corn, and not mud is taken away, and that the buckets or troughs are hidden from sight. Below, within the stomach of the poor bark, three or four labourers are at work, helping to feed the elevator. They shovel the corn up towards its maw, so that at every swallow he should take in all that he can hold. Thus the troughs, as they ascend, are kept full, and when they reach the upper building they empty themselves into a shoot, over which a porter stands guard, moderating the shoot by a door, which the weight of his finger can open and close. Through this doorway the corn runs into a measure, and is weighed. By measures of forty bushels each, the tale is kept. There stands the apparatus, with the figures plainly marked, over against the porter's eye; and as the sum mounts nearly up to forty bushels he closes the door till the grains run thinly through, hardly a handful at a time, so that the balance is exactly struck. Then the teller standing by marks down his figure, and the record is made. The exact porter touches the string of another door, and the forty bushels of corn run out at the bottom of the measure, disappear down another shoot, slanting also towards the water, and deposit themselves in the canal-boat. The transit of the bushels of corn from the larger vessel to the smaller will have taken less than a minute, and the cost of that transit will have been—a farthing.

But I have spoken of the rivers of wheat, and I must explain what are those rivers. In the working of the elevator, which I have just attempted to describe, the two vessels were supposed to be lying at the same wharf, on the same side of the building, in the same water, the smaller vessel inside the larger one. When this is the case the corn runs direct from the weighing measure into the shoot that communicates with the canal boat. But there is not room or time for confining the work to one side of the building. There is water on both sides, and the corn or wheat is elevated on the one side, and re-shipped on the other. To effect this the corn is carried across the breadth of the building; but, nevertheless, it is never handled or moved in its direction on trucks or carriages requiring the use of men's muscles for its motion. Across the floor of the building are two gutters, or channels, and through these small troughs on a pliable band circulate very quickly. They which run one way, in one channel, are laden; they which return by the other channel are empty. The corn pours itself into these, and they again pour it into the shoot which commands the other water. And thus rivers of corn are running through these buildings night and day. The secret of all the motion and arrangement consists of course in the elevation. The corn is lifted up; and when lifted up can move itself and arrange itself, and weigh itself, and load itself.

I should have stated that all this wheat which passes through Buffalo comes loose, in bulk. Nothing is known of sacks or bags. To any spectator at Buffalo this becomes immediately a matter of course; but this should be explained, as we in England are not accustomed to see wheat travelling in this open, unguarded, and plebeian manner. Wheat with us is aristocratic, and travels always in its private carriage.

Over and beyond the elevators there is nothing specially worthy of remark at Buffalo. It is a fine city, like all other American cities of its class. The streets are broad, the "blocks" are high, and cars on tramways run all day, and nearly all night as well.

XII

Buffalo to New York

WE had now before us only two points of interest before we should reach New York,—the Falls of Trenton, and West Point on the Hudson River. We were too late in the year to get up to Lake George, which lies in the State of New York, north of Albany, and is, in fact, the southern continuation of Lake Champlain. Lake George, I know, is very lovely, and I would fain have seen it; but visitors to it must have some hotel accommodation, and the hotel was closed when we were near enough to visit it. I was in its close neighbourhood three years since in June; but then the hotel was not yet opened. A visitor to Lake George must be very exact in his time. July and August are the months,—with perhaps the grace of a week in September.

The hotel at Trenton was also closed, as I was told. But even if there were no hotel at Trenton, it can be visited without difficulty. It is within a carriage drive of Utica, and there is moreover a direct railway from Utica, with a station at the Trenton Falls. Utica is a town on the line of railway from Buffalo to New York viâ Albany, and is like all the other towns we had visited. There are broad streets, and avenues of trees, and large shops, and excellent houses. A general air of fat prosperity pervades them all, and is strong at Utica as elsewhere.

I remember to have been told thirty years ago that a traveller might go far and wide in search of the picturesque, without finding a spot more romantic in its loveliness than Trenton Falls. The name of the river is Canada Creek West; but as that is hardly euphonious, the course of the water which forms the falls has been called after the town or parish. This course is nearly two miles in length, and along the space of these two miles it is impossible to say where the greatest beauty exists. To see Trenton aright one must be careful not to have too much water. A sufficiency is no doubt desirable, and it may be that at the close of summer, before any of the autumnal rains have fallen, there may occasionally be an insufficiency. But if there be too much, the passage up the rocks along the river is impossible. The way on which the tourist should walk becomes the bed of the stream, and the great charm of the place cannot be enjoyed. That charm consists in descending into the ravine of the river, down amidst the rocks through which it has cut its channel, and in walking up the bed against the stream, in climbing the sides of the various falls, and sticking close to the river till an envious block is reached, which comes sheer down into the water, and prevents further progress. This is nearly two miles above the steps by which the descent is made; and not a foot of this distance but is wildly beautiful. When the river is very low there is a pathway even beyond that block; but when this is the case there can hardly be enough of water to make the fall satisfactory.

There is no one special cataract at Trenton which is in itself either wonderful or pre-eminently beautiful. It is the position, form, colour, and rapidity of the river which give the charm. It runs through a deep ravine, at the bottom of which the water has cut for itself a channel through the rocks, the sides of which rise sometimes with the sharpness of the walls of a stone sarcophagus. They are rounded too towards the bed, as I have seen the bottom of a sarcophagus. Along the side of the right bank of the river there is a passage, which when the freshets come is altogether covered. This passage is sometimes very narrow, but in the narrowest parts an iron chain is affixed into the rock. It is slippery and wet, and it is well for ladies when visiting the place to be provided with outside india-rubber shoes, which keep a hold upon the stone. If I remember rightly there are two actual cataracts, one not far above the steps by which the descent is made into the channel, and the other close under a summer-house, near to which the visitors reascend into the wood. But these cataracts, though by no means despicable as cataracts, leave comparatively a slight impression. They tumble down with sufficient violence, and the usual fantastic disposition of their forces; but simply as cataracts, within a day's journey of Niagara, they would be nothing. Up beyond the summer-house the passage along the river can be continued for another mile, but it is rough, and the climbing in some places rather difficult for ladies. Every man, however, who has the use of his legs, should do it, for the succession of rapids, and the twistings of the channels, and the forms of the rocks are as wild and beautiful as the imagination can desire. The banks of the river are closely wooded on each side; and though this circumstance does not at first seem to add much to the beauty, seeing that the ravine is so deep that the absence of wood above would hardly be noticed, still there are broken clefts ever and anon through which the colours of the foliage show themselves, and straggling boughs and rough roots break through the rocks here and there, and add to the wildness and charm of the whole.

The walk back from the summer-house through the wood is very lovely; but it would be a disappointing walk to visitors who had been prevented by a flood in the river from coming up the channel, for it indicates plainly how requisite it is that the river should be seen from below and not from above. The best view of the larger fall itself is that seen from the wood. And here again I would point out that any male visitor should walk the channel of the river up and down. The descent is too slippery and difficult for bipeds laden with petticoats. We found a small hotel open at Trenton, at which we got a comfortable dinner, and then in the evening were driven back to Utica.

Albany is the capital of the State of New York, and our road from Trenton to West Point lay through that town; but these political State capitals have no interest in themselves. The State legislature was not sitting, and we went on, merely remarking that the manner in which the railway cars are made to run backward and forward through the crowded streets of the town must cause a frequent loss of human life. One is led to suppose that children in Albany can hardly have a chance of coming to maturity. Such accidents do not become the subject of long-continued and strong comment in the States as they do with us; but, nevertheless, I should have thought that such a state of things as we saw there would have given rise to some remark on the part of the philanthropists. I cannot myself say that I saw anybody killed, and therefore should not be justified in making more than this passing remark on the subject.

When first the Americans of the northern States began to talk much of their country, their claims as to fine scenery were confined to Niagara and the Hudson River. Of Niagara, I have spoken, and all the world has acknowledged that no claim made on that head can be regarded as exaggerated. As to the Hudson, I am not prepared to say so much generally, though there is one spot upon it which cannot be beaten for sweetness. I have been up and down the Hudson by water, and confess that the entire river is pretty. But there is much of it that is not pre-eminently pretty among rivers. As a whole it cannot be named with the Upper Mississippi, with the Rhine, with the Moselle, or with the Upper Rhone. The palisades just out of New York are pretty, and the whole passage through the mountains from West Point up to Catskill and Hudson is interesting. But the glory of the Hudson is at West Point itself; and thither on this occasion we went direct by railway, and there we remained for two days. The Catskill mountains should be seen by a detour off from the river. We did not visit them because, here again, the hotel was closed. I will leave them therefore for the new handbook which Mr. Murray will soon bring out.

Of West Point there is something to be said independently of its scenery. It is the Sandhurst of the States. Here is their military school, from which officers are drafted to their regiments, and the tuition for military purposes is, I imagine, of a high order. It must, of course, be borne in mind that West Point, even as at present arranged, is fitted to the wants of the old army, and not to that of the army now required. It can go but a little way to supply officers for 500,000 men; but would do much towards supplying them for 40,000. At the time of my visit to West Point the regular army of the northern States had not even then swelled itself to the latter number.

I found that there were 220 students at West Point; that about forty graduate every year, each of whom receives a commission in the army; that about 120 pupils are admitted every year; and that in the course of every year about eighty either resign, or are called upon to leave on account of some deficiency, or fail in their final examination. The result is simply this, that one third of those who enter succeeds, and that two thirds fail. The number of failures seemed to me to be terribly large,—so large as to give great ground of hesitation to a parent in accepting a nomination for the college. I especially inquired into the particulars of these dismissals and resignations, and was assured that the majority of them take place in the first year of the pupillage. It is soon seen whether or no a lad has the mental and physical capacities necessary for the education and future life required of him, and care is taken that those shall be removed early as to whom it may be determined that the necessary capacity is clearly wanting. If this is done,—and I do not doubt it,—the evil is much mitigated. The effect otherwise would be very injurious. The lads remain till they are perhaps one and twenty, and have then acquired aptitudes for military life, but no other aptitudes. At that age the education cannot be commenced anew, and, moreover, at that age the disgrace of failure is very injurious. The period of education used to be five years, but has now been reduced to four. This was done in order that a double class might be graduated in 1861 to supply the wants of the war. I believe it is considered that but for such necessity as that, the fifth year of education can be ill spared.

The discipline, to our English ideas, is very strict. In the first place no kind of beer, wine, or spirits is allowed at West Point. The law upon this point may be said to be very vehement, for it debars even the visitors at the hotel from the solace of a glass of beer. The hotel is within the bounds of the College, and as the lads might become purchasers at the bar, there is no bar allowed. Any breach of this law leads to instant expulsion; or, I should say rather, any detection of such breach. The officer who showed us over the College assured me that the presence of a glass of wine in a young man's room would secure his exclusion, even though there should be no evidence that he had tasted it. He was very firm as to this; but a little bird of West Point, whose information, though not official or probably accurate in words, seemed to me to be worthy of reliance in general, told me that eyes were wont to wink when such glasses of wine made themselves un-necessarily visible. Let us fancy an English mess of young men from seventeen to twenty-one, at which a mug of beer would be a felony, and a glass of wine high treason! But the whole management of the young with the Americans differs much from that in vogue with us. We do not require so much at so early an age, either in knowledge, in morals, or even in manliness. In America, if a lad be under control, as at West Point, he is called upon for an amount of labour, and a degree of conduct, which would be considered quite transcendental and out of the question in England. But if he be not under control, if at the age of eighteen he be living at home, or be from his circumstances exempt from professorial power, he is a full-fledged man with his pipe appar-atus and his bar acquaintances.

And then I was told at West Point how needful and yet how painful it was that all should be removed who were in any way deficient in credit to the establishment. "Our rules are very exact," my informant told me; "but the carrying out of our rules is a task not always easy." As to this also I had already heard something from that little bird of West Point, but of course I wisely assented to my informant, remark-ing that discipline in such an establishment was essentially necessary. The little bird had told me that discipline at West Point had been rendered terribly difficult by political interference. "A young man will be dismissed by the unanimous voice of the Board, and will be sent away. And then, after a week or two, he will be sent back, with an order from Washington, that another trial shall be given him. The lad will march back into the college with all the honours of a victory, and will be conscious of a triumph over the superintendent and his officers." "And is that common?" I asked. "Not at the present moment," I was told. "But it was common before the war. While Mr. Buchanan, and Mr. Pierce, and Mr. Polk were Presidents, no officer or board of officers then at West Point was able to dismiss a lad whose father was a Southerner, and who had friends among the Government."

Not only was this true of West Point, but the same allegation is true as to all matters of patronage throughout the United States. During the three or four last Presidencies, and I believe back to the time of Jackson, there has been an organized system of dishonesty in the management of all beneficial places under the control of the Government. I doubt whether any despotic court of Europe has been so corrupt in the distribution of places,—that is in the selection of public officers,—as has been the assemblage of statesmen at Washington. And this is the evil which the country is now expiating with its blood and treasure. It has allowed its knaves to stand in the high places; and now it finds that knavish works have brought about evil results. But of this I shall be constrained to say something further hereafter.

We went into all the schools of the College, and made ourselves fully aware that the amount of learning imparted was far above our comprehension. It always occurs to me in looking through the new schools of the present day, that I ought to be thankful to persons who know so much for condescending to speak to me at all in plain English. I said a word to the gentleman who was with me about horses, seeing a lot of lads going to their riding lesson. But he was down upon me, and crushed me instantly beneath the weight of my own ignorance. He walked me up to the image of a horse, which he took to pieces bit by bit, taking off skin, muscle, flesh, nerves and bones, till the animal was a heap of atoms, and assured me that the anatomy of the horse throughout was one of the necessary studies of the place. We afterwards went to see the riding. The horses themselves were poor enough. This was accounted for by the fact that such of them as had been found fit for military service had been taken for the use of the army.

There is a gallery in the College in which are hung sketches and pictures by former students. I was greatly struck with the merit of many of these. There were some copies from well-known works of art of very high excellence, when the age is taken into account of those by whom they were done. I don't know how far the art of drawing, as taught generally and with no special tendency to military instruction, may be necessary for military training; but if it be necessary I should imagine that more is done in that direction at West Point than at Sandhurst. I found, however, that much of that in the gallery which was good had been done by lads who had not obtained their degree, and who had shown an aptitude for drawing, but had not shown any aptitude for other pursuits necessary to their intended career.

And then we were taken to the chapel, and there saw, displayed as trophies, two of our own dear old English flags. I have seen many a banner hung up in token of past victory, and many a flag taken on the field of battle mouldering by degrees into dust on some chapel's wall,—but they have not been the flags of England. Till this day I had never seen our own colours in any position but one of self-assertion and independent power. From the tone used by the gentleman who showed them to me, I could gather that he would have passed them by had he not foreseen that he could not do so without my notice. "I don't know that we are right to put them there," he said. "Quite right," was my reply, "as long as the world does such things." In private life it is vulgar to triumph over one's friends, and malicious to triumph over one's enemies. We have not got so far yet in public life, but I hope we are advancing towards it. In the mean time I did not begrudge the Americans our two flags. If we keep flags and cannons taken from our enemies, and show them about as signs of our own prowess after those enemies have become friends, why should not others do so as regards us? It clearly would not be well for the world that we should always beat other nations and never be beaten. I did not begrudge that chapel our two flags. But nevertheless the sight of them made me sick in the stomach and uncomfortable. As an Englishman I do not want to be ascendant over any one. But it makes me very ill when any one tries to be ascendant over me. I wish we could send back with our compliments all the trophies that we hold, carriage paid, and get back in return those two flags and any other flag or two of our own that may be doing similar duty about the world. I take it that the parcel sent away would be somewhat more bulky than that which would reach us in return.

The discipline at West Point seemed, as I have said, to be very severe; but it seemed also that that severity could not in all cases be maintained. The hours of study also were long, being nearly continuous throughout the day. "English lads of that age could not do it," I said; thus confessing that English lads must have in them less power of sustained work than those of America. "They must do it here," said

my informant, "or else leave us." And then he took us off to one of the
young gentleman's quarters, in order that we might see the nature of
their rooms. We found the young gentleman fast asleep on his bed, and
felt uncommonly grieved that we should have thus intruded on him.
As the hour was one of those allocated by my informant in the distribution of the day to private study, I could not but take the present
occupation of the embryo warrior as an indication that the amount of
labour required might be occasionally too much even for an American
youth. "The heat makes one so uncommonly drowsy," said the young
man. I was not the least surprised at the exclamation. The air of the
apartment had been warmed up to such a pitch by the hot-pipe
apparatus of the building that prolonged life to me would, I should
have thought, be out of the question in such an atmosphere. "Do you
always have it as hot as this?" I asked. The young man swore that it
was so, and with considerable energy expressed his opinion that all his
health and spirits and vitality were being baked out of him. He seemed
to have a strong opinion on the matter, for which I respected him; but
it had never occurred to him, and did not then occur to him, that
anything could be done to moderate that deathly flow of hot air which
came up to him from the neighbouring infernal regions. He was pale in
the face, and all the lads there were pale. American lads and lasses are
all pale. Men at thirty and women at twenty-five have had all sembl-
ance of youth baked out of them. Infants even are not rosy, and the
only shades known on the cheeks of children are those composed of
brown, yellow, and white. All this comes of those damnable hot-air
pipes with which every tenement in America is infested. "We cannot do
without them," they say. "Our cold is so intense that we must heat our
houses throughout. Open fire-places in a few rooms would not keep
our toes and fingers from the frost." There is much in this. The
assertion is no doubt true, and thereby a great difficulty is created. It is
no doubt quite within the power of American ingenuity to moderate
the heat of these stoves, and to produce such an atmosphere as may be
most conducive to health. In hospitals no doubt this will be done;
perhaps is done at present,—though even in hospitals I have thought
the air hotter than it should be. But hot-air-drinking is like dram-
drinking. There is the machine within the house capable of supplying
any quantity, and those who consume it unconsciously increase their
draughts, and take their drams stronger and stronger, till a breath of
fresh air is felt to be a blast direct from Boreas.

West Point is at all points a military colony, and as such belongs
exclusively to the Federal Government as separate from the Govern-

ment of any individual State. It is the purchased property of the United States as a whole, and is devoted to the necessities of a military college. No man could take a house there, or succeed in getting even permanent lodgings, unless he belonged to or were employed by the establishment. There is no intercourse by road between West Point and other towns or villages on the river side, and any such intercourse even by water is looked upon with jealousy by the authorities. The wish is that West Point should be isolated and kept apart for military instruction to the exclusion of all other purposes whatever,— especially love-making purposes. The coming over from the other side of the water of young ladies by the ferry is regarded as a great hindrance. They will come, and then the military students will talk to them. We all know to what such talking leads! A lad when I was there had been tempted to get out of barracks in plain clothes, in order that he might call on a young lady at the hotel;—and was in consequence obliged to abandon his commission and retire from the Academy. Will that young lady ever again sleep quietly in her bed? I should hope not. An opinion was expressed to me that there should be no hotel in such a place;—that there should be no ferry, no roads, no means by which the attention of the students should be distracted;—that these military Rasselases should live in a happy military valley from which might be excluded both strong drinks and female charms,—those two poisons from which youthful military ardour is supposed to suffer so much.

It always seems to me that such training begins at the wrong end. I will not say that nothing should be done to keep lads of eighteen from strong drinks. I will not even say that there should not be some line of moderation with reference to feminine allurements. But as a rule the restraint should come from the sense, good feeling, and education of him who is restrained. There is no embargo on the beer-shops either at Harrow or at Oxford,—and certainly none upon the young ladies. Occasional damage may accrue from habits early depraved, or a heart too early and too easily susceptible; but the injury so done is not, I think, equal to that inflicted by a Draconian code of morals, which will probably be evaded, and will certainly create a desire for its evasion.

Nevertheless, I feel assured that West Point, taken as a whole, is an excellent military academy, and that young men have gone forth from it, and will go forth from it, fit for officers as far as training can make men fit. The fault, if fault there be, is that which is to be found in so many of the institutions of the United States; and is one so allied to a virtue that no foreigner has a right to wonder that it is regarded in the light of a virtue by all Americans. There has been an attempt to make the place too perfect. In the desire to have the establishment self-sufficient at all points, more has been attempted than human nature can achieve. The lad is taken to West Point, and it is presumed that from the moment of his reception, he shall expend every energy of his mind and body in making himself a soldier. At fifteen he is not to be a boy, at twenty he is not to be a young man. He is to be a gentleman, a soldier, and an officer. I believe that those who leave the College for the army are gentlemen, soldiers, and officers, and therefore the result is good. But they are also young men; and it seems that they have become so, not in accordance with their training, but in spite of it.

But I have another complaint to make against the authorities of West Point, which they will not be able to answer so easily as that already preferred. What right can they have to take the very prettiest spot on the Hudson—the prettiest spot on the continent—one of the prettiest spots which Nature, with all her vagaries, ever formed—and shut it up from all the world for purposes of war? Would not any plain, however ugly, do for military exercises? Cannot broadsword, goose-step, and double quick time be instilled into young hands and legs in any field of thirty, forty, or fifty acres? I wonder whether these lads appreciate the fact that they are studying fourteen hours a day amidst the sweetest river, rock, and mountain scenery that the imagination can conceive. Of course it will be said that the world at large is not excluded from West Point, that the ferry to the place is open, and that there is even a hotel there, closed against no man or woman who will consent to become a teetotaller for the period of his visit. I must admit that this is so; but still one feels that one is only admitted as a guest. I want to go and live at West Point, and why should I be prevented? The Government had a right to buy it of course, but Government should not buy up the prettiest spots on a country's surface. If I were an American I should make a grievance of this; but Americans will suffer things from their Government which no Englishmen would endure.

It is one of the peculiarities of West Point that every thing there is in good taste. The Point itself consists of a bluff of land so formed that the river Hudson is forced to run round three sides of it. It is consequently a peninsula, and as the surrounding country is mountainous on both sides of the river, it may be imagined that the site is good. The views both up and down the river are lovely, and the mountains behind break themselves so as to make the landscape perfect. But this is not all. At West Point there is much of buildings, much of military arrangement in the way of cannons, forts, and artillery yards. All these things are so contrived as to group themselves well into pictures. There is no picture of architectural grandeur; but everything stands well and where it should stand, and the eye is not hurt at any spot. I regard West Point as a delightful place, and was much gratified by the kindness I received there.

From West Point we went direct to New York.

XIII

An Apology for the War

I THINK it may be received as a fact that the northern States, taken
together, sent a full tenth of their able-bodied men into the ranks of
the army in the course of the summer and autumn of 1861. The South,
no doubt, sent a much larger proportion; but the effect of such a drain
upon the South would not be the same, because the slaves were left at
home to perform the agricultural work of the country. I very much
doubt whether any other nation ever made such an effort in so short a
time. To a people who can do this it may well be granted that they are
in earnest; and I do not think it should be lightly decided by any
foreigner that they are wrong. The strong and unanimous impulse of a
great people is seldom wrong. And let it be borne in mind that in this
case both people may be right,—the people both of North and South.
Each may have been guided by a just and noble feeling; though each
was brought to its present condition by bad government and dishonest
statesmen.

There can be no doubt that, since the commencement of the war, the
American feeling against England has been very bitter. All Americans
to whom I spoke on the subject admitted that it was so. I, as an
Englishman, felt strongly the injustice of this feeling, and lost no
opportunity of showing or endeavouring to show that the line of
conduct pursued by England towards the States was the only line
which was compatible with her own policy and just interests, and also
with the dignity of the States' Government. I heard much of the tender

sympathy of Russia. Russia sent a flourishing general message, saying that she wished the North might win, and ending with some good general advice, proposing peace. It was such a message as strong nations send to those which are weaker. Had England ventured on such council the diplomatic paper would probably have been returned to her. It is, I think, manifest that an absolute and disinterested neutrality has been the only course which could preserve England from deserved rebuke,—a neutrality on which her commercial necessity for importing cotton or exporting her own manufactures should have no effect. That our Government would preserve such a neutrality I have always insisted, and I believe it has been done with a pure and strict disregard to any selfish views on the part of Great Britain. So far I think England may feel that she has done well in this matter. But I must confess that I have not been so proud of the tone of all our people at home, as I have been of the decisions of our statesmen. It seems to me that some of us never tire in abusing the Americans, and calling them names for having allowed themselves to be driven into this civil war. We tell them that they are fools and idiots; we speak of their doings as though there had been some plain course by which the war might have been avoided; and we throw it in their teeth that they have no capability for war. We tell them of the debt which they are creating, and point out to them that they can never pay it. We laugh at their attempt to sustain loyalty, and speak of them as a steady father of a family is wont to speak of some unthrifty prodigal who is throwing away his estate and hurrying from one ruinous debauchery to another. And, alas! we too frequently allow to escape from us some expression of that satisfaction which one rival tradesman has in the downfall of another. "Here you are with all your boasting," is what we say. "You were going to whip all creation the other day; and it has come to this! Brag is a good dog, but Holdfast is a better. Pray remember that, if ever you find yourselves on your legs again." That little advice about the two dogs is very well, and was not altogether inapplicable. But this is not the time in which it should be given. Putting aside slight asperities, we will all own that the people of the States have been and are our friends, and that as friends we cannot spare them. For one Englishman who brings home to his own heart a feeling of cordiality for France—a belief in the affection of our French alliance—there are ten who do so with reference to the States. Now, in these days of their trouble, I think that we might have borne with them more tenderly.

And how was it possible that they should have avoided this war? I will not now go into the cause of it, or discuss the course which it has taken, but will simply take up the fact of the rebellion. The South rebelled against the North, and such being the case, was it possible that the North should yield without a war? It may very likely be well that Hungary should be severed from Austria, or Poland from Russia, or Venice from Austria. Taking Englishmen in a lump they think that such separation would be well. The subject people do not speak the language of those that govern them, or enjoy kindred interests. But yet when military efforts are made by those who govern Hungary, Poland, and Venice, to prevent such separation, we do not say that Russia and Austria are fools. We are not surprised that they should take up arms against the rebels, but would be very much surprised indeed if they did not do so. We know that nothing but weakness would prevent their doing so. But if Austria and Russia insist on tying to themselves a people who do not speak their language or live in accordance with their habits, and are not considered unreasonable in so insisting, how much more thoroughly would they carry with them the sympathy of their neighbours in preventing any secession by integral parts of their own nationalities? Would England let Ireland walk off by herself if she wished it? In 1843 she did wish it. Three-fourths of the Irish population would have voted for such a separation; but England would have prevented such secession *vi et armis* had Ireland driven her to the necessity of such prevention.

I will put it to any reader of history whether, since government commenced, it has not been regarded as the first duty of government to prevent a separation of the territories governed, and whether also it has not been regarded as a point of honour with all nationalities to preserve uninjured each its own greatness and its own power? I trust that I may not be thought to argue that all governments or even all nationalities should succeed in such endeavours. Few kings have fallen in my day in whose fate I have not rejoiced; none, I take it, except that poor citizen King of the French. And I can rejoice that England lost her American colonies, and shall rejoice when Spain has been deprived of Cuba. But I hold that citizen King of the French in small esteem, seeing that he made no fight, and I know that England was bound to struggle when the Boston people threw her tea into the water. Spain keeps a tighter hand on Cuba than we thought she would some ten years since, and therefore she stands higher in the world's respect.

It may be well that the South should be divided from the North. I am inclined to think that it would be well—at any rate for the North; but the South must have been aware that such division could only be effected in two ways; either by agreement,— in which case the proposition must have been brought forward by the South and discussed by the North,—or by violence. They chose the latter way, as being the readier and the surer, as most seceding nations have done. O'Connell, when struggling for the secession of Ireland, chose the other, and nothing came of it. The South chose violence, and prepared for it secretly and with great adroitness. If that be not rebellion there never has been rebellion since history began; and if civil war was ever justified in one portion of a nation by turbulence in another, it has now been justified in the northern States of America.

What was the North to do; this foolish North, which has been so liberally told by us that she has taken up arms for nothing, that she is fighting for nothing, and will ruin herself for nothing? When was she to take the first step towards peace? Surely every Englishman will remember that when the earliest tidings of the coming quarrel reached us on the election of Mr. Lincoln, we all declared that any division was impossible;—it was a mere madness to speak of it. The States, which were so great in their unity, would never consent to break up all their prestige and all their power by a separation! Would it have been well for the North then to say, "If the South wish it we will certainly separate?" After that, when Mr. Lincoln assumed the power to which he had been elected, and declared with sufficient manliness, and sufficient dignity also, that he would make no war upon the South, but would collect the customs and carry on the government, did we turn round and advise him that he was wrong? No. The idea in England then was that his message was, if anything, too mild. "If he means to be President of the whole Union," England said, "he must come out with something stronger than that." Then came Mr. Seward's speech, which was, in truth, weak enough. Mr. Seward had run Mr. Lincoln very hard for the President's chair on the republican interest, and was—most unfortunately, as I think—made Secretary of State by Mr. Lincoln, or by his party. The Secretary of State holds the highest office in the United States Government under the President. He cannot be compared to our Prime Minister, seeing that the President himself exercises political power, and is responsible for its exercise. Mr. Seward's speech simply amounted to a declaration that separation was a thing of which the Union would neither hear, speak, nor, if possible, think. Things looked very like it; but no; they could never come to that! The world was too good, and especially the American world. Mr. Seward had no specific against secession; but let every free man strike his breast, look up to heaven, determine to be good, and all would go right. A great deal had been expected from Mr. Seward, and when this speech came out, we in England were a little disappointed, and nobody presumed even then that the North would let the South go.

It will be argued by those who have gone into the details of American politics that an acceptance of the Crittenden compromise at this point would have saved the war. What is or was the Crittenden compromise I will endeavour to explain hereafter; but the terms and meaning of that compromise can have no bearing on the subject. The republican party who were in power disapproved of that compromise, and could not model their course upon it. The republican party may have been right or may have been wrong; but surely it will not be argued that any political party elected to power by a majority should follow the policy of a minority, lest that minority should rebel. I can conceive of no government more lowly placed than one which deserts the policy of the majority which supports it, fearing either the tongues or arms of a minority.

As the next scene in the play, the State of South Carolina bombarded Fort Sumter. Was that to be the moment for a peaceable separation? Let us suppose that O'Connell had marched down to the Pigeon House at Dublin, and had taken it—in 1843, let us say—would that have been an argument to us for allowing Ireland to set up for herself? Is that the way of men's minds, or of the minds of nations? The powers of the President were defined by law, as agreed upon among all the States of the Union, and against that power and against that law, South Carolina raised her hand, and the other States joined her in rebellion. When circumstances had come to that, it was no longer possible that the North should shun the war. To my thinking the rights of rebellion are holy. Where would the world have been, or where would the world hope to be, without rebellion? But let rebellion look the truth in the face, and not blanch from its own consequences. She has to judge her own opportunities and to decide on her own fitness. Success is the test of her judgment. But rebellion can never be successful except by overcoming the power against which she raises herself. She has no right to expect bloodless triumphs; and if she be not the stronger in the encounter which she creates, she must bear the penalty of her rashness. Rebellion is justified by being better served than constituted authority, but cannot be justified otherwise. Now and again it may happen that rebellion's cause is so good that constituted authority will fall to the ground at the first glance of her sword. This was so the other day in Naples, when Garibaldi blew away the king's armies with a breath. But this is not so often. Rebellion knows that it must fight, and the legalized power against which rebels rise must of necessity fight also.

I cannot see at what point the North first sinned; nor do I think that had the North yielded, England would have honoured her for her meekness. Had she yielded without striking a blow she would have been told that she had suffered the Union to drop asunder by her supineness. She would have been twitted with cowardice, and told that she was no match for southern energy. It would then have seemed to those who sat in judgment on her that she might have righted everything by that one blow from which she had abstained. But having struck that one blow, and having found that it did not suffice, could she then withdraw, give way, and own herself beaten? Has it been so usually with Anglo-Saxon pluck? In such case as that would there have been no mention of those two dogs, Brag and Holdfast? The man of the northern States knows that he has bragged,—bragged as loudly as his English forefathers. In that matter of bragging the British lion and the Star-spangled banner may abstain from throwing mud at each other. And now the northern man wishes to show that he can hold fast also. Looking at all this I cannot see that peace has been possible to the North.

As to the question of secession and rebellion being one and the same thing, the point to me does not seem to bear an argument. The confederation of States had a common army, a common policy, a common capital, a common government, and a common debt. If one might secede, any or all might secede, and where then would be their property, their debt, and their servants? A confederation with such a license attached to it would have been simply playing at national power. If New York had seceded—a State which stretches from the Atlantic to British North America—it would have cut New England off from the rest of the Union. Was it legally within the power of New York to place the six States of New England in such a position? And why should it be assumed that so suicidal a power of destroying a nationality should be inherent in every portion of the nation? The States are bound together by a written compact, but that compact gives each State no such power. Surely such a power would have been specified had it been intended that it should be given. But there are axioms in politics as in mathematics, which recommend themselves to the mind at once, and require no argument for their proof. Men who are not argumentative perceive at once that they are true. A part cannot be greater than the whole.

I think it is plain that the remnant of the Union was bound to take up arms against those States which had illegally torn themselves off from her; and if so, she could only do so with such weapons as were at her hand. The United States' army had never been numerous or well appointed; and of such officers and equipments as it possessed, the more valuable part was in the hands of the Southerners. It was clear enough that she was ill-provided, and that in going to war she was undertaking a work as to which she had still to learn many of the rudiments. But Englishmen should be the last to twit her with such ignorance. It is not yet ten years since we were all boasting that swords and guns were useless things, and that military expenditure might be cut down to any minimum figure that an economizing Chancellor of the Exchequer could name. Since then we have extemporized two, if not three armies. There are our volunteers at home; and the army which holds India can hardly be considered as one with that which is to maintain our prestige in Europe and the West. We made some natural blunders in the Crimea, but in making those blunders we taught ourselves the trade. It is the misfortune of the northern States that they must learn these lessons in fighting their own countrymen. In the course of our history we have suffered the same calamity more than once. The Roundheads, who beat the Cavaliers and created English liberty, made themselves soldiers on the bodies of their countrymen. But England was not ruined by that civil war; nor was she ruined by those which preceded it. From out of these she came forth stronger than she entered them,—stronger, better, and more fit for a great destiny in the history of nations. The northern States had nearly five hundred thousand men under arms when the winter of 1861 commenced, and for that enormous multitude all commissariat requirements were well supplied. Camps and barracks sprang up through the country as though by magic. Clothing was obtained with a rapidity that has, I think, never been equalled. The country had not been prepared for the fabrication of arms, and yet arms were put into the men's hands almost as quickly as the regiments could be mustered. The eighteen millions of the northern States lent themselves to the effort as one man. Each State gave the best it had to give. Newspapers were as rabid against each other as ever, but no newspaper could live which did not support the war. "The South has rebelled against the law, and the law shall be supported." This has been the cry and the heartfelt feeling of all men; and it is a feeling which cannot but inspire respect.

We have heard much of the tyranny of the present Government of the United States, and of the tyranny also of the people. They have both been very tyrannical. The "habeas corpus" has been suspended by the word of one man. Arrests have been made on men who have been hardly suspected of more than secession principles. Arrests have, I believe, been made in cases which have been destitute even of any fair ground for such suspicion. Newspapers have been stopped for advocating views opposed to the feelings of the North, as freely as newspapers were ever stopped in France for opposing the Emperor. A man has not been safe in the streets who was known to be a Secessionist. It must be at once admitted that opinion in the northern States was not free when I was there. But has opinion ever been free anywhere on all subjects? In the best-built strongholds of freedom have there not always been questions on which opinion has not been free; and must it not always be so? When the decision of a people on any matter has become, so to say, unanimous,—when it has shown itself to be so general as to be clearly the expression of the nation's voice as a single chorus,—that decision becomes holy, and may not be touched. Could any newspaper be produced in England which advocated the overthrow of the Queen? And why may not the passion for the Union be as strong with the northern States, as the passion for the Crown is strong with us? The Crown with us is in no danger, and therefore the matter is at rest. But I think we must admit that in any nation, let it be ever so free, there may be points on which opinion must be held under restraint. And as to those summary arrests, and the suspension of the "habeas corpus," is there not something to be said for the States' Government on that head also? Military arrests are very dreadful, and the soul of a nation's liberty is that personal freedom from arbitrary interference which is signified to the world by those two unintelligible Latin words. A man's body shall not be kept in duress at any man's will; but shall be brought up into open court, with uttermost speed, in order that the law may say whether or no it should be kept in duress. That I take it is the meaning of "habeas corpus," and it is easy to see that the suspension of that privilege destroys all freedom, and places the liberty of every individual at the mercy of him who has the power to suspend it. Nothing can be worse than this; and such suspension, if extended over any long period of years, will certainly make a nation weak, mean-spirited, and poor. But in a period of civil war, or even of a widely-extended civil commotion, things cannot work in their accustomed grooves. A lady does not willingly get out of her bedroom-window with nothing on but her nightgown; but when her house is on fire she is very thankful for an opportunity of doing so. It is not long since the "habeas corpus" was suspended in parts of Ireland, and absurd arrests were made almost daily when that suspension first took effect. It was grievous that there should be necessity for such a step, and it is very grievous now that such necessity should be felt in the northern States. But I do not think that it becomes Englishmen to bear hardly upon Americans generally for what has been done in that matter. Mr. Seward, in an official letter to the British Minister at Washington—which letter, through official dishonesty, found its way to the press—claimed for the President the right of suspending the "habeas corpus" in the States whenever it might seem good to him to do so. If this be in accordance with the law of the land, which I think must be doubted, the law of the land is not favourable to freedom. For myself, I conceive that Mr. Lincoln and Mr. Seward have been wrong in their law, and that no such right is given to the President by the Constitution of the United States. This I will attempt to prove in some subsequent chapter. But I think it must be felt by all who have given any thought to the constitution of the States, that let what may be the letter of the law, the Presidents of the United States have had no such power. It is because the States have been no longer united that Mr. Lincoln has had the power, whether it be given to him by the law or no.

And then as to the debt; it seems to me very singular that we in England should suppose that a great commercial people would be ruined by a national debt. As regards ourselves, I have always looked on our national debt as the ballast in our ship. We have a great deal of ballast, but then the ship is very big. The States also are taking in ballast at a rather rapid rate;—and we too took it in quickly when we were about it. But I cannot understand why their ship should not carry, without shipwreck, that which our ship has carried without damage, and, as I believe, with positive advantage to its sailing. The ballast, if carried honestly, will not, I think, bring the vessel to grief. The fear is lest the ballast should be thrown overboard.

So much I have said, wishing to plead the cause of the northern States before the bar of English opinion, and thinking that there is ground for a plea in their favour. But yet I cannot say that their bitterness against Englishmen has been justified, or that their tone towards England has been dignified. Their complaint is that they have received no sympathy from England; but it seems to me that a great nation should not require an expression of sympathy during its struggle. Sympathy is for the weak rather than for the strong. When I hear two powerful men contending together in argument, I do not sympathize with him who has the best of it; but I watch the precision of his logic, and acknowledge the effects of his rhetoric. There has been a whining weakness in the complaints made by Americans against England, which has done more to lower them as a people in my judgment than any other part of their conduct during the present crisis. When we were at war with Russia, the feeling of the States was strongly against us. All their wishes were with our enemies. When the Indian mutiny was at its worst, the feeling of France was equally adverse to us. The joy expressed by the French newspapers was almost ecstatic. But I do not think that on either occasion we bemoaned ourselves sadly on the want of sympathy shown by our friends. On each occasion we took the opinion expressed for what it was worth, and managed to live it down. We listened to what was said, and let it pass by. When in each case we had been successful, there was an end of our friends' croakings.

But in the northern States of America the bitterness against England has amounted almost to a passion. The players, those chroniclers of the time, have had no hits so sure as those which have been aimed at Englishmen as cowards, fools, and liars. No paper has dared to say that England has been true in her American policy. The name of an Englishman has been made a byword for reproach. In private intercourse private amenities have remained. I, at any rate, may boast that such has been the case as regards myself. But even in private life I have been unable to keep down the feeling that I have always been walking over smothered ashes.

It may be that, when the civil war in America is over, all this will pass by, and there will be nothing left of international bitterness but its memory. It is sincerely to be hoped that this may be so;—that even the memory of the existing feeling may fade away and become unreal. I for one cannot think that two nations, situated as are the States and England, should permanently quarrel and avoid each other. But words have been spoken which will, I fear, long sound in men's ears, and thoughts have sprung up which will not easily allow themselves to be extinguished.

XIV

New York

SPEAKING of New York as a traveller I have two faults to find with it. In the first place there is nothing to see; and in the second place there is no mode of getting about to see anything. Nevertheless New York is a most interesting city. It is the third biggest city in the known world;—for those Chinese congregations of unwinged ants are not cities in the known world. In no other city is there a population so mixed and cosmopolitan in their modes of life. And yet in no other city that I have seen are there such strong and ever-visible characteristics of the social and political bearings of the nation to which it belongs. New York appears to me as infinitely more American than Boston, Chicago, or Washington. It has no peculiar attribute of its own, as have those three cities; Boston in its literature and accomplished intelligence, Chicago in its internal trade, and Washington in its congressional and State politics. New York has its literary aspirations, its commercial grandeur, and,—heaven knows,—it has its politics also. But these do not strike the visitor as being specially characteristic of the city. That it is pre-eminently American is its glory or its disgrace,—as men of different ways of thinking may decide upon it. Free institutions, general education, and the ascendancy of dollars are the words written on every paving-stone along Fifth Avenue, down Broadway, and up Wall Street. Every man can vote, and values the privilege. Every man can read, and uses the privilege. Every man worships the dollar, and is down before his shrine from morning to night.

As regards voting and reading no American will be angry with me for saying so much of him; and no Englishman, whatever may be his ideas as to the franchise in his own country, will conceive that I have said aught to the dishonour of an American. But as to that dollar-worshipping, it will of course seem that I am abusing the New Yorkers. We all know what a wretchedly wicked thing money is! How it stands between us and heaven! How it hardens our hearts, and makes vulgar our thoughts! Dives has ever gone to the devil, while Lazarus has been laid up in heavenly lavender. The hand that employs itself in compelling gold to enter the service of man has always been stigmatized as the ravisher of things sacred. The world is agreed about that, and therefore the New Yorker is in a bad way. There are very few citizens in any town known to me which under this dispensation are in a good way, but the New Yorker is in about the worst way of all. Other men, the world over, worship regularly at the shrine with matins and vespers, nones and complines, and whatever other daily services may be known to the religious houses; but the New Yorker is always on his knees.

That is the amount of the charge which I bring against New York; and now having laid on my paint thickly, I shall proceed, like an unskilful artist, to scrape a great deal of it off again. New York has been a leading commercial city in the world for not more than fifty or sixty years. As far as I can learn, its population at the close of the last century did not exceed 60,000, and ten years later it had not reached 100,000. In 1860 it had reached nearly 800,000 in the city of New York itself. To this number must be added the numbers of Brooklyn, Williamsburgh, and the city of New Jersey, in order that a true conception may be had of the population of this American metropolis, seeing that those places are as much a part of New York as Southwark is of London. By this the total will be swelled to considerably above a million. It will no doubt be admitted that this growth has been very fast, and that New York may well be proud of it. Increase of population is, I take it, the only trustworthy sign of a nation's success or of a city's success. We boast that London has beaten the other cities of the world, and think that that boast is enough to cover all the social sins for which London has to confess her guilt. New York beginning with 60,000 sixty years since has now a million souls;—a million mouths, all of which eat a sufficiency of bread, all of which speak *ore rotundo*, and almost all of which can read. And this has come of its love of dollars.

For myself I do not believe that Dives is so black as he is painted, or that his peril is so imminent. To reconcile such an opinion with holy

writ might place me in some difficulty were I a clergyman. Clergymen
in these days are surrounded by difficulties of this nature, finding it
necessary to explain away many old-established teachings which
narrowed the Christian Church, and to open the door wide enough to
satisfy the aspirations and natural hopes of instructed men. The
brethren of Dives are now so many and so intelligent that they will no
longer consent to be damned, without looking closely into the matter
themselves. I will leave them to settle the matter with the Church,
merely assuring them of my sympathies in their little difficulties in any
case in which mere money causes the hitch.

To eat his bread in the sweat of his brow was man's curse in Adam's
day, but is certainly man's blessing in our day. And what is eating
one's bread in the sweat of one's brow but making money? I will
believe no man who tells me that he would not sooner earn two loaves
than one;—and if two, then two hundred. I will believe no man who
tells me that he would sooner earn one dollar a day than two;—and if
two then two hundred. That is, in the very nature of the argument,—
cæteris paribus. When a man tells me that he would prefer one honest
loaf to two that are dishonest, I will, in all possible cases, believe him.
So also a man may prefer one quiet loaf to two that are unquiet. But
under circumstances that are the same, and to a man who is sane, a
whole loaf is better than half, and two loaves are better than one. The
preachers have preached well, but on this matter they have preached
in vain. Dives has never believed that he will be damned because he is
Dives. He has never even believed that the temptations incident to his
position have been more than a fair counterpoise, or even so much as a
fair counterpoise, to his opportunities for doing good. All men who
work desire to prosper by their work, and they so desire by the nature
given to them from God. Wealth and progress must go on hand in
hand together, let the accidents which occasionally divide them for a
time happen as often as they may. The progress of the Americans has
been caused by their aptitude for money-making, and that continual
kneeling at the shrine of the coined goddess has carried them across
from New York to San Francisco. Men who kneel at that shrine are
called on to have ready wits, and quick hands, and not a little aptitude
for self-denial. The New Yorker has been true to his dollar, because his
dollar has been true to him.

But not on this account can I, nor on this account will any
Englishman, reconcile himself to the savour of dollars which pervades
the atmosphere of New York. The _ars celare artem_ is wanting. The
making of money is the work of man; but he need not take his work to

bed with him, and have it ever by his side at table, amidst his family, in church, while he disports himself, as he declares his passion to the girl of his heart, in the moments of his softest bliss, and at the periods of his most solemn ceremonies. That many do so elsewhere than in New York,—in London, for instance, in Paris, among the mountains of Switzerland, and the steppes of Russia, I do not doubt. But there is generally a veil thrown over the object of the worshipper's idolatry. In New York one's ear is constantly filled with the fanatic's voice as he prays, one's eyes are always on the familiar altar. The frankincense from the temple is ever in one's nostrils. I have never walked down Fifth Avenue alone without thinking of money. I have never walked there with a companion without talking of it. I fancy that every man there, in order to maintain the spirit of the place, should bear on his forehead a label stating how many dollars he is worth, and that every label should be expected to assert a falsehood.

I do not think that New York has been less generous in the use of its money than other cities, or that the men of New York generally are so. Perhaps I might go farther and say that in no city has more been achieved for humanity by the munificence of its richest citizens than in New York. Its hospitals, asylums, and institutions for the relief of all ailments to which flesh is heir, are very numerous, and beyond praise in the excellence of their arrangements. And this has been achieved in a great degree by private liberality. Men in America are not as a rule anxious to leave large fortunes to their children. The millionaire when making his will very generally gives back a considerable portion of the wealth which he has made to the city in which he made it. The rich citizen is always anxious that the poor citizen shall be relieved. It is a point of honour with him to raise the character of his municipality, and to provide that the deaf and dumb, the blind, the mad, the idiots, the old, and the incurable shall have such alleviation in their misfortune as skill and kindness can afford.

Nor is the New Yorker a hugger-mugger with his money. He does not hide up his dollars in old stockings and keep rolls of gold in hidden pots. He does not even invest it where it will not grow but only produce small though sure fruit. He builds houses, he speculates largely, he spreads himself in trade to the extent of his wings,—and not seldom somewhat further. He scatters his wealth broadcast over strange fields, trusting that it may grow with an increase of an hundred-fold, but bold to bear the loss should the strange field prove itself barren. His regret at losing his money is by no means commensurate with his desire to make it. In this there is a living spirit which to me divests the dollar-worshipping idolatry of something of its ugliness. The hand when closed on the gold is instantly reopened. The idolator is anxious to get, but he is anxious also to spend. He is energetic to the last, and has no comfort with his stock unless it breeds with transatlantic rapidity of procreation.

So much I say, being anxious to scrape off some of that daub of black paint with which I have smeared the face of my New Yorker; but not desiring to scrape it all off. For myself, I do not love to live amidst the clink of gold, and never have "a good time," as the Americans say, when the price of shares and percentages come up in conversation. That state of men's minds here which I have endeavoured to explain tends, I think, to make New York disagreeable. A stranger there who has no great interest in percentages soon finds himself anxious to escape. By degrees he perceives that he is out of his element, and had better go away. He calls at the bank, and when he shows himself ignorant as to the price at which his sovereigns should be done, he is conscious that he is ridiculous. He is like a man who goes out hunting for the first time at forty years of age. He feels himself to be in the wrong place, and is anxious to get out of it. Such was my experience of New York, at each of the visits that I paid to it.

But, yet, I say again, no other American city is so intensely American as New York. It is generally considered that the inhabitants of New England, the Yankees properly so called, have the American characteristics of physiognomy in the fullest degree. The lantern jaws, the thin and lithe body, the dry face on which there has been no tint of the rose since the baby's long-clothes were first abandoned, the harsh, thick hair, the thin lips, the intelligent eyes, the sharp voice with the nasal twang—not altogether harsh, though sharp and nasal,—all these traits are supposed to belong especially to the Yankee. Perhaps it was so once, but at present they are, I think, more universally common in New York than in any other part of the States. Go to Wall Street, the front of the Astor House, and the regions about Trinity Church, and you will find them in their fullest perfection.

What circumstances of blood or food, of early habit or subsequent education, have created for the latter-day American his present physiognomy? It is as completely marked, as much his own, as is that of any race under the sun that has bred in and in for centuries. But the American owns a more mixed blood than any other race known. The chief stock is English, which is itself so mixed that no man can trace its ramifications. With this are mingled the bloods of Ireland, Holland, France, Sweden, and Germany. All this has been done within but a few years, so that the American may be said to have no claim to any national type of face. Nevertheless, no man has a type of face so clearly national as the American. He is acknowledged by it all over the continent of Europe, and on his own side of the water is gratified by knowing that he is never mistaken for his English visitor. I think it comes from the hot-air pipes and from dollar worship. In the Jesuit his mode of dealing with things divine has given a peculiar cast of countenance; and why should not the American be similarly moulded by his special aspirations? As to the hot-air pipes, there can, I think be no doubt that to them is to be charged the murder of all rosy cheeks throughout the States. If the effect was to be noticed simply in the dry faces of the men about Wall Street, I should be very indifferent to the matter. But the young ladies of Fifth Avenue are in the same category. The very pith and marrow of life is baked out of their young bones by the hot-air chambers to which they are accustomed. Hot air is the great destroyer of American beauty.

In saying that there is very little to be seen in New York, I have also said that there is no way of seeing that little. My assertion amounts to this,—that there are no cabs. To the reading world at large this may not seem to be much, but let the reading world go to New York, and it will find out how much the deficiency means. In London, in Paris, in Florence, in Rome, in the Havana, or at Grand Cairo, the cab-driver or attendant does not merely drive the cab or belabour the donkey, but he is the visitor's easiest and cheapest guide. In London, the Tower, Westminster Abbey, and Madame Tussaud, are found by the stranger without difficulty, and almost without a thought, because the cab-driver knows the whereabouts and the way. Space is moreover annihilated, and the huge distances of the English metropolis are brought within the scope of mortal power. But in New York there is no such institution.

In New York there are street omnibuses as we have,—there are street cars such as last year we declined to have,—and there are very excellent public carriages; but none of these give you the accommodation of a cab, nor can all of them combined do so. The omnibuses, though clean and excellent, were to me very unintelligible. They have no conductor to them. To know their different lines and usages a man should have made a scientific study of the city. To those going up and down Broadway I became accustomed, but in them I was never quite at my ease. The money has to be paid through a little hole behind the driver's back, and should, as I learned at last, be paid immediately on entrance. But in getting up to do this I always stumbled about, and it would happen that when with considerable difficulty I had settled my own account, two or three ladies would enter, and would hand me, without a word, some coins with which I had no lifelong familiarity in order that I might go through the same ceremony on their account. The change I would usually drop into the straw, and then there would arise trouble and unhappiness. Before I became aware of that law as to instant payment, bells used to be rung at me which made me uneasy. I knew I was not behaving as a citizen should behave, but could not compass the exact points of my delinquency. And then when I desired to escape, the door being strapped up tight, I would halloo vainly at the driver through the little hole; whereas, had I known my duty, I should have rung a bell, or pulled a strap, according to the nature of the omnibus in question. In a month or two all these things may possibly be learned;—but the visitor requires his facilities for locomotion at the first moment of his entrance into the city. I heard it asserted by a lecturer in Boston, Mr. Wendell Phillips, whose name is there a household word, that citizens of the United States carried brains in their fingers as well as in their heads, whereas "common people," by which Mr. Phillips intended to designate the remnant of mankind beyond the United States, were blessed with no such extended cerebral development. Having once learned this fact from Mr. Phillips, I understood why it was that a New York omnibus should be so disagreeable to me, and at the same time so suitable to the wants of the New Yorkers.

And then there are street cars—very long omnibuses—which run on rails but are dragged by horses. They are capable of holding forty passengers each, and as far as my experience goes carry an average load of sixty. The fare of the omnibus is six cents or three pence. That of the street car five cents or two pence halfpenny. They run along the different avenues, taking the length of the city. In the upper or new part of the town their course is simple enough, but as they descend to the Bowery, Peckslip, and Pearl Street, nothing can be conceived more difficult or devious than their courses. The Broadway omnibus, on the other hand, is a straightforward honest vehicle in the lower part of the town, becoming, however, dangerous and miscellaneous when it ascends to Union Square and the vicinities of fashionable life.

The street cars are manned with conductors, and therefore are free from many of the perils of the omnibus, but they have perils of their own. They are always quite full. By that I mean that every seat is crowded, that there is a double row of men and women standing down the centre, and that the driver's platform in front is full, and also the conductor's platform behind. That is the normal condition of a street car in the Third Avenue. You, as a stranger in the middle of the car, wish to be put down at, let us say, 89th Street. In the map of New York now before me the cross streets running from east to west are numbered up northwards as far as 154th Street. It is quite useless for you to give the number as you enter. Even an American conductor, with brains all over him, and an anxious desire to accommodate as is the case with all these men, cannot remember. You are left therefore in misery to calculate the number of the street as you move along, vainly endeavouring through the misty glass to decipher the small numbers which after a day or two you perceive to be written on the lamp posts.

But I soon gave up all attempts at keeping a seat in one of these cars. It became my practice to sit down on the outside iron rail behind, and as the conductor generally sat in my lap I was in a measure protected. As for the inside of these vehicles, the women of New York, were, I must confess, too much for me. I would no sooner place myself on a seat, than I would be called on by a mute, unexpressive, but still impressive stare into my face, to surrender my place. From cowardice if not from gallantry I would always obey; and as this led to discomfort and an irritated spirit, I preferred nursing the conductor on the hard bar in the rear.

And here if I seem to say a word against women in America, I beg that it may be understood that I say that word only against a certain class; and even as to that class I admit that they are respectable, intelligent, and, as I believe, industrious. Their manners, however, are to me more odious than those of any other human beings that I ever met elsewhere. Nor can I go on with that which I have to say without carrying my apology further, lest perchance I should be misunderstood by some American women whom I would not only exclude from my censure, but would include in the very warmest eulogium which words of mine could express as to those of the female sex whom I love and admire the most. I have known, do know, and mean to continue to know as far as in me may lie, American ladies as bright, as beautiful, as graceful, as sweet, as mortal limits for brightness, beauty, grace, and sweetness will permit. They belong to the aristocracy of the land, by whatever means they may have become aristocrats. In America one does not inquire as to their birth, their training, or their old names. The fact of their aristocratic power comes out in every word and look. It is not only so with those who have travelled or with those who are rich. I have found female aristocrats with families and slender means, who have as yet made no grand tour across the ocean. These women are charming beyond expression. It is not only their beauty. Had he been speaking of such, Wendell Phillips would have been right in saying that they have brains all over them. So much for those who are bright and beautiful; who are graceful and sweet! And now a word as to those who to me are neither bright nor beautiful; and who can be to none either graceful or sweet.

It is a hard task that of speaking ill of any woman, but it seems to me that he who takes upon himself to praise incurs the duty of dispraising also where dispraise is, or to him seems to be, deserved. The trade of a novelist is very much that of describing the softness, sweetness, and loving dispositions of women; and this he does, copying as best he can from nature. But if he only sings of that which is sweet, whereas that which is not sweet too frequently presents itself, his song will in the end be untrue and ridiculous. Women are entitled to much observance from men, but they are entitled to no observance which is incompatible with truth. Women, by the conventional laws of society, are allowed to exact much from men, but they are allowed to exact nothing for which they should not make some adequate return. It is well that a man should kneel in spirit before the grace and weakness of a woman, but it is not well that he should kneel either in spirit or body if there be neither grace or weakness. A man should yield everything to a woman for a word, for a smile,—to one look of entreaty. But if there be no look of entreaty, no word, no smile, I do not see that he is called upon to yield much.

The happy privileges with which women are at present blessed, have come to them from the spirit of chivalry. That spirit has taught men to endure in order that women may be at their ease; and has generally taught women to accept the ease bestowed on them with grace and thankfulness. But in America the spirit of chivalry has sunk deeper among men than it has among women. It must be borne in mind that in that country material well-being and education are more extended than with us; and that, therefore, men there have learned to be chivalrous who with us have hardly progressed so far. The conduct of men to women throughout the States is always gracious. They have learned the lesson. But it seems to me that the women have not advanced as far as the men have done. They have acquired a sufficient perception of the privileges which chivalry gives them, but no perception of that return which chivalry demands from them. Women of the class to which I allude are always talking of their rights; but seem to have a most indifferent idea of their duties. They have no scruple at demanding from men everything that a man can be called on to relinquish in a woman's behalf, but they do so without any of that grace which turns the demand made into a favour conferred.

I have seen much of this in various cities of America, but much more of it in New York than elsewhere. I have heard young Americans complain of it, swearing that they must change the whole tenor of their habits towards women. I have heard American ladies speak of it with loathing and disgust. For myself, I have entertained on sundry occasions that sort of feeling for an American woman which the close vicinity of an unclean animal produces. I have spoken of this with reference to street cars, because in no position of life does an unfortunate man become more liable to these anti-feminine atrocities than in the centre of one of these vehicles. The woman, as she enters, drags after her a misshapen, dirty mass of battered wirework, which she calls her crinoline, and which adds as much to her grace and comfort as a log of wood does to a donkey when tied to the animal's leg in a paddock. Of this she takes much heed, not managing it so that it may be conveyed up the carriage with some decency, but striking it about against men's legs, and heaving it with violence over people's knees. The touch of a real woman's dress is in itself delicate; but these blows from a harpy's fins are loathsome. If there be two of them they talk loudly together, having a theory that modesty has been put out of court by women's rights. But, though not modest, the woman I describe is ferocious in her propriety. She ignores the whole world around her, and as she sits with raised chin and face flattened by affectation, she pretends to declare aloud that she is positively not aware that any man is even near her. She speaks as though to her, in her womanhood, the neighbourhood of men was the same as that of dogs or cats. They are there, but she does not hear them, see them, or even acknowledge them by any courtesy of motion. But her own face always gives her the lie. In her assumption of indifference she displays her nasty consciousness, and in each attempt at a would-be propriety is guilty of an immodesty. Who does not know the timid retiring face of the young girl who when alone among men unknown to her feels that it becomes her to keep herself secluded? As many men as there are around her, so many knights has such a one, ready bucklered for her service, should occasion require such services. Should it not, she passes on unmolested,— but not, as she herself will wrongly think, unheeded. But as to her of whom I am speaking, we may say that every twist of her body, and every tone of her voice is an unsuccessful falsehood. She looks square at you in the face, and you rise to give her your seat. You rise from a deference to your own old convictions, and from that courtesy which you have ever paid to a woman's dress, let it be worn with ever such hideous deformities. She takes the place from which you have moved without a word or a bow. She twists herself round, banging your shins with her wires, while her chin is still raised, and her face is still flattened, and she directs her friend's attention to another seated man, as though that place were also vacant, and necessarily at her disposal. Perhaps the man opposite has his own ideas about chivalry. I have seen such a thing, and have rejoiced to see it.

You will meet these women daily, hourly,—everywhere in the streets. Now and again you will find them in society, making themselves even more odious there than elsewhere. Who they are, whence they come, and why they are so unlike that other race of women of which I have spoken, you will settle for yourself. Do we not all say of our chance acquaintances after half an hour's conversation,—nay, after half an hour spent in the same room without conversation,—that this woman is a lady, and that that other woman is not? They jostle each other even among us, but never seem to mix. They are closely allied; but neither imbues the other with her attributes. Both shall be equally well-born, or both shall be equally ill-born; but still it is so. The contrast exists in England; but in America it is much stronger. In England women become ladylike or vulgar. In the States they are either charming or odious.

See that female walking down Broadway. She is not exactly such a one as her I have attempted to describe on her entrance into the street car; for this lady is well-dressed, if fine clothes will make well-dressing. The machinery of her hoops is not battered, and altogether she is a personage much more distinguished in all her expenditures. But yet she is a copy of the other woman. Look at the train which she drags behind her over the dirty pavement, where dogs have been, and chewers of tobacco, and everything concerned with filth except a scavenger. At every hundred yards some unhappy man treads upon the silken swab which she trails behind her,—loosening it dreadfully at the girth one would say; and then see the style of face and the expression of features with which she accepts the sinner's half-muttered apology. The world, she supposes, owes her everything because of her silken train,—even room enough in a crowded thoroughfare to drag it along unmolested. But, according to her theory, she owes the world nothing in return. She is a woman with perhaps a hundred dollars on her back, and having done the world the honour of wearing them in the world's presence, expects to be repaid by the world's homage and chivalry. But chivalry owes her nothing,—

nothing, though she walk about beneath a hundred times a hundred dollars,—nothing even though she be a woman. Let every woman learn this,—that chivalry owes her nothing unless she also acknowledge her debt to chivalry. She must acknowledge it and pay it; and then chivalry will not be backward in making good her claims upon it.

All this has come of the street cars. But as it was necessary that I should say it somewhere, it is as well said on that subject as on any other. And now to continue with the street cars. They run, as I have said, the length of the town, taking parallel lines. They will take you from the Astor House, near the bottom of the town, for miles and miles northward,—half-way up the Hudson river,—for, I believe, five pence. They are very slow, averaging about five miles an hour; but they are very sure. For regular inhabitants, who have to travel five or six miles perhaps to their daily work, they are excellent. I have nothing really to say against the street cars. But they do not fill the place of cabs.

There are, however, public carriages, roomy vehicles dragged by two horses, clean and nice, and very well suited to ladies visiting the city. But they have none of the attributes of the cab. As a rule they are not to be found standing about. They are very slow. They are very dear. A dollar an hour is the regular charge; but one cannot regulate one's motion by the hour. Going out to dinner and back costs two dollars, over a distance which in London would cost two shillings. As a rule, the cost is four times that of a cab; and the rapidity half that of a cab. Under these circumstances I think I am justified in saying that there is no mode of getting about in New York to see anything.

And now as to the other charge against New York, of there being nothing to see. How should there be anything there to see of general interest? In other large cities, cities as large in name as New York, there are works of art, fine buildings, ruins, ancient churches, picturesque costumes, and the tombs of celebrated men. But in New York there are none of these things. Art has not yet grown up there. One or two fine figures by Crawford are in the town,—especially that of the sorrowing Indian at the rooms of the Historical Society; but art is a luxury in a city which follows but slowly on the heels of wealth and civilization. Of fine buildings,—which indeed are comprised in art,—there are none deserving special praise or remark. It might well have been that New York should ere this have graced herself with something grand in architecture; but she has not done so. Some good architectural effect there is, and much architectural comfort. Of ruins of course there can be none; none at least of such ruins as travellers admire, though perhaps some of that sort which disgraces rather than decorates. Churches there are plenty, but none that are ancient. The costume is the same as our own; and I need hardly say that it is not picturesque. And the time for the tombs of celebrated men has not yet come. A great man's ashes are hardly of value till they have all but ceased to exist.

The visitor to New York must seek his gratification and obtain his instruction from the habits and manners of men. The American, though he dresses like an Englishman, and eats roast beef with a silver fork,—or sometimes with a steel knife,—as does an Englishman, is not like an Englishman in his mind, in his aspirations, in his tastes, or in his politics. In his mind he is quicker, more universally intelligent, more ambitious of general knowledge, less indulgent of stupidity and ignorance in others, harder, sharper, brighter with the surface brightness of steel, than is an Englishman; but he is more brittle, less enduring, less malleable, and I think less capable of impressions. The mind of the Englishman has more imagination, but that of the American more incision. The American is a great observer, but he observes things material rather than things social or picturesque. He is a constant and ready speculator; but all speculations, even those which come of philosophy, are with him more or less material. In his aspirations the American is more constant than an Englishman,—or I should rather say he is more constant in aspiring. Every citizen of the United States intends to do something. Every one thinks himself capable of some effort. But in his aspirations he is more limited than an Englishman. The ambitious American never soars so high as the ambitious Englishman. He does not even see up to so great a height; and when he has raised himself somewhat above the crowd becomes sooner dizzy with his own altitude. An American of mark, though always anxious to show his mark, is always fearful of a fall. In his tastes the American imitates the Frenchman. Who shall dare to say that he is wrong, seeing that in general matters of design and luxury the French have won for themselves the foremost name? I will not say that the American is wrong, but I cannot avoid thinking that he is so. I detest what is called French taste; but the world is against me. When I complained to a landlord of an hotel out in the West that his furniture was useless; that I could not write at a marble table whose outside rim was curved into fantastic shapes; that a gold clock in my bedroom which did not go would give me no aid in washing myself; that a heavy, immoveable curtain shut out the light; and that papier-maché chairs with small fluffy velvet seats were bad to sit on,—he answered me completely by telling me that his house had been furnished not in accordance with the taste of England, but with that of France. I acknowledged the rebuke, gave up my pursuits of literature and cleanliness, and hurried out of the house as quickly as I could. All America is now furnishing itself by the rules which guided that hotel-keeper. I do not merely allude to actual household furniture,—to chairs, tables, and detestable gilt clocks. The taste of America is becoming French in its conversation, French in its comforts and French in its discomforts, French in its eating, and French in its dress, French in its manners, and will become French in its art. There are those who will say that English taste is taking the same direction. I do not think so. I strongly hope that it is not so. And therefore I say that an Englishman and an American differ in their tastes.

But of all differences between an Englishman and an American that in politics is the strongest, and the most essential. I cannot here, in one paragraph, define that difference with sufficient clearness to make my definition satisfactory; but I trust that some idea of that difference may be conveyed by the general tenor of my book. The American and the Englishman are both Republicans. The governments of the States and of England are probably the two purest republican governments in the world. I do not, of course, here mean to say that the governments are more pure than others, but that the systems are more absolutely republican. And yet no men can be much further asunder in politics than the Englishman and the American. The American of the present day puts a ballot-box into the hands of every citizen and takes his stand upon that and that only. It is the duty of an American citizen to vote, and when he has voted he need trouble himself no further till the time for voting shall come round again. The candidate for whom he has voted represents his will, if he have voted with the majority, and in that case he has no right to look for further influence. If he have voted with the minority, he has no right to look for any influence at all. In either case he has done his political work, and may go about his business till the next year or the next two or four years shall have come round. The Englishman, on the other hand, will have no ballot-box, and is by no means inclined to depend exclusively upon voters or upon voting. As far as voting can show it, he desires to get the sense of the country; but he does not think that that sense will be shown by universal suffrage. He thinks that property amounting to a thousand pounds will show more of that sense than property amounting to a hundred; but he will not on that account go to work

and apportion votes to wealth. He thinks that the educated can show
more of that sense than the uneducated; but he does not therefore lay
down any rule about reading, writing, and arithmetic, or apportion
votes to learning. He prefers that all these opinions of his shall bring
themselves out and operate by their own intrinsic weight. Nor does he
at all confine himself to voting in his anxiety to get the sense of the
country. He takes it in any way that it will show itself, uses it for what it
is worth,—or perhaps for more than it is worth,—and welds it into
that gigantic lever by which the political action of the country is
moved. Every man in Great Britain, whether he possess any actual
vote or no, can do that which is tantamount to voting every day of his
life, by the mere expression of his opinion. Public opinion in America
has hitherto been nothing, unless it has managed to express itself by a
majority of ballot-boxes. Public opinion in England is everything, let
votes go as they may. Let the people want a measure, and there is no
doubt of their obtaining it. Only the people must want it;—as they did
want Catholic emancipation, reform, and corn-law repeal;—and as
they would want war if it were brought home to them that their
country was insulted.

In attempting to describe this difference in the political action of the
two countries, I am very far from taking all praise for England or
throwing any reproach on the States. The political action of the States
is undoubtedly the more logical and the clearer. That indeed of
England is so illogical and so little clear that it would be quite impossible for any other nation to assume it, merely by resolving to do so.
Whereas the political action of the States might be assumed by any
nation to-morrow, and all its strength might be carried across the
water in a few written rules as are the prescriptions of a physician or
the regulations of an infirmary. With us the thing has grown of habit,
has been fostered by tradition, has crept up uncared for and in some
parts unnoticed. It can be written in no book, can be described in no
words, can be copied by no statesmen, and I almost believe can be
understood by no people but that to whose peculiar uses it has been
adapted.

In speaking as I have here done of American taste and American
politics I must allude to a special class of Americans who are to be met
more generally in New York than elsewhere,—men who are educated,
who have generally travelled, who are almost always agreeable, but
who as regards their politics are to me the most objectionable of all
men. As regards taste they are objectional to me also. But that is a
small thing; and as they are quite as likely to be right as I am I will say

nothing against their taste. But in politics it seems to me that these
men have fallen into the bitterest and perhaps into the basest of errors.
Of the man who begins his life with mean political ideas, having
sucked them in with his mother's milk, there may be some hope. The
evil is at any rate the fault of his forefathers rather than of himself. But
who can have hope of him who having been thrown by birth and
fortune into the running river of free political activity, has allowed
himself to be drifted into the stagnant level of general political servility? There are very many such Americans. They call themselves
republicans, and sneer at the idea of a limited monarchy, but they
declare that there is no republic so safe, so equal for all men, so purely
democratic as that now existing in France. Under the French empire
all men are equal. There is no aristocracy; no oligarchy; no oversha-
dowing of the little by the great. One superior is admitted;—admitted
on earth, as a superior is also admitted in heaven. Under him everything is level, and—provided he be not impeded—everything is free.
He knows how to rule, and the nation, allowing him the privilege of
doing so, can go along its course safely;—can eat, drink, and be merry.
If few men can rise high, so also can few men fall low. Political equality
is the one thing desirable in a commonwealth, and by this arrangement political equality is obtained. Such is the modern creed of many
an educated republican of the States.

To me it seems that such a political state is about the vilest to which
a man can descend. It amounts to a tacit abandonment of the struggle
which men are making for political truth and political beneficence, in
order that bread and meat may be eaten in peace during the score of
years or so that are at the moment passing over us. The politicians of
this class have decided for themselves that the *summum bonum* is to be
found in bread and the circus games. If they be free to eat, free to rest,
free to sleep, free to drink little cups of coffee while the world passes
before them on a boulevard, they have that freedom which they covet.
But equality is necessary as well as freedom. There must be no tower-
ing trees in this parterre to overshadow the clipped shrubs, and
destroy the uniformity of a growth which should never mount more
than two feet above the earth. The equality of this politician would
forbid any to rise above him instead of inviting all to rise up to him. It is
the equality of fear and of selfishness, and not the equality of courage
and philanthropy. And brotherhood too must be invoked,—fraternity
as we may better call it in the jargon of the school. Such politicians tell
one much of fraternity, and define it too. It consists in a general raising
of the hat to all mankind; in a daily walk that never hurries itself into a

jostling trot, inconvenient to passengers on the pavement;—in a pla-
cid voice, a soft smile, and a small cup of coffee on a boulevard. It
means all this, but I could never find that it meant any more. There is a
nation for which one is almost driven to think that such political
aspirations as these are suitable; but that nation is certainly not the
States of America.

And yet one finds many American gentlemen who have allowed
themselves to be drifted into such a theory. They have begun the world
as republican citizens, and as such they must go on. But in their travels
and their studies, and in the luxury of their life, they have learned to
dislike the rowdiness of their country's politics. They want things to be
soft and easy;—as republican as you please, but with as little noise as
possible. The President is there for four years. Why not elect him for
eight, for twelve, or for life?—for eternity if it were possible to find one
who could continue to live? It is to this way of thinking that Americans
are driven, when the polish of Europe has made the roughness of their
own elections odious to them.

"Have you seen any of our great insteetootions, sir?" That of course is
a question, which is put to every Englishman who has visited New
York, and the Englishman who intends to say that he has seen New
York, should visit many of them. I went to schools, hospitals, lunatic
asylums, institutes for deaf and dumb, water works, historical
societies, telegraph offices, and large commercial establishments. I
rather think that I did my work in a thorough and conscientious
manner, and I owe much gratitude to those who guided me on such
occasions. Perhaps I ought to describe all these institutions; but were I
to do so, I fear that I should inflict fifty or sixty very dull pages on my
readers. If I could make all that I saw as clear and intelligible to others
as it was made to me who saw it, I might do some good. But I know
that I should fail. I marvelled much at the developed intelligence of
a room full of deaf and dumb pupils, and was greatly astonished at
the performance of one special girl, who seemed to be brighter and
quicker, and more rapidly easy with her pen than girls generally are
who can hear and talk; but I cannot convey my enthusiasm to others.
On such a subject a writer may be correct, may be exhaustive, may be
statistically great; but he can hardly be entertaining, and the chances
are that he will not be instructive.

In all such matters, however, New York is pre-eminently great. All
through the States suffering humanity receives so much attention that
humanity can hardly be said to suffer. The daily recurring boast of
"our glorious insteetootions, sir," always provokes the ridicule of an

Englishman. The words have become ridiculous, and it would, I think, be well for the nation if the term "Institution" could be excluded from its vocabulary. But, in truth, they are glorious. The country in this respect boasts, but it has done that which justifies a boast. The arrangements for supplying New York with water are magnificent. The drainage of the new part of the city is excellent. The hospitals are almost alluring. The lunatic asylum which I saw was perfect,— though I did not feel obliged to the resident physician for introducing me to all the worst patients as countrymen of my own. "An English lady, Mr. Trollope. I'll introduce you. Quite a hopeless case. Two old women. They've been here fifty years. They're English. Another gentleman from England, Mr. Trollope. A very interesting case! Confirmed inebriety."

And as to the schools, it is almost impossible to mention them with too high a praise. I am speaking here specially of New York, though I might say the same of Boston, or of all New England. I do not know any contrast that would be more surprising to an Englishman, up to that moment ignorant of the matter, than that which he would find by visiting first of all a free school in London, and then a free school in New York. If he would also learn the number of children that are educated gratuitously in each of the two cities, and also the number in each which altogether lack education, he would, if susceptible of statistics, be surprised also at that. But seeing and hearing are always more effective than mere figures. The female pupil at a free school in London is, as a rule, either a ragged pauper, or a charity girl, if not degraded at least stigmatized by the badges and dress of the Charity. We Englishmen know well the type of each, and have a fairly correct idea of the amount of education which is imparted to them. We see the result afterwards when the same girls become our servants, and the wives of our grooms and porters. The female pupil at a free school in New York is neither a pauper nor a charity girl. She is dressed with the utmost decency. She is perfectly cleanly. In speaking to her, you cannot in any degree guess whether her father has a dollar a day, or three thousand dollars a year. Nor will you be enabled to guess by the manner in which her associates treat her. As regards her own manner to you, it is always the same as though her father were in all respects your equal. As to the amount of her knowledge, I fairly confess that it is terrific. When, in the first room which I visited, a slight slim creature was had up before me to explain to me the properties of the hypothenuse I fairly confess that, as regards education, I backed down, and that I resolved to confine my criticisms to manner, dress, and general

behaviour. In the next room I was more at my ease, finding that
ancient Roman history was on the tapis. "Why did the Romans run
away with the Sabine women?" asked the mistress, herself a young
woman of about three-and-twenty. "Because they were pretty," sim-
pered out a little girl with a cherry mouth. The answer did not give
complete satisfaction; and then followed a somewhat abstruse explanation on the subject of population. It was all done with good faith
and a serious intent, and showed what it was intended to show,—that
the girls there educated had in truth reached the consideration of
important subjects, and that they were leagues beyond that terrible
repetition of A B C, to which, I fear, that most of our free metropolitan
schools are still necessarily confined. You and I, reader, were we called
on to superintend the education of girls of sixteen, might not select as
favourite points either the hypothenuse, or the ancient methods of
populating young colonies. There may be, and to us on the European
side of the Atlantic there will be, a certain amount of absurdity in the
transatlantic idea that all knowledge is knowledge, and that it should
be imparted if it be not knowledge of evil. But as to the general result,
no fair-minded man or woman can have a doubt. That the lads and
girls in these schools are excellently educated comes home as a fact to
the mind of any one who will look into the subject. That girl could not
have got as far as the hypothenuse without a competent and abiding
knowledge of much that is very far beyond the outside limits of what
such girls know with us. It was at least manifest in the other examination that the girls knew as well as I did who were the Romans, and who
were the Sabine women. That all this is of use, was shown in the very
gestures and bearings of the girl. *Emollit mores*, as Colonel Newcome
used to say. That young woman whom I had watched while she cooked
her husband's dinner upon the banks of the Mississippi, had doubtless
learned all about the Sabine women, and I feel assured that she cooked
her husband's dinner all the better for that knowledge,—and faced the
hardships of the world with a better front than she would have done
had she been ignorant on the subject.

In order to make a comparison between the schools of London and
those of New York, I have called them both free schools. They are in
fact more free in New York than they are in London, because in New
York every boy and girl, let his parentage be what it may, can attend
these schools without any payment. Thus an education as good as the
American mind can compass, prepared with every care, carried on by
highly paid tutors, under ample surveillance, provided with all that is
most excellent in the way of rooms, desks, books, charts, maps, and

implements, is brought actually within the reach of everybody. I need not point out to Englishmen how different is the nature of schools in London. It must not, however, be supposed that these are charity schools. Such is not their nature. Let us say what we may as to the beauty of charity as a virtue, the recipient of charity in its customary sense among us is ever more or less degraded by the position. In the States that has been fully understood, and the schools to which I allude, are carefully preserved from any such taint. Throughout the States a separate tax is levied for the maintenance of these schools, and as the tax-payer supports them, he is of course entitled to the advantage which they confer. The child of the non-tax-payer is also entitled, and to him the boon, if strictly analysed, will come in the shape of a charity. But under the system as it is arranged, this is not analysed. It is understood that the school is open to all in the ward to which it belongs, and no inquiry is made whether the pupil's parent has or has not paid anything towards the school's support. I found this theory carried out so far that at the deaf and dumb school, where some of the poorer children are wholly provided for by the institution, care is taken to clothe them in dresses of different colours and different make, in order that nothing may attach to them which has the appearance of a badge. Political economists will see something of evil in this. But philanthropists will see very much that is good.

It is not without a purpose that I have given this somewhat glowing account of a girls' school in New York so soon after my little picture of New York women, as they behave themselves in the streets and street cars. It will, of course, be said that those women of whom I have spoken, by no means in terms of admiration, are the very girls whose education has been so excellent. This of course is so; but I beg to remark that I have by no means said that an excellent school education will produce all female excellences. The fact, I take it is this,—that seeing how high in the scale these girls have been raised, one is anxious that they should be raised higher. One is surprised at their pert vulgarity and hideous airs, not because they are so low in our general estimation but because they are so high. Women of the same class in London are humble enough, and therefore rarely offend us who are squeamish. They show by their gestures that they hardly think themselves good enough to sit by us; they apologise for their presence; they conceive it to be their duty to be lowly in their gestures. The question is which is best, the crouching and crawling or the impudent unattractive self-composure. Not, my reader, which action on her part may the better conduce to my comfort or to yours! That is by no means the

question. Which is the better for the woman herself? That I take it is
the point to be decided. That there is something better than either we
shall all agree;—but to my thinking the crouching and crawling is the
lowest type of all.

At that school I saw some five or six hundred girls collected in one
room, and heard them sing. The singing was very pretty, and it was all
very nice; but I own that I was rather startled, and to tell the truth
somewhat abashed, when I was invited to "say a few words to them."
No idea of such a suggestion had dawned upon me, and I felt myself
quite at a loss. To be called up before five hundred men is bad enough,
but how much worse before that number of girls! What could I say but
that they were all very pretty. As far as I can remember I did say that
and nothing else. Very pretty they were, and neatly dressed, and
attractive; but among them all there was not a pair of rosy cheeks.
How should there be, when every room in the building was heated up
to the condition of an oven by those damnable hot-air pipes!

In England a taste for very large shops has come up during the last
twenty years. A firm is not doing a good business, or at any rate a
distinguished business, unless he can assert in his trade card that he
occupies at least half a dozen houses—Nos. 105, 106, 107, 108, 109,
and 110. The old way of paying for what you want over the counter is
gone; and when you buy a yard of tape or a new carriage,—for either of
which articles you will probably visit the same establishment,—you
go through about the same amount of ceremony as when you sell a
thousand pounds out of the stocks in propriâ personâ. But all this is
still further exaggerated in New York. Mr. Stewart's store there is
perhaps the handsomest institution in the city, and his hall of audience
for new carpets is a magnificent saloon. "You have nothing like that in
England," my friend said to me as he walked me through it in triumph.
"I wish we had nothing approaching to it," I answered. For I confess
to a liking for the old-fashioned private shops. Harper's establishment
for the manufacture and sale of books is also very wonderful. Everything is done on the premises, down to the very colouring of the paper
which lines the covers, and places the gilding on their backs. The firm
prints, engraves, electroplates, sews, binds, publishes, and sells
wholesale and retail. I have no doubt that the authors have rooms in
the attics where the other slight initiatory step is taken towards the
production of literature.

New York is built upon an island, which is I believe about ten miles
long, counting from the southern point at the battery up to Carmans-
ville, to which place the city is presumed to extend northwards. This

island is called Manhattan,—a name which I have always thought
would have been more graceful for the city than that of New York. It is
formed by the Sound or East river, which divides the continent from
Long Island, by the Hudson river which runs into the Sound or rather
joins it at the city foot, and by a small stream called the Haarlem river
which runs out of the Hudson and meanders away into the Sound at
the north of the city, thus cutting the city off from the main land. The
breadth of the island does not much exceed two miles, and therefore
the city is long, and not capable of extension in point of breadth. In its
old days it clustered itself round about the Point, and stretched itself
up from there along the quays of the two waters. The streets down in
this part of the town are devious enough, twisting themselves about
with delightful irregularity; but as the city grew there came the taste
for parallelograms, and the upper streets are rectangular and numbered. Broadway, the street of New York with which the world is
generally best acquainted, begins at the southern point of the town and
goes northward through it. For some two miles and a half it walks
away in a straight line, and then it turns to the left towards the
Hudson, and becomes in fact a continuation of another street called
the Bowery, which comes up in a devious course from the south-east
extremity of the island. From that time Broadway never again takes a
straight course, but crosses the various Avenues in an oblique direction till it becomes the Bloomingdale road, and under that name takes
itself out of town. There are eleven so-called Avenues, which descend
in absolutely straight lines from the northern, and at present unsettled,
extremity of the new town, making their way southward till they lose
themselves among the old streets. These are called First Avenue,
Second Avenue, and so on. The town had already progressed two
miles up northwards from the Battery before it had caught the parallel-
ogrammic fever from Philadelphia, for at about that distance we find
"First Street." First Street runs across the Avenues from water to
water, and then Second Street. I will not name them all, seeing that
they go up to 154th Street! They do so at least on the map, and I believe
on the lamp-posts. But the houses are not yet built in order beyond
50th or 60th Street. The other hundred streets, each of two miles long,
with the Avenues which are mostly unoccupied for four or five miles, is
the ground over which the young New Yorkers are to spread themselves. I do not in the least doubt that they will occupy it all, and that
154th Street will find itself too narrow a boundary for the population.

I have said that there was some good architectural effect in New
York, and I alluded chiefly to that of the Fifth Avenue. The Fifth

Avenue is the Belgrave Square, the Park Lane, and the Pall Mall of New York. It is certainly a very fine street. The houses in it are magnificent, not having that aristocratic look which some of our detached London residences enjoy, or the palatial appearance of an old-fashioned hotel in Paris, but an air of comfortable luxury and commercial wealth which is not excelled by the best houses of any other town that I know. They are houses, not hotels or palaces; but they are very roomy houses, with every luxury that complete finish can give them. Many of them cover large spaces of ground, and their rent will sometimes go up as high as 800*l.* and 1000*l.* a year. Generally the best of these houses are owned by those who live in them, and rent is not therefore paid. But this is not always the case, and the sums named above may be taken as expressing their value. In England a man should have a very large income indeed who could afford to pay 1000*l.* a year for his house in London. Such a one would as a matter of course have an establishment in the country, and be an Earl or a Duke or a millionaire. But it is different in New York. The resident there shows his wealth chiefly by his house, and though he may probably have a villa at Newport or a box somewhere up the Hudson he has no second establishment. Such a house therefore will not represent a total expenditure of above 4000*l.* a year.

There are churches on each side of Fifth Avenue,—perhaps five or six within sight at one time,—which add much to the beauty of the street. They are well-built, and in fairly good taste. These, added to the general well-being and splendid comfort of the place, give it an effect better than the architecture of the individual houses would seem to warrant. I own that I have enjoyed the vista as I have walked up and down Fifth Avenue, and have felt that the city had a right to be proud of its wealth. But the greatness and beauty and glory of wealth have on such occasions been all in all with me. I know no great man, no celebrated statesman, no philanthropist of peculiar note who has lived in Fifth Avenue. That gentleman on the right made a million of dollars by inventing a shirt-collar; this one on the left electrified the world by a lotion; as to the gentleman at the corner there,—there are rumours about him and the Cuban slave-trade; but my informant by no means knows that they are true. Such are the aristocracy of Fifth Avenue. I can only say that if I could make a million dollars by a lotion, I should certainly be right to live in such a house as one of those.

The suburbs of New York are, by the nature of the localities, divided from the city by water. New Jersey and Hoboken are on the other side of the Hudson, and in another State. Williamsburgh and Brooklyn are in Long Island, which is a part of the State of New York. But these places are as easily reached as Lambeth is reached from Westminster. Steam ferries ply every three or four minutes, and into these boats coaches, carts, and waggons of any size or weight are driven. In fact they make no other stoppage to the commerce than that occasioned by the payment of a few cents. Such payment no doubt is a stoppage, and therefore it is that New Jersey, Brooklyn, and Williamsburgh are, at any rate in appearance, very dull and uninviting. They are, however, very populous. Many of the quieter citizens prefer to live there; and I am told that the Brooklyn tea-parties consider themselves to be, in æsthetic feeling, very much ahead of anything of the kind in the more opulent centres of the city. In beauty of scenery Staten Island is very much the prettiest of the suburbs of New York. The view from the hill side in Staten Island down upon New York harbour is very lovely. It is the only really good view of that magnificent harbour which I have been able to find. As for appreciating such beauty when one is entering a port from sea, or leaving it for sea, I do not believe in any such power. The ship creeps up or creeps out while the mind is engaged on other matters. The passenger is uneasy either with hopes or fears; and then the grease of the engines offends one's nostrils. But it is worth the tourist's while to look down upon New York harbour from the hill side in Staten Island. When I was there Fort Lafayette looked black in the centre of the channel, and we knew that it was crowded with the victims of secession. Fort Tomkins was being built, to guard the pass,—worthy of a name of richer sound; and Fort something else was bristling with new cannon. Fort Hamilton, on Long Island, opposite, was frowning at us; and immediately around us a regiment of volunteers was receiving regimental stocks and boots from the hands of its officers. Everything was bristling with war; and one could not but think that not in this way had New York raised herself so quickly to her present greatness.

But the glory of New York is the Central Park;—its glory in the mind of all New Yorkers of the present day. The first question asked of you is whether you have seen the Central Park, and the second is as to what you think of it. It does not do to say simply that it is fine, grand, beautiful, and miraculous. You must swear by cock and pie that it is more fine, more grand, more beautiful, more miraculous than anything else of the kind anywhere. Here you encounter, in its most annoying form, that necessity for eulogium which presses you everywhere. For, in truth, taken as it is at present, the Central Park is not fine, nor grand, nor beautiful. As to the miracle, let that pass. It is perhaps as miraculous as some other great latter-day miracles.

But the Central Park is a very great fact, and affords a strong additional proof of the sense and energy of the people. It is very large, being over three miles long, and about three quarters of a mile in breadth. When it was found that New York was extending itself, and becoming one of the largest cities of the world, a space was selected between Fifth and Seventh Avenues, immediately outside the limits of the city as then built, but nearly in the centre of the city as it is intended to be built. The ground around it became at once of great value; and I do not doubt that the present fashion of the Fifth Avenue about Twentieth Street will in course of time move itself up to the Fifth Avenue as it looks, or will look, over the Park at Seventieth, Eightieth, and Ninetieth Streets. The great waterworks of the city bring the Croton River, whence New York is supplied, by an aqueduct over the Haarlem river into an enormous reservoir just above the Park; and hence it has come to pass that there will be water not only for sanitary and useful purposes, but also for ornament. At present the Park, to English eyes, seems to be all road. The trees are not grown up, and the new embankments, and new lakes, and new ditches, and new paths give to the place anything but a picturesque appearance. The Central Park is good for what it will be, rather than for what it is. The summer heat is so very great that I doubt much whether the people of New York will ever enjoy such verdure as our parks show. But there will be a pleasant assemblage of walks and water-works, with fresh air, and fine shrubs and flowers, immediately within the reach of the citizens. All that art and energy can do will be done, and the Central Park doubtless will become one of the great glories of New York. When I was expected to declare that St. James's Park, Green Park, Hyde Park, and Kensington Gardens, altogether, were nothing to it, I confess that I could only remain mute.

Those who desire to learn what are the secrets of society in New York, I would refer to the Potiphar Papers. The Potiphar Papers are perhaps not as well known in England as they deserve to be. They were published, I think, as much as seven or eight years ago; but are probably as true now as they were then. What I saw of society in New York was quiet and pleasant enough; but doubtless I did not climb into that circle in which Mrs. Potiphar held so distinguished a position. It may be true that gentlemen habitually throw fragments of their supper and remnants of their wine onto their host's carpets; but if so I did not see it.

As I progress in my work I feel that duty will call upon me to write a separate chapter on hotels in general, and I will not, therefore, here say much about those in New York. I am inclined to think that few towns in the world, if any, afford on the whole better accommodation, but there are many in which the accommodation is cheaper. Of the railways also I ought to say something. The fact respecting them which is most remarkable is that of their being continued into the centre of the town through the streets. The cars are not dragged through the city by locomotive engines, but by horses; the pace therefore is slow, but the convenience to travellers in being brought nearer to the centre of trade must be much felt. It is as though passengers from Liverpool and passengers from Bristol were carried on from Euston Square and Paddington along the New Road, Portland Place, and Regent Street to Pall Mall, or up the City Road to the Bank. As a general rule, however, the railways, railway cars, and all about them are ill-managed. They are monopolies, and the public, through the press, has no restraining power upon them as it has in England. A parcel sent by express over a distance of forty miles will not be delivered within twenty-four hours. I once made my plaint on this subject at the bar or office of an hotel, and was told that no remonstrance was of avail. "It is a monopoly," the man told me, "and if we say anything, we are told that if we do not like it we need not use it." In railway matters and postal matters time and punctuality are not valued in the States as they are with us, and the public seem to acknowledge that they must put up with defects,—that they must grin and bear them in America, as the public no doubt do in Austria where such affairs are managed by a government bureau.

In the beginning of this chapter I spoke of the population of New York, and I cannot end it without remarking that out of that population more than one-eighth is composed of Germans. It is, I believe, computed that there are about 120,000 Germans in the city, and that only two other German cities in the world, Vienna and Berlin, have a larger German population than New York. The Germans are good citizens and thriving men, and are to be found prospering all over the northern and western parts of the Union. It seems that they are excellently well adapted to colonization, though they have in no instance become the dominant people in a colony, or carried with them their own language or their own laws. The French have done so in Algeria, in some of the West India islands, and quite as essentially into Lower Canada, where their language and laws still prevail. And yet it is, I think, beyond doubt that the French are not good colonists, as are the Germans.

Of the ultimate destiny of New York as one of the ruling commercial cities of the world, it is, I think, impossible to doubt. Whether or no it will ever equal London in population I will not pretend to say. Even should it do so, should its numbers so increase as to enable it to say that it had done so, the question could not very well be settled. When it comes to pass that an assemblage of men in one so-called city have to be counted by millions, there arises the impossibility of defining the limits of that city, and of saying who belong to it and who do not. An arbitrary line may be drawn, but that arbitrary line, though perhaps false when drawn as including too much, soon becomes more false as including too little. Ealing, Acton, Fulham, Putney, Norwood, Sydenham, Blackheath, Woolwich, Greenwich, Stratford, Highgate, and Hampstead, are, in truth, component parts of London, and very shortly Brighton will be as much so.

XV

The Constitution of the State of New York

As New York is the most populous State of the Union, having the largest representation in Congress,—on which account it has been called the Empire State,—I propose to mention, as shortly as may be, the nature of its separate Constitution as a State. Of course it will be understood that the constitutions of the different States are by no means the same. They have been arranged according to the judgment of the different people concerned, and have been altered from time to time to suit such altered judgment. But as the States together form one nation, and on such matters as foreign affairs, war, customs, and post-office regulations, are bound together as much as are the English counties, it is, of course, necessary that the constitution of each should in most matters assimilate itself to those of the others. These constitutions are very much alike. A Governor, with two houses of legislature, generally called the Senate and the House of Representatives, exists in each State. In the State of New York the lower house is called the Assembly. In most States the Governor is elected annually; but in some States for two years, as in New York. In Pennsylvania he is elected for three years. The House of Representatives or the Assembly is, I think, always elected for one session only; but as, in many of the States, the Legislature only sits once in two years, the election recurs of course at the same interval. The franchise in all the States is nearly universal, but in no State is it perfectly so. The Governor, Lieutenant-Governor, and other officers are elected by vote of the people as well as the members of the Legislature. Of course it will be understood that each State makes laws for itself,—that they are in nowise dependent on the Congress assembled at Washington for their laws,—unless for laws which refer to matters between the United States as a nation and other nations, or between one State and another. Each State declares with what punishment crimes shall be visited; what taxes shall be levied for the use of the State; what laws shall be passed as to education; what shall be the State judiciary. With reference to the judiciary, however, it must be understood, that the United States as a nation have separate national law courts before which come all cases litigated between State and State, and all cases which do not belong in every respect to any one individual State. In a subsequent chapter I will endeavour to explain this more fully. In endeavouring to understand the constitution of the United States it is essentially necessary that we should remember that we have always to deal with two different political arrangements,—that which refers to the nation as a whole, and that which belongs to each State as a separate governing power in itself. What is law in one State is not law in another. Nevertheless there is a very great likeness throughout these various constitutions; and any political student who shall have thoroughly mastered one, will not have much to learn in mastering the others.

This State, now called New York, was first settled by the Dutch in 1614, on Manhattan Island. They established a government in 1629, under the name of the New Netherlands. In 1664 Charles II. granted the province to his brother, James II., then Duke of York, and possession was taken of the country on his behalf by one Colonel Nichols. In 1673 it was recaptured by the Dutch, but they could not hold it, and the Duke of York again took possession by patent. A legislative body was first assembled during the reign of Charles II., in 1683; from which it will be seen that parliamentary representation was introduced into the American colonies at a very early date. The declaration of independence was made by the revolted colonies in 1776, and in 1777 the first constitution was adopted by the State of New York. In 1822 this was changed for another; and the one of which I now purport to state some of the details was brought into action in 1847. In this constitution there is a provision that it shall be overhauled and remodelled, if needs be, once in twenty years. Article XIII. Sec. 2.—"At the general election to be held in 1866, and in each twentieth year thereafter, the question, 'Shall there be a convention to revise the Constitution and amend the same?' shall be decided by the electors qualified to vote for members of the Legislature." So that the New Yorkers cannot be twitted with the presumption of finality in reference to their legislative arrangements.

The present constitution begins with declaring the inviolability of trial by jury and of habeas corpus,—"unless when, in cases of rebellion or invasion, the public safety may require its suspension." It does not say by whom it may be suspended, or who is to judge of the public safety, but, at any rate, it may be presumed that such suspension was supposed to come from the powers of the State which enacted the law. At the present moment the habeas corpus is suspended in New York, and this suspension has proceeded not from the powers of the State, but from the Federal Government, without the sanction even of the Federal Congress.

"Every citizen may freely speak, write, and publish his sentiments on all subjects, being responsible for the abuse of that right; and no law shall be passed to restrain or abridge the liberty of speech or of the press." Art. I. Sec. 8. But at the present moment liberty of speech and of the press is utterly abrogated in the State of New York, as it is in other States. I mention this not as a reproach against either the State or the Federal Government, but to show how vain all laws are for the protection of such rights. If they be not protected by the feelings of the people,—if the people are at any time, or from any cause, willing to abandon such privileges, no written laws will preserve them.

In Art. I. Sec. 14, there is a proviso that no land—land, that is, used for agricultural purposes—shall be let on lease for a longer period than twelve years. "No lease or grant of agricultural land for a longer period than twelve years hereafter made, in which shall be reserved any rent or service of any kind, shall be valid." I do not understand the intended virtue of this proviso, but it shows very clearly how different are the practices with reference to land in England and America. Farmers in the States almost always are the owners of the land which they farm, and such tenures as those, by which the occupiers of land generally hold their farms with us, are almost unknown. There is no such relation as that of landlord and tenant as regards agricultural holdings.

Every male citizen of New York may vote who is twenty-one, who has been a citizen for ten days, who has lived in the State for a year, and for four months in the county in which he votes. He can vote for all "officers that now are, or hereafter may be, elective by the people." Art. II. Sec. 1. "But," the section goes on to say, "no man of colour, unless he shall have been for three years a citizen of the State, and for one year next preceding any election shall have been possessed of a freehold estate of the value of 250 dollars (50*l.*), and shall have been actually rated, and paid a tax thereon, shall be entitled to vote at such election." This is the only embargo with which universal suffrage is laden in the State of New York.

The third article provides for the election of the Senate and the Assembly. The Senate consists of thirty-two members. And it may here be remarked that large as is the State of New York, and great as is its population, its Senate is less numerous than that of many other States. In Massachusetts, for instance, there are forty senators, though the population of Massachusetts is barely one third that of New York. In Virginia there are fifty senators, whereas the free population is not one third of that of New York. As a consequence the Senate of New York is said to be filled with men of a higher class than are generally found in the Senates of other States. Then follows in the article a list of the districts which are to return the Senators. These districts consist of one, two, three, or in one case four counties, according to the population.

The article does not give the number of members of the Lower House, nor does it even state what amount of population shall be held as entitled to a member. It merely provides for the division of the State into districts which shall contain an equal number, not of population, but of voters. The House of Assembly does consist of 128 members.

It is then stipulated that every member of both houses shall receive three dollars a day, or twelve shillings, for their services during the sitting of the legislature; but this sum is never to exceed 300 dollars, or sixty pounds in one year, unless an extra Session be called. There is also an allowance for the travelling expenses of members. It is, I presume, generally known that the members of the Congress at Washington are all paid, and that the same is the case with reference to the legislatures of all the States.

No member of the New York legislature can also be a member of the Washington Congress, or hold any civil or military office under the general States Government.

A majority of each House must be present, or as the article says, "shall constitute a quorum to do business." Each House is to keep a journal of its proceedings. The doors are to be open,—except when the public welfare shall require secrecy. A singular proviso this in a country boasting so much of freedom! For no speech or debate in either

House shall the legislature be called in question in any other place. The legislature assembles on the first Tuesday in January, and sits for about three months. Its seat is at Albany.

The executive power, (Art. IV.) is to be vested in a Governor and a Lieutenant-Governor, both of whom shall be chosen for two years. The Governor must be a citizen of the United States, must be thirty years of age, and have lived for the last four years in the State. He is to be commander-in-chief of the military and naval forces of the State,— as is the President of those of the Union. I see that this is also the case in inland States, which one would say can have no navies. And with reference to some States it is enacted that the Governor is commander-in-chief of the army, navy, and militia, showing that some army over and beyond the militia may be kept by the State. In Tennessee, which is an inland State, it is enacted that the Governor shall be "commander-in-chief of the army and navy of this State, and of the militia, except when they shall be called into the service of the United States." In Ohio the same is the case, except that there is no mention of militia. In New York there is no proviso with reference to the service of the United States. I mention this as it bears with some strength on the question of the right of secession, and indicates the jealousy of the individual States with reference to the Federal Government. The Governor can convene extra Sessions of one House or of both. He makes a message to the legislature when it meets,—a sort of Queen's speech; and he receives for his services a compensation, to be established by law. In New York this amounts to 800*l.* a year. In some States this is as low as 200*l.*, and 300*l.* In Virginia it is 1000*l.* In California 1200*l.*

The Governor can pardon, except in cases of treason. He has also a veto upon all bills sent up by the legislature. If he exercise this veto he returns the bill to the legislature with his reasons for so doing. If the bill on reconsideration by the Houses be again passed by a majority of two thirds in each House, it becomes law in spite of the Governor's veto. The veto of the President at Washington is of the same nature. Such are the powers of the Governor. But though they are very full, the Governor of each State does not practically exercise any great political power, nor is he, even politically, a great man. You might live in a State during the whole term of his government and hardly hear of him. There is vested in him by the language of the constitution a much wider power than that intrusted to the Governors of our colonies. But in our colonies everybody talks, and thinks, and knows about the Governor. As far as the limits of the colony the Governor is a great man. But this is not the case with reference to the Governors in the different States.

The next article provides that the Governor's ministers, viz., the Secretary of State, the Comptroller, Treasurer, and Attorney-General, shall be chosen every two years at a general election. In this respect the State constitution differs from that of the national constitution. The President at Washington names his own ministers,—subject to the approbation of the Senate. He makes many other appointments with the same limitation. As regards these nominations in general, the Senate, I believe, is not slow to interfere; but with reference to the ministers it is understood that the names sent in by the President shall stand. Of the Secretary of State, Comptroller, &c., belonging to the different States, and who are elected by the people, in a general way one never hears. No doubt they attend their offices and take their pay, but they are not political personages.

The next article, No. VI., refers to the Judiciary, and is very complicated. After considerable study I have failed to understand it. The judges are elected by vote, and remain in office for, I believe, a term of eight years. In Sect. 20 of this article it is provided that—"No judicial officer, except Justices of the Peace, shall receive to his own use any fees or perquisites of office." How pleasantly this enactment must sound in the ears of the justices of the peace.

Article VII. refers to fiscal matters, and is more especially interesting as showing how greatly the State of New York has depended on its canals for its wealth. These canals are the property of the State; and by this article it seems to be provided that they shall not only maintain themselves, but maintain to a considerable extent the State expenditure also, and stand in lieu of taxation. It is provided, section 6, that the "legislature shall not sell, lease, or otherwise dispose of any of the canals of the State; but that they shall remain the property of the State, and under its management for ever." But in spite of its canals the State does not seem to be doing very well, for I see that in 1860, its income was 4,780,000 dollars, and its expenditure 5,100,000, whereas its debt was 32,500,000 dollars. Of all the States, Pennsylvania is the most indebted, Virginia is the second on the list, and New York the third. New Hampshire, Connecticut, Vermont, Delaware, and Texas, owe no State debts. All the other State ships have taken in ballast.

The militia is supposed to consist of all men capable of bearing arms, under forty-five years of age. But no one need be enrolled, who from scruples of conscience is averse to bearing arms. At the present moment such scruples do not seem to be very general. Then follows, in Article XI., a detailed enactment as to the choosing of militia officers. It may be perhaps sufficient to say that the privates are to choose the captains and the subalterns; the captains and subalterns are to choose the field officers; and the field officers the brigadier-generals and inspectors of brigade. The Governor, however, with the consent of the Senate shall nominate all major-generals. Now that real soldiers have unfortunately become necessary the above plan has not been found to work well.

Such is the Constitution of the State of New York, which has been intended to work and does work quite separately from that of the United States. It will be seen that the purport has been to make it as widely democratic as possible,—to provide that all power of all description shall come directly from the people, and that such power shall return to the people at short intervals. The Senate and the Governor each remain for two years, but not for the same two years. If a new Senate commence its work in 1861, a new Governor will come in in 1862. But, nevertheless, there is in the form of Government as thus established an absence of that close and immediate responsibility which attends our ministers. When a man has been voted in, it seems that responsibility is over for the period of the required service. He has been chosen, and the country which has chosen him is to trust that he will do his best. I do not know that this matters much with reference to the legislature or governments of the different States, for their State legislatures and governments are but puny powers; but in the legislature and government at Washington it does matter very much. But I shall have another opportunity of speaking on that subject.

Nothing has struck me so much in America as the fact that these State legislatures are puny powers. The absence of any tidings whatever of their doings across the water is a proof of this. Who has heard of the legislature of New York or of Massachusetts? It is boasted here that their insignificance is a sign of the well-being of the people;—that the smallness of the power necessary for carrying on the machine shows how beautifully the machine is organized, and how well it works. "It is better to have little governors than great governors," an American said to me once. "It is our glory that we know how to live without having great men over us to rule us." That glory, if ever it were a glory, has come to an end. It seems to me that all these troubles have come upon the States because they have not placed high men in high places. The less of laws and the less of control the better, providing a people can go right with few laws and little control. One may say that no laws and no control would be best of all,—provided that none were needed. But this is not exactly the position of the American people.

The two professions of law-making and of governing have become unfashionable, low in estimation, and of no repute in the States. The municipal powers of the cities have not fallen into the hands of the leading men. The word politician has come to bear the meaning of political adventurer and almost of political blackleg. If A calls B a politician A intends to vilify B by so calling him. Whether or no the best citizens of a State will ever be induced to serve in the State legislature by a nobler consideration than that of pay, or by a higher tone of political morals than that now existing, I cannot say. It seems to me that some great decrease in the numbers of the State legislators should be a first step towards such a consummation. There are not many men in each State who can afford to give up two or three months of the year to the State service for nothing; but it may be presumed that in each State there are a few. Those who are induced to devote their time by the payment of 60*l.*, can hardly be the men most fitted for the purpose of legislation. It certainly has seemed to me that the members of the State legislatures and of the State governments are not held in that respect and treated with that confidence to which, in the eyes of an Englishman, such functionaries should be held as entitled.

XVI

Boston

From New York we returned to Boston by Hartford, the capital, or one of the capitals of Connecticut. This proud little State is composed of two old provinces, of which Hartford and Newhaven were the two metropolitan towns. Indeed there was a third colony called Saybrook, which was joined to Hartford. As neither of the two could of course give way when Hartford and Newhaven were made into one, the houses of legislature and the seat of government are changed about, year by year. Connecticut is a very proud little State, and has a pleasant legend of its own stanchness in the old colonial days. In 1662 the colonies were united, and a charter was given to them by Charles II. But some years later, in 1686, when the bad days of James II. had come, this charter was considered to be too liberal, and order was given that it should be suspended. One Sir Edmund Andross had been appointed governor of all New England, and sent word from Boston to Connecticut that the charter itself should be given up to him. This the men of Connecticut refused to do. Whereupon Sir Edmund with a military following presented himself at their assembly, declared their governing powers to be dissolved, and after much palaver caused the charter itself to be laid upon the table before him. The discussion had been long, having lasted through the day into the night, and the room had been lighted with candles. On a sudden each light disappeared, and Sir Edmund with his followers were in the dark. As a matter of course, when the light was restored the charter was gone, and Sir

Edmund, the governor-general, was baffled, as all governors-general and all Sir Edmunds always are in such cases. The charter was gone, a gallant Captain Wadsworth having carried it off and hidden it in an oak tree. The charter was renewed when William III. came to the throne, and now hangs triumphantly in the State House at Hartford. The charter oak has, alas! succumbed to the weather, but was standing a few years since. The men of Hartford are very proud of their charter, and regard it as the parent of their existing liberties quite as much as though no national revolution of their own had intervened.

And indeed the northern States of the Union, especially those of New England, refer all their liberties to the old charters which they held from the mother-country. They rebelled, as they themselves would seem to say, and set themselves up as a separate people, not because the mother-country had refused to them by law sufficient liberty and sufficient self-control, but because the mother-country infringed the liberties and powers of self-control which she herself had given. The mother-country, so these States declare, had acted the part of Sir Edmund Andross, had endeavoured to take away their charters. So they also put out the lights, and took themselves to an oak tree of their own,—which is still standing, though winds from the infernal regions are now battering its branches. Long may it stand!

Whether the mother-country did or did not infringe the charters she had given, I will not here inquire. As to the nature of those alleged infringements, are they not written down to the number of twenty-seven in the Declaration of Independence? The twenty-seven paragraphs may all be seen. They mostly begin with He. "He" has done this, and "He" has done that. The "He" is poor George III., whose twenty-seven mortal sins against his transatlantic colonies are thus recapitulated. It would avail nothing to argue now whether those deeds were sins or virtues; nor would it have availed then. The child had grown up and was strong, and chose to go alone into the world. The young bird was fledged, and flew away. Poor George III. with his cackling was certainly not efficacious in restraining such a flight. But it is gratifying to see how this new people, when they had it in their power to change all their laws, to throw themselves upon any Utopian theory that the folly of a wild philanthropy could devise, to discard as abominable every vestige of English rule and English power,—it is gratifying to see that when they could have done all this, they did not do so, but preferred to cling to things English. Their old colonial limits were still to be the borders of their States. Their old charters were still to be regarded as the sources from whence their State powers had come. The old laws were to remain in force. The precedents of the English courts were to be held as legal precedents in the courts of the new nation,—and are now so held. It was still to be England,—but England without a King making his last struggle for political power. This was the idea of the people, and this was their feeling; and that idea has been carried out, and that feeling has remained.

In the constitution of the State of New York nothing is said about the religion of the people. It was regarded as a subject with which the constitution had no concern whatever. But as soon as we come among the stricter people of New England we find that the constitution-makers have not been able absolutely to ignore the subject. In Connecticut it is enjoined that as it is the duty of all men to worship the Supreme Being, and their right to render that worship in the mode most consistent with their consciences, no person shall be by law compelled to join or be classed with any religious association. The line of argument is hardly logical, the conclusion not being in accordance with, or hanging on the first of the two premises. But nevertheless the meaning is clear. In a free country no man shall be made to worship after any special fashion; but it is decreed by the constitution that every man is bound by duty to worship after some fashion. The article then goes on to say how they who do worship are to be taxed for the support of their peculiar church. I am not quite clear whether the New Yorkers have not managed this difficulty with greater success. When we come to the old Bay State,—to Massachusetts,—we find the Christian religion spoken of in the Constitution as that which in some one of its forms should receive the adherence of every good Christian.

Hartford is a pleasant little town, with English-looking houses, and an English-looking country around it. Here, as everywhere through the States, one is struck by the size and comfort of the residences. I sojourned there at the house of a friend, and could find no limit to the number of spacious sitting-rooms which it contained. The modest dining-room and drawing-room which suffice with us for men of seven or eight hundred a year would be regarded as very mean accommodation by persons of similar incomes in the States.

I found that Hartford was all alive with trade, and that wages were high, because there are there two factories for the manufacture of arms. Colt's pistols come from Hartford, as do also Sharpe's rifles. Wherever arms can be prepared, or gunpowder; where clothes or blankets fit for soldiers can be made, or tents or standards, or things appertaining in any way to warfare, there trade was still brisk. No being is more costly in his requirements than a soldier, and no soldier so costly as the American. He must eat and drink of the best, and have good boots and warm bedding, and good shelter. There were during the Christmas of 1861 above half a million of soldiers so to be provided,—the President, in his message made in December to Congress, declared the number to be above six hundred thousand— and therefore in such places as Hartford trade was very brisk. I went over the rifle factory, and was shown everything, but I do not know that I brought away much with me that was worth any reader's attention. The best of rifles, I have no doubt, were being made with the greatest rapidity, and all were sent to the army as soon as finished. I saw some murderous-looking weapons, with swords attached to them instead of bayonets, but have since been told by soldiers that the old-fashioned bayonet is thought to be more serviceable.

Immediately on my arrival in Boston I heard that Mr. Emerson was going to lecture at the Tremont Hall on the subject of the war, and I resolved to go and hear him. I was acquainted with Mr. Emerson, and by reputation knew him well. Among us in England he is regarded as transcendental, and perhaps even as mystic in his philosophy. His 'Representative Men' is the work by which he is best known on our side of the water, and I have heard some readers declare that they could not quite understand Mr. Emerson's 'Representative Men.' For myself, I confess that I had broken down over some portions of that book. Since I had become acquainted with him I had read others of his writings, especially his book on England, and had found that he improved greatly on acquaintance. I think that he has confined his mysticism to the book above named. In conversation he is very clear, and by no means above the small practical things of the world. He would, I fancy, know as well what interest he ought to receive for his money as though he were no philosopher; and I am inclined to think that if he held land he would make his hay while the sun shone, as might any common farmer. Before I had met Mr. Emerson, when my idea of him was formed simply on the 'Representative Men,' I should have thought that a lecture from him on the war would have taken his hearers all among the clouds. As it was, I still had my doubts, and was inclined to fear that a subject which could only be handled usefully at such a time before a large audience by a combination of common sense, high principles, and eloquence, would hardly be safe in Mr. Emerson's hands. I did not doubt the high principles, but feared much that there would be a lack of common sense. So many have talked on that subject, and have shown so great a lack of common sense! As to the eloquence, that might be there, or might not.

Mr. Emerson is a Massachusetts man, very well known in Boston, and a great crowd was collected to hear him. I suppose there were some three thousand persons in the room. I confess that when he took his place before us my prejudices were against him. The matter in hand required no philosophy. It required common sense, and the very best of common sense. It demanded that he should be impassioned, for of what interest can any address be on a matter of public politics without passion? But it demanded that the passion should be winnowed, and free from all rhodomontade. I fancied what might be said on such a subject as to that overlauded star-spangled banner, and how the star-spangled flag would look when wrapped in a mist of mystic Platonism.

But from the beginning to the end there was nothing mystic—no Platonism; and, if I remember rightly, the star-spangled banner was altogether omitted. To the national eagle he did allude. "Your American eagle," he said, "is very well. Protect it here and abroad. But beware of the American peacock." He gave an account of the war from the beginning, showing how it had arisen, and how it had been conducted; and he did so with admirable simplicity and truth. He thought the North were right about the war; and as I thought so also, I was not called upon to disagree with him. He was terse and perspicuous in his sentences, practical in his advice, and, above all things, true in what he said to his audience of themselves. They who know America will understand how hard it is for a public man in the States to practise such truth in his addresses. Fluid compliments and high-flown national eulogium are expected. In this instance none were forthcoming. The North had risen with patriotism to make this effort, and it was now warned that in doing so it was simply doing its national duty. And then came the subject of slavery. I had been told that Mr. Emerson was an abolitionist, and knew that I must disagree with him on that head, if on no other. To me it has always seemed that to mix up the question of general abolition with this war must be the work of a man too ignorant to understand the real subject of the war, or too false to his country to regard it. Throughout the whole lecture I was waiting for Mr. Emerson's abolition doctrine, but no abolition doctrine came. The words abolition and compensation were mentioned, and then there was an end of the subject. If Mr. Emerson be an abolitionist he expressed his views very mildly on that occasion. On the whole the lecture was excellent, and that little advice about the peacock was in itself worth an hour's attention.

That practice of lecturing is "quite an institution" in the States. So it is in England, my readers will say. But in England it is done in a different way, with a different object and with much less of result. With us, if I am not mistaken, lectures are mostly given gratuitously by the lecturer. They are got up here and there with some philanthropical object, and in the hope that an hour at the disposal of young men and women may be rescued from idleness. The subjects chosen are social, literary, philanthropic, romantic, geographical, scientific, religious,—anything rather than political. The lecture-rooms are not usually filled to overflowing, and there is often a question whether the real good achieved is worth the trouble taken. The most popular lectures are given by big people, whose presence is likely to be attractive; and the whole thing, I fear we must confess, is not pre-eminently successful. In the northern States of America the matter stands on a very different footing. Lectures there are more popular than either theatres or concerts. Enormous halls are built for them. Tickets for long courses are taken with avidity. Very large sums are paid to popular lecturers, so that the profession is lucrative,—more so, I am given to understand, than is the cognate profession of literature. The whole thing is done in great style. Music is introduced. The lecturer stands on a large raised platform, on which sit around him the bald and hoary-headed and superlatively wise. Ladies come in large numbers; especially those who aspire to soar above the frivolities of the world. Politics is the subject most popular, and most general. The men and women of Boston could no more do without their lectures, than those of Paris could without their theatres. It is the decorous diversion of the best ordered of her citizens. The fast young men go to clubs, and the fast young women to dances, as fast young men and women do in other places that are wicked; but lecturing is the favourite diversion of the steady-minded Bostonian. After all, I do not know that the result is very good. It does not seem that much will be gained by such lectures on either side of the Atlantic,—except that respectable killing of an evening which might otherwise be killed less respectably. It is but an industrious idleness, an attempt at a royal road to information, that habit of attending lectures. Let any man or woman say what he has brought away from any such attendance. It is attractive, that idea of being studious without any of the labour of study; but I fear it is illusive. If an evening can be so passed without ennui, I believe that that may be regarded as the best result to be gained. But then it so often happens that the evening is not passed without ennui! Of course in saying this, I am not alluding to lectures given in special places as a course of special study. Medical lectures, no doubt, are a necessary part of medical education. As many as two or three thousand often attend these political lectures in Boston, but I do not know whether on that account the popular subjects are much better understood. Nevertheless I resolved to hear more, hoping that I might in that way teach myself to understand what were the popular politics in New England. Whether or no I may have learned this in any other way I do not perhaps know; but at any rate I did not learn it in this way.

The next lecture which I attended was also given in the Tremont Hall, and on this occasion also the subject of the war was to be treated. The special treachery of the rebels was, I think, the matter to be taken in hand. On this occasion also the room was full, and my hopes of a pleasant hour ran high. For some fifteen minutes I listened, and I am bound to say that the gentleman discoursed in excellent English. He was master of that wonderful fluency which is peculiarly the gift of an American. He went on from one sentence to another with rhythmic tones and unerring pronunciation. He never faltered, never repeated his words, never fell into those vile half-muttered hems and haws by which an Englishman in such a position so generally betrays his timidity. But during the whole time of my remaining in the room he did not give expression to a single thought. He went on from one soft platitude to another, and uttered words from which I would defy any one of his audience to carry away with them anything. And yet it seemed to me that his audience was satisfied. I was not satisfied, and managed to escape out of the room.

The next lecturer to whom I listened was Mr. Everett. Mr. Everett's reputation as an orator is very great, and I was especially anxious to hear him. I had long since known that his power of delivery was very marvellous; that his tones, elocution, and action were all great; and that he was able to command the minds and sympathies of his audience in a remarkable manner. His subject also was the war;—or rather the causes of the war, and its qualification. Had the North given to the South cause of provocation? Had the South been fair and honest in its dealings to the North? Had any compromise been possible by which the war might have been avoided, and the rights and dignity of the North preserved? Seeing that Mr. Everett is a northern man and was lecturing to a Boston audience, one knew well how these questions would be answered, but the manner of the answering would be everything. This lecture was given at Roxboro', one of the suburbs of

Boston. So I went out to Roxboro' with a party, and found myself honoured by being placed on the platform among the bald-headed ones and the superlatively wise. This privilege is naturally gratifying, but it entails on him who is so gratified the inconvenience of sitting at the lecturer's back, whereas it is perhaps better for the listener to be before his face.

I could not but be amused by one little scenic incident. When we all went upon the platform, some one proposed that the clergymen should lead the way out of the waiting-room in which we bald-headed ones and superlatively wise were assembled. But to this the manager of the affair demurred. He wanted the clergymen for a purpose, he said. And so the profane ones led the way, and the clergymen, of whom there might be some six or seven, clustered in around the lecturer at last. Early in his discourse Mr. Everett told us what it was that the country needed at this period of her trial. Patriotism, courage, the bravery of the men, the good wishes of the women, the self-denial of all,—"and," continued the lecturer, turning to his immediate neighbours, "the prayers of these holy men whom I see around me." It had not been for nothing that the clergymen were detained.

Mr. Everett lectures without any book or paper before him, and continues from first to last as though the words came from him on the spur of the moment. It is known, however, that it is his practice to prepare his orations with great care and commit them entirely to memory, as does an actor. Indeed he repeats the same lecture over and over again, I am told, without the change of a word or of an action. I did not like Mr. Everett's lecture. I did not like what he said, or the seeming spirit in which it was framed. But I am bound to admit that his power of oratory is very wonderful. Those among his countrymen who have criticised his manner in my hearing have said that he is too florid, that there is an affectation in the motion of his hands, and that the intended pathos of his voice sometimes approaches too near the precipice over which the fall is so deep and rapid, and at the bottom of which lies absolute ridicule. Judging for myself, I did not find it so. My position for seeing was not good, but my ear was not offended. Critics also should bear in mind that an orator does not speak chiefly to them or for their approval. He who writes, or speaks, or sings for thousands, must write, speak, or sing as those thousands would have him. That to a dainty connoisseur will be false music, which to the general ear shall be accounted as the perfection of harmony. An eloquence altogether suited to the fastidious and hypercritical, would probably fail to carry off the hearts and interest the sympathies of the young and eager. As regards manners, tone, and choice of words, I think that the oratory of Mr. Everett places him very high. His skill in his work is perfect. He never falls back upon a word. He never repeats himself. His voice is always perfectly under command. As for hesitation or timidity, the days for those failings have long passed by with him. When he makes a point, he makes it well, and drives it home to the intelligence of every one before him. Even that appeal to the holy men around him sounded well,—or would have done so had I not been present at that little arrangement in the ante-room. On the audience at large it was manifestly effective.

But nevertheless the lecture gave me but a poor idea of Mr. Everett as a politician, though it made me regard him highly as an orator. It was impossible not to perceive that he was anxious to utter the sentiments of the audience rather than his own;—that he was making himself an echo, a powerful and harmonious echo of what he conceived to be public opinion in Boston at that moment;—that he was neither leading nor teaching the people before him, but allowing himself to be led by them, so that he might best play his present part for their delectation. He was neither bold nor honest, as Emerson had been, and I could not but feel that every tyro of a politician before him would thus recognize his want of boldness and of honesty. As a statesman, or as a critic of statecraft and of other statesmen, he is wanting in backbone. For many years Mr. Everett has been not even inimical to southern politics and southern courses, nor was he among those who, during the last eight years previous to Mr. Lincoln's election, fought the battle for northern principles. I do not say that on this account he is now false to advocate the war. But he cannot carry men with him when, at his age, he advocates it by arguments opposed to the tenour of his long political life. His abuse of the South and of southern ideas was as virulent as might be that of a young lad now beginning his political career, or of one who had through life advocated abolition principles. He heaped reproaches on poor Virginia, whose position as the chief of the border States has given to her hardly the possibility of avoiding a Scylla of ruin on the one side, or a Charybdis of rebellion on the other. When he spoke as he did of Virginia, ridiculing the idea of her sacred soil, even I, Englishman as I am, could not but think of Washington, of Jefferson, of Randolph, and of Madison. He should not have spoken of Virginia as he did speak; for no man could have known better Virginia's difficulties. But Virginia was at a discount in Boston, and Mr. Everett was speaking to a Boston audience. And then he referred to England and to Europe. Mr. Everett has been minister to England, and knows the people. He is a student of history, and must, I think, know that England's career has not been unhappy or unprosperous. But England also was at a discount in Boston, and Mr. Everett was speaking to a Boston audience. They are sending us their advice across the water, said Mr. Everett. And what is their advice to us? That we should come down from the high place we have built for ourselves, and be even as they are. They screech at us from the low depths in which they are wallowing in their misery, and call on us to join them in their wretchedness. I am not quoting Mr. Everett's very words, for I have not them by me; but I am not making them stronger, nor so strong as he made them. As I thought of Mr. Everett's reputation, and of his years of study,—of his long political life and unsurpassed sources of information,—I could not but grieve heartily when I heard such words fall from him. I could not but ask myself whether it were impossible that under the present circumstances of her constitution this great nation of America should produce an honest, high-minded statesman. When Lincoln and Hamlin, the existing President and Vice-President of the States, were in 1860 as yet but the candidates of the republican party, Bell and Everett also were the candidates of the old whig, conservative party. Their express theory was this,—that the question of slavery should not be touched. Their purpose was to crush agitation and restore harmony by an impartial balance between the North and South: a fine purpose,—the finest of all purposes, had it been practicable. But such a course of compromise was now at a discount in Boston, and Mr. Everett was speaking to a Boston audience. As an orator, Mr. Everett's excellence is, I think, not to be questioned; but as a politician I cannot give him a high rank.

After that I heard Mr. Wendell Phillips. Of him, too, as an orator all the world of Massachusetts speaks with great admiration, and I have no doubt so speaks with justice. He is, however, known as the hottest and most impassioned advocate of abolition. Not many months since the cause of abolition as advocated by him, was so unpopular in Boston, that Mr. Phillips was compelled to address his audience surrounded by a guard of policemen. Of this gentleman, I may at any rate say that he is consistent, devoted, and disinterested. He is an abolitionist by profession, and seeks to find in every turn of the tide of politics some stream on which he may bring himself nearer to his object. In the old days, previous to the election of Mr. Lincoln, in days so old that they are now nearly eighteen months past, Mr. Phillips was an anti-Union man. He advocated strongly the disseverance of the

Union, so that the country to which he belonged might have hands
clean from the taint of slavery. He had probably acknowledged to
himself, that while the North and South were bound together no hope
existed of emancipation, but that if the North stood alone the South
would become too weak to foster and keep alive the "social institution." In which, if such were his opinions, I am inclined to agree with
him. But now he is all for the Union, thinking that a victorious North
can compel the immediate emancipation of southern slaves. As to
which I beg to say that I am bold to differ from Mr. Phillips altogether.

It soon became evident to me that Mr. Phillips was unwell, and
lecturing at a disadvantage. His manner was clearly that of an accustomed orator, but his voice was weak, and he was not up to the effect
which he attempted to make. His hearers were impatient, repeatedly
calling upon him to speak out, and on that account I tried hard to feel
kindly towards him and his lecture. But I must confess that I failed. To
me it seemed that the doctrine he preached was one of rapine, bloodshed, and social destruction. He would call upon the Government and
upon Congress to enfranchise the slaves at once,—now during the
war,—so that the Southern power might be destroyed by a concurrence of misfortunes. And he would do so at once, on the spur of the
moment, fearing lest the South should be before him, and themselves
emancipate their own bondsmen. I have sometimes thought that there
is no being so venomous, so bloodthirsty as a professed philanthropist;
and that when the philanthropist's ardour lies negro-wards, it then
assumes the deepest die of venom and bloodthirstiness. There are four
millions of slaves in the southern States, none of whom have any
capacity for self-maintenance or self-control. Four millions of slaves,
with the necessities of children, with the passions of men, and the
ignorance of savages! And Mr. Phillips would emancipate these at a
blow; would, were it possible for him to do so, set them loose upon the
soil to tear their masters, destroy each other, and make such a hell
upon the earth as has never even yet come from the uncontrolled
passions and unsatisfied wants of men. But Congress cannot do this.
All the members of Congress put together cannot, according to the
constitution of the United States, emancipate a single slave in South
Carolina; not if they were all unanimous. No emancipation in a Slave
State can come otherwise than by the legislative enactment of that
State. But it was then thought that in this coming winter of 1860–61
the action of Congress might be set aside. The North possessed an
enormous army under the control of the President. The South was in
rebellion, and the President could pronounce, and the army perhaps

enforce the confiscation of all property held in slaves. If any who held them were not disloyal, the question of compensation might be settled afterwards. How those four million slaves should live, and how white men should live among them, in some States or parts of States not equal to the blacks in number;—as to that Mr. Phillips did not give us his opinion.

And Mr. Phillips also could not keep his tongue away from the abominations of Englishmen and the miraculous powers of his own countrymen. It was on this occasion that he told us more than once how Yankees carried brains in their fingers, whereas "common people"—alluding by that name to Europeans—had them only, if at all, inside their brain-pans. And then he informed us that Lord Palmerston had always hated America. Among the Radicals there might be one or two who understood and valued the institutions of America, but it was a well-known fact that Lord Palmerston was hostile to the country. Nothing but hidden enmity,—enmity hidden or not hidden,—could be expected from England. That the people of Boston, or of Massachusetts, or of the North generally, should feel sore against England is to me intelligible. I know how the minds of men are moved in masses to certain feelings, and that it ever must be so. Men in common talk are not bound to weigh their words, to think, and speculate on their results, and be sure of the premises on which their thoughts are founded. But it is different with a man who rises before two or three thousand of his countrymen to teach and instruct them. After that I heard no more political lectures in Boston.

Of course I visited Bunker's Hill, and went to Lexington and Concord. From the top of the monument on Bunker's Hill there is a fine view of Boston Harbour, and seen from thence the harbour is picturesque. The mouth is crowded with islands and jutting necks and promontories; and though the shores are in no place rich enough to make the scenery grand, the general effect is good. The monument, however, is so constructed that one can hardly get a view through the windows at the top of it, and there is no outside gallery round it. Immediately below the monument is a marble figure of Major Warren, who fell there,—not from the top of the monument, as some one was led to believe when informed that on that spot the Major had fallen. Bunker's Hill, which is little more than a mound, is at Charleston,—a dull, populous, respectable, and very unattractive suburb of Boston.

Bunker's Hill has obtained a considerable name, and is accounted great in the annals of American history. In England we have all heard of Bunker's Hill, and some of us dislike the sound as much as French-men do that of Waterloo. In the States men talk of Bunker's Hill as we may, perhaps, talk of Agincourt and such favourite fields. But, after all, little was done at Bunker's Hill, and, as far as I can learn, no victory was gained there by either party. The road from Boston to the town of Concord, on which stands the village of Lexington, is the true scene of the earliest and greatest deeds of the men of Boston. The monument at Bunker's Hill stands high and commands attention, while those at Lexington and Concord are very lowly and command no attention. But it is of that road and what was done on it that Mas-sachusetts should be proud. When the colonists first began to feel that they were oppressed, and a half resolve was made to resist that oppression by force, they began to collect a few arms and some gunpowder at Concord, a small town about eighteen miles from Bos-ton. Of this preparation the English Governor received tidings, and determined to send a party of soldiers to seize the arms. This he endeavoured to do secretly; but he was too closely watched, and word was sent down over the waters by which Boston was then surrounded that the colonists might be prepared for the soldiers. At that time Boston Neck, as it was and is still called, was the only connection between the town and the main land, and the road over Boston Neck did not lead to Concord. Boats therefore were necessarily used, and there was some difficulty in getting the soldiers to the nearest point. They made their way, however, to the road, and continued their route as far as Lexington without interruption. Here, however, they were attacked, and the first blood of that war was shed. They shot three or four of the—rebels, I suppose I should in strict language call them, and then proceeded on to Concord. But at Concord they were stopped and repulsed, and along the road back from Concord to Lexington they were driven with slaughter and dismay. And thus the rebellion was commenced which led to the establishment of a people which, let us Englishmen say and think what we may of them at this present moment, has made itself one of the five great nations of the earth, and has enabled us to boast that the two out of the five who enjoy the greatest liberty and the widest prosperity, speak the English language and are known by English names. For all that has come and is like to come, I say again, long may that honour remain. I could not but feel that that road from Boston to Concord deserves a name in the world's history greater, perhaps, than has yet been given to it.

Concord is at present to be noted as the residence of Mr. Emerson and of Mr. Hawthorne, two of those many men of letters of whose

presence Boston and its neighbourhood have reason to be proud. Of
Mr. Emerson I have already spoken. The author of the 'Scarlet
Letter' I regard as certainly the first of American novelists. I know
what men will say of Mr. Cooper,—and I also am an admirer of
Cooper's novels. But I cannot think that Mr. Cooper's powers were
equal to those of Mr. Hawthorne, though his mode of thought may
have been more genial, and his choice of subjects more attractive in
their day. In point of imagination, which, after all, is the novelist's
greatest gift, I hardly know any living author who can be accounted
superior to Mr. Hawthorne.

Very much has, undoubtedly, been done in Boston to carry out that
theory of Colonel Newcome's—*Emollit mores*, by which the Colonel
meant to signify his opinion that a competent knowledge of reading,
writing, and arithmetic, with a taste for enjoying those accomplish-
ments, goes very far towards the making of a man, and will by no
means mar a gentleman. In Boston nearly every man, woman, and
child has had his or her manners so far softened; and though they may
still occasionally be somewhat rough to the outer touch, the inward
effect is plainly visible. With us, especially among our agricultural
population, the absence of that inner softening is as visible.

I went to see a public library in the city, which, if not founded by Mr.
Bates whose name is so well known in London as connected with the
house of Messrs. Baring, has been greatly enriched by him. It is by his
money that it has been enabled to do its work. In this library there is a
certain number of thousands of volumes—a great many volumes, as
there are in most public libraries. There are books of all classes, from
ponderous unreadable folios, of which learned men know the title-
pages, down to the lightest literature. Novels are by no means
eschewed,—are rather, if I understood aright, considered as one of the
staples of the library. From this library any book, excepting such rare
volumes as in all libraries are considered holy, is given out to any
inhabitant of Boston, without any payment, on presentation of a
simple request on a prepared form. In point of fact, it is a gratuitous
circulating library open to all Boston, rich or poor, young or old. The
books seemed in general to be confided to young children, who came as
messengers from their fathers and mothers, or brothers and sisters. No
question whatever is asked, if the applicant is known or the place of his
residence undoubted. If there be no such knowledge, or there be any
doubt as to the residence, the applicant is questioned, the object being
to confine the use of the library to the *bonâ fide* inhabitants of the city.
Practically the books are given to those who ask for them, whoever

they may be. Boston contains over 200,000 inhabitants, and all those 200,000 are entitled to them. Some twenty men and women are kept employed from morning to night in carrying on this circulating library; and there is, moreover, attached to the establishment a large reading-room supplied with papers and magazines, open to the public of Boston on the same terms.

Of course I asked whether a great many of the books were not lost, stolen, and destroyed; and of course I was told that there were no losses, no thefts, and no destruction. As to thefts, the librarian did not seem to think that any instance of such an occurrence could be found. Among the poorer classes a book might sometimes be lost when they were changing their lodgings, but anything so lost was more than replaced by the fines. A book is taken out for a week, and if not brought back at the end of that week, when the loan can be renewed if the reader wishes, a fine, I think of two cents, is incurred. The children, when too late with the books, bring in the two cents as a matter of course, and the sum so collected fully replaces all losses. It was all *coleur de rose*; the librarianesses looked very pretty and learned, and, if I remember aright, mostly wore spectacles; the head librarian was enthusiastic; the nice instructive books were properly dogs-eared; my own productions were in enormous demand; the call for books over the counter was brisk, and the reading-room was full of readers.

It has, I dare say, occurred to other travellers to remark that the proceedings at such institutions, when visited by them on their travels, are always rose coloured. It is natural that the bright side should be shown to the visitor. It may be that many books are called for and returned unread, that many of those taken out are so taken by persons who ought to pay for their novels at circulating libraries, that the librarian and librarianesses get very tired of their long hours of attendance,—for I found that they were very long;—and that many idlers warm themselves in that reading-room: nevertheless the fact remains,—the library is public to all the men and women in Boston, and books are given out without payment to all who may choose to ask for them. Why should not the great Mr. Mudie emulate Mr. Bates, and open a library in London on the same system?

The librarian took me into one special room, of which he himself kept the key, to show me a present which the library had received from the English Government. The room was filled with volumes of two sizes, all bound alike, containing descriptions and drawings of all the patents taken out in England. According to this librarian such a work would be invaluable as to American patents; but he conceived that the subject had become too confused to render any such an undertaking possible. "I never allow a single volume to be used for a moment without the presence of myself or one of my assistants," said the librarian; and then he explained to me, when I asked him why he was so particular, that the drawings would, as a matter of course, be cut out and stolen if he omitted his care. "But they may be copied," I said. "Yes; but if Jones merely copies one, Smith may come after him and copy it also. Jones will probably desire to hinder Smith from having any evidence of such a patent." As to the ordinary borrowing and returning of books, the poorest labourer's child in Boston might be trusted as honest; but when a question of trade came up, of commercial competition, then the librarian was bound to bethink himself that his countrymen are very smart. "I hope," said the librarian, "you will let them know in England how grateful we are for their present." And I hereby execute that librarian's commission.

I shall always look back to social life in Boston with great pleasure. I met there many men and women whom to know is a distinction, and with whom to be intimate is a great delight. It was a Puritan city, in which strict old Roundhead sentiments and laws used to prevail but now-a-days ginger is hot in the mouth there, and in spite of the war there were cakes and ale. There was a law passed in Massachusetts in the old days that any girl should be fined and imprisoned who allowed a young man to kiss her. That law has now, I think, fallen into abeyance, and such matters are regulated in Boston much as they are in other large towns further eastward. It still, I conceive, calls itself a Puritan city, but it has divested its Puritanism of austerity, and clings rather to the politics and public bearing of its old fathers than to their social manners and pristine severity of intercourse. The young girls are, no doubt, much more comfortable under the new dispensation,—and the elderly men also, as I fancy. Sunday, as regards the outer streets, is sabbatical. But Sunday evenings within doors I always found to be, what my friends in that country call "quite a good time." It is not the thing in Boston to smoke in the streets during the day; but the wisest, the sagest, and the most holy,—even those holy men whom the lecturer saw around him,—seldom refuse a cigar in the dining-room as soon as the ladies have gone. Perhaps even the wicked weed would make its appearance before that sad eclipse, thereby postponing, or perhaps absolutely annihilating, the melancholy period of widowhood to both parties, and would light itself under the very eyes of those who in sterner cities will lend no countenance to such lightings. Ah me, it was very pleasant! I confess I like this

abandonment of the stricter rules of the more decorous world. I fear
that there is within me an aptitude to the milder debaucheries which
makes such deviations pleasant. I like to drink and I like to smoke, but
I do not like to turn women out of the room. Then comes the question
whether one can have all that one likes together. In some small circles
in New England I found people simple enough to fancy that they
could. In Massachusetts the Maine Liquor Law is still the law of the
land, but, like that other law to which I have alluded, it has fallen very
much out of use. At any rate it had not reached the houses of the
gentlemen with whom I had the pleasure of making acquaintance. But
here I must guard myself from being misunderstood. I saw but one
drunken man through all New England, and he was very respectable.
He was, however, so uncommonly drunk that he might be allowed to
count for two or three. The Puritans of Boston are, of course, simple in
their habits and simple in their expenses. Champagne and canvas-
back ducks I found to be the provisions most in vogue among those
who desired to adhere closely to the manners of their forefathers. Upon
the whole I found the ways of life which had been brought over in the
'Mayflower' from the stern sects of England, and preserved through
the revolutionary war for liberty, to be very pleasant ways, and I made
up my mind that a Yankee Puritan can be an uncommonly pleasant
fellow. I wish that some of them did not dine so early; for when a man
sits down at half-past two, that keeping up of the after-dinner recrea-
tions till bedtime becomes hard work.

   In Boston the houses are very spacious and excellent, and they are
always furnished with those luxuries which it is so difficult to introduce
into an old house. They have hot and cold water pipes into every room,
and baths attached to the bed-chambers. It is not only that comfort is
increased by such arrangements, but that much labour is saved. In an
old English house it will occupy a servant the best part of the day
to carry water up and down for a large family. Everything also is
spacious, commodious, and well lighted. I certainly think that in
house building the Americans have gone beyond us, for even our new
houses are not commodious as are theirs. One practice which they
have in their cities would hardly suit our limited London spaces. When
the body of the house is built, they throw out the dining-room behind.
It stands alone, as it were, with no other chamber above it, and
removed from the rest of the house. It is consequently behind the
double drawing-rooms which form the ground-floor, and is
approached from them, and also from the back of the hall. The second
entrance to the dining-room is thus near the top of the kitchen stairs,

which no doubt is its proper position. The whole of the upper part of
the house is thus kept for the private uses of the family. To me this plan
of building recommended itself as being very commodious.

I found the spirit for the war quite as hot at Boston now (in
November), if not hotter than it was when I was there ten weeks
earlier; and I found also, to my grief, that the feeling against England
was as strong. I can easily understand how difficult it must have been,
and still must be, to Englishmen at home to understand this, and see
how it has come to pass. It has not arisen, as I think, from the old
jealousy of England. It has not sprung from that source which for years
has induced certain newspapers, especially the 'New York Herald' to
vilify England. I do not think that the men of New England have ever
been, as regards this matter, in the same boat with the 'New York
Herald.' But when this war between the North and South first broke
out, even before there was as yet a war, the northern men had taught
themselves to expect what they called British sympathy, meaning
British encouragement. They regarded, and properly regarded, the
action of the South as a rebellion, and said among themselves that so
staid and conservative a nation as Great Britain would surely countenance them in quelling rebels. If not,—should it come to pass that
Great Britain should show no such countenance and sympathy for
Northern law, if Great Britain did not respond to her friend as she was
expected to respond, then it would appear that Cotton was king, at
least in British eyes. The war did come, and Great Britain regarded the
two parties as beligerents, standing, as far as she was concerned, on
equal grounds. This it was that first gave rise to that fretful anger
against England which has gone so far towards ruining the northern
cause. We know how such passions are swelled by being ventilated,
and how they are communicated from mind to mind till they become
national. Politicians—American politicians I here mean—have their
own future careers ever before their eyes, and are driven to make
capital where they can. Hence it is that such men as Mr. Seward in the
cabinet, and Mr. Everett out of it, can reconcile it to themselves to
speak as they have done of England. It was but the other day that Mr.
Everett spoke in one of his orations of the hope that still existed that the
flag of the United States might still float over the whole continent of
North America. What would he say of an English statesman who
should speak of putting up the Union Jack on the State House in
Boston? Such words tell for the moment on the hearers, and help to
gain some slight popularity; but they tell for more than a moment on
those who read them and remember them.

And then came the capture of Messrs. Slidell and Mason. I was at Boston when those men were taken óut of the 'Trent' by the 'San Jacinto,' and brought to Fort Warren in Boston Harbour. Captain Wilkes was the officer who had made the capture, and he immediately was recognized as a hero. He was invited to banquets and fêted. Speeches were made to him as speeches are commonly made to high officers who come home after many perils victorious from the wars. His health was drunk with great applause, and thanks were voted to him by one of the Houses of Congress. It was said that a sword was to be given to him, but I do not think that the gift was consummated. Should it not have been a policeman's truncheon? Had he at the best done anything beyond a policeman's work? Of Captain Wilkes no one would complain for doing policeman's duty. If his country were satisfied with the manner in which he did it, England, if she quarrelled at all, would not quarrel with him, It may now and again become the duty of a brave officer to do work of so low a calibre. It is a pity that an ambitious sailor should find himself told off for so mean a task, but the world would know that it is not his fault. No one could blame Captain Wilkes for acting policeman on the seas. But who ever before heard of giving a man glory for achievements so little glorious? How Captain Wilkes must have blushed when those speeches were made to him, when that talk about the sword came up, when the thanks arrived to him from Congress! An officer receives his country's thanks when he has been in great peril, and has borne himself gallantly through his danger; when he has endured the brunt of war, and come through it with victory; when he has exposed himself on behalf of his country and singed his epaulets with an enemy's fire. Captain Wilkes tapped a merchantman on the shoulder in the high seas, and told him that his passengers were wanted. In doing this he showed no lack of spirit, for it might be his duty; but where was his spirit when he submitted to be thanked for such work?

And then there arose a clamour of justification among the lawyers; judges and ex-judges flew to Wheaton, Phillimore, and Lord Stowell. Before twenty-four hours were over, every man and every woman in Boston were armed with precedents. Then there was the burning of the 'Caroline.' England had improperly burned the 'Caroline' on Lake Erie, or rather in one of the American ports on Lake Erie, and had then begged pardon. If the States had been wrong, they would beg pardon; but whether wrong or right, they would not give up Slidell and Mason. But the lawyers soon waxed stronger. The men were manifestly ambassadors, and as such contraband of war. Wilkes was quite right, only he should have seized the vessel also. He was quite right, for though Slidell and Mason might not be ambassadors, they were undoubtedly carrying despatches. In a few hours there began to be a doubt whether the men could be ambassadors, because if called ambassadors, then the power that sent the embassy must be presumed to be recognized. That Captain Wilkes had taken no despatches was true; but the Captain suggested a way out of this difficulty by declaring that he had regarded the two men themselves as an incarnated embodiment of despatches. At any rate, they were clearly contraband of war. They were going to do an injury to the North. It was pretty to hear the charming women of Boston, as they became learned in the law of nations: "Wheaton is quite clear about it," one young girl said to me. It was the first I had ever heard of Wheaton, and so far was obliged to knock under. All the world, ladies and lawyers, expressed the utmost confidence in the justice of the seizure, but it was clear that all the world was in a state of the profoundest nervous anxiety on the subject. To me it seemed to be the most suicidal act that any party in a life-and-death struggle ever committed. All Americans on both sides had felt, from the beginning of the war, that any assistance given by England to one or the other would turn the scale. The Government of Mr. Lincoln must have learned by this time that England was at least true in her neutrality; that no desire for cotton would compel her to give aid to the South as long as she herself was not ill-treated by the North. But it seemed as though Mr. Seward, the President's prime minister, had no better work on hand than that of showing in every way his indifference as to courtesy with England. Insults offered to England would, he seemed to think, strengthen his hands. He would let England know that he did not care for her. When our minister, Lord Lyons, appealed to him regarding the suspension of the habeas corpus, Mr. Seward not only answered him with insolence, but instantly published his answer in the papers. He instituted a system of passports, especially constructed so as to incommode Englishmen proceeding from the States across the Atlantic. He resolved to make every Englishman in America feel himself in some way punished because England had not assisted the North. And now came the arrest of Slidell and Mason out of an English mail-steamer; and Mr. Seward took care to let it be understood that, happen what might, those two men should not be given up.

Nothing during all this time astonished me so much as the estimation in which Mr. Seward was then held by his own party. It is, perhaps, the worst defect in the Constitution of the States, that no incapacity on the part of a minister, no amount of condemnation expressed against him by the people or by Congress, can put him out of office during the term of the existing Presidency. The President can dismiss him; but it generally happens that the President is brought in on a "platform," which has already nominated for him his Cabinet as thoroughly as they have nominated him. Mr. Seward ran Mr. Lincoln very hard for the position of candidate for the Presidency on the Republican interest. On the second voting of the Republican delegates at the Convention at Chicago, Mr. Seward polled 184 to Mr. Lincoln's 181. But as a clear half of the total number of votes was necessary— that is 233 out of 465—there was necessarily a third polling, and Mr. Lincoln won the day. On that occasion Mr. Chase and Mr. Cameron, both of whom became members of Mr. Lincoln's Cabinet, were also candidates for the White House on the Republican side. I mention this here to show, that though the President can in fact dismiss his ministers, he is in a great manner bound to them, and that a minister in Mr. Seward's position is hardly to be dismissed. But from the 1st of November, 1861, till the day on which I left the States, I do not think that I heard a good word spoken of Mr. Seward as a minister even by one of his own party. The Radical or Abolitionist Republicans all abused him. The Conservative or Anti-abolition Republicans, to whose party he would consider himself as belonging, spoke of him as a mistake. He had been prominent as Senator from New York, and had been Governor of the State of New York, but had none of the aptitudes of a statesman. He was there, and it was a pity. He was not so bad as Mr. Cameron, the Minister for War; that was the best his own party could say for him, even in his own State of New York. As to the Democrats, their language respecting him was as harsh as any that I have heard used towards the southern leaders. He seemed to have no friend, no one who trusted him;—and yet he was the President's chief minister, and seemed to have in his own hands the power of misman-aging all foreign relations as he pleased. But, in truth, the States of America, great as they are, and much as they have done, have not produced Statesmen. That theory of governing by the little men rather than by the great, has not been found to answer, and such follies as those of Mr. Seward have been the consequence.

At Boston, and indeed elsewhere, I found that there was even then,—at the time of the capture of Mason and Slidell, no true conception of the neutrality of England with reference to the two parties. When any argument was made, showing that England who had carried those messengers from the South, would undoubtedly have also carried messengers from the North, the answer always was—"But the Southerners are all rebels. Will England regard us who are by treaty her friend, as she does a people that is in rebellion against its own government?" That was the old story over again, and as it was a very long story, it was hardly of use to go back through all its details. But the fact was that unless there had been such absolute neutrality— such equality between the parties in the eyes of England—even Captain Wilkes would not have thought of stopping the 'Trent,' or the Government at Washington of justifying such a proceeding. And it must be remembered that the Government at Washington had justified that proceeding. The Secretary of the Navy had distinctly done so in his official report; and that report had been submitted to the President and published by his order. It was because England was neutral between the North and South that Captain Wilkes claimed to have the right of seizing those two men. It had been the President's intention, some month or so before this affair, to send Mr. Everett and other gentlemen over to England with objects as regards the North, similar to those which had caused the sending of Slidell and Mason with reference to the South. What would Mr. Everett have thought had he been refused a passage from Dover to Calais, because the carrying of him would have been towards the South a breach of neutrality? It would never have occurred to him that he could become subject to such stoppage. How should we have been abused for southern sympathies had we so acted? We, forsooth, who carry passengers about the world, from China and Australia, round to Chili and Peru, who have the charge of the world's passengers and letters, and as a nation incur out of our pocket annually a loss of some half-million of pounds sterling for the privilege of doing so, are to inquire the business of every American traveller before we let him on board, and be stopped in our work if we take anybody on one side whose journeyings may be conceived by the other side to be to them prejudicial! Not on such terms will Englishmen be willing to spread civilization across the ocean! I do not pretend to understand Wheaton and Phillimore, or even to have read a single word of any international law. I have refused to read any such, knowing that it would only confuse and mislead me. But I have my common sense to guide me. Two men living in one street, quarrel and shy brickbats at each other, and make the whole street very uncomfortable. Not only is no one to interfere with them, but they are to have the privilege of deciding that their brickbats have the right of way, rather than the ordinary intercourse of the neighbourhood! If that be national law, national law must be changed. It might do for some centuries back, but it cannot do now. Up to this period my sympathies had been with the North. I thought, and still think, that the North had no alternative, that the war had been forced upon them, and that they had gone about their work with patriotic energy. But this stopping of an English mail-steamer was too much for me.

What will they do in England? was now the question. But for any knowledge as to that, I had to wait till I reached Washington.

XVII

Cambridge and Lowell

THE two places of most general interest in the vicinity of Boston are Cambridge and Lowell. Cambridge is to Massachusetts, and, I may almost say, is to all the northern States, what Cambridge and Oxford are to England. It is the seat of the University which gives the highest education to be attained by the highest classes in that country. Lowell also is in little to Massachusetts and to New England what Manchester is to us in so great a degree. It is the largest and most prosperous cotton-manufacturing town in the States.

Cambridge is not above three or four miles from Boston. Indeed, the town of Cambridge properly so called begins where Boston ceases. The Harvard College—that is its name, taken from one of its original founders—is reached by horse-cars in twenty minutes from the city. An Englishman feels inclined to regard the place as a suburb of Boston; but if he so expresses himself, he will not find favour in the eyes of the men of Cambridge.

The University is not so large as I had expected to find it. It consists of Harvard College, as the undergraduates' department, and of professional schools of law, medicine, divinity, and science. In the few words that I will say about it I will confine myself to Harvard College proper, conceiving that the professional schools connected with it have not in themselves any special interest. The average number of undergraduates does not exceed 450, and these are divided into four classes. The average number of degrees taken annually by bachelors of

244

art is something under 100. Four years' residence is required for a degree, and at the end of that period a degree is given as a matter of course if the candidate's conduct has been satisfactory. When a young man has pursued his studies for that period, going through the required examinations and lectures, he is not subjected to any final examination as is the case with a candidate for a degree at Oxford and Cambridge. It is, perhaps, in this respect that the greatest difference exists between the English Universities and Harvard College. With us a young man may, I take it, still go through his three or four years with a small amount of study. But his doing so does not insure him his degree. If he have utterly wasted his time he is plucked, and late but heavy punishment comes upon him. At Cambridge in Massachusetts the daily work of the men is made more obligatory; but if this be gone through with such diligence as to enable the student to hold his own during the four years, he has his degree as a matter of course. There are no degrees conferring special honour. A man cannot go out "in honours" as he does with us. There are no "firsts" or "double firsts;" no "wranglers;" no "senior opts" or "junior opts." Nor are there prizes of fellowships and livings to be obtained. It is, I think, evident from this that the greatest incentives to high excellence are wanting at Harvard College. There is neither the reward of honour nor of money. There is none of that great competition which exists at our Cambridge for the high place of Senior Wrangler; and, consequently, the degree of excellence attained is no doubt lower than with us. But I conceive that the general level of the University education is higher there than with us; that a young man is more sure of getting his education, and that a smaller percentage of men leaves Harvard College utterly uneducated than goes in that condition out of Oxford or Cambridge. The education at Harvard College is more diversified in its nature, and study is more absolutely the business of the place than it is at our Universities.

The expense of education at Harvard College is not much lower than at our colleges; with us there are, no doubt, more men who are absolutely extravagant than at Cambridge, Massachusetts. The actual authorized expenditure in accordance with the rules is only 50*l.* per annum, *i.e.* 249 dollars; but this does not, by any means, include everything. Some of the richer young men may spend as much as 300*l.* per annum, but the largest number vary their expenditure from 100*l.* to 180*l.* per annum; and I take it the same thing may be said of our Universities. There are many young men at Harvard College of very small means. They will live on 70*l.* per annum, and will earn a great portion of that by teaching in the vacations. There are thirty-six scholarships attached to the University varying in value from 20*l*. to 60*l*. per annum; and there is also a beneficiary fund for supplying poor scholars with assistance during their collegiate education. Many are thus brought up at Cambridge who have no means of their own, and I think I may say that the consideration in which they are held among their brother students is in no degree affected by their position. I doubt whether we can say so much of the sizars and bible clerks at our Universities.

At Harvard College there is, of course, none of that old-fashioned, time-honoured, delicious, mediæval life which lends so much grace and beauty to our colleges. There are no gates, no porter's lodges, no butteries, no halls, no battels, and no common rooms. There are no proctors, no bulldogs, no bursers, no deans, no morning and evening chapel, no quads, no surplices, no caps and gowns. I have already said that there are no examinations for degrees and no honours; and I can easily conceive that in the absence of all these essentials many an Englishman will ask what right Harvard College has to call itself a University.

I have said that there are no honours,—and in our sense there are none. But I should give offence to my American friends if I did not explain that there are prizes given—I think, all in money, and that they vary from 50 to 10 dollars. These are called *deturs*. The degrees are given on Commencement Day, at which occasion certain of the expectant graduates are selected to take parts in a public literary exhibition. To be so selected seems to be tantamount to taking a degree in honours. There is also a dinner on Commencement Day,—at which, however, "no wine or other intoxicating drink shall be served."

It is required that every student shall attend some place of Christian worship on Sundays; but he, or his parents for him, may elect what denomination of church he shall attend. There is a University chapel on the University grounds which belongs, if I remember right, to the Episcopalian Church. The young men for the most part live in College, having rooms in the College buildings; but they do not board in those rooms. There are establishments in the town under the patronage of the University, at which dinner, breakfast, and supper are provided; and the young men frequent one of these houses or another as they, or their friends for them, may arrange. Every young man not belonging to a family resident within a hundred miles of Cambridge, and whose parents are desirous to obtain the protection thus provided, is placed, as regards his pecuniary management, under the care of a patron, and this patron acts by him as a father does in England by a boy at school. He pays out his money for him and keeps him out of debt. The arrangement will not recommend itself to young men at Oxford quite so powerfully as it may do to the fathers of some young men who have been there. The rules with regard to the lodging and boarding-houses are very stringent. Any festive entertainment is to be reported to the President. No wine or spirituous liquors may be used, &c. It is not a picturesque system, this; but it has its advantages.

There is a handsome library attached to the College, which the young men can use; but it is not as extensive as I had expected. The University is not well off for funds by which to increase it. The new museum in the College is also a handsome building. The edifices used for the undergraduates' chambers and for the lecture-rooms are by no means handsome. They are very ugly red-brick houses standing here and there without order. There are seven such, and they are called Brattle House, College House, Divinity Hall, Hollis Hall, Holsworthy Hall, Massachusetts Hall, and Stoughton Hall. It is almost astonishing that buildings so ugly should have been erected for such a purpose. These, together with the library, the museum, and the chapel, stand on a large green, which might be made pretty enough if it were kept well mown like the gardens of our Cambridge colleges; but it is much neglected. Here, again, the want of funds—the res angusta domi—must be pleaded as an excuse. On the same green, but at some little distance from any other building, stands the President's pleasant house.

The immediate direction of the College is of course mainly in the hands of the President, who is supreme. But for the general management of the Institution there is a Corporation, of which he is one. It is stated in the laws of the University that the Corporation of the University and its Overseers constitute the Government of the University. The Corporation consists of the President, five Fellows, so called, and a Treasurer. These Fellows are chosen, as vacancies occur, by themselves, subject to the concurrence of the Overseers. But these Fellows are in nowise like to the Fellows of our colleges, having no salaries attached to their offices. The Board of Overseers consists of the State Governor, other State officers, the President and Treasurer of Harvard College, and thirty other persons,—men of note, chosen by vote. The Faculty of the College, in which is vested the immediate care and government of the undergraduates, is composed of the President and the Professors. The Professors answer to the tutors of our colleges, and upon them the education of the place depends. I cannot complete this short notice of Harvard College without saying that it is happy in the possession of that distinguished natural philosopher, Professor Agassiz. M. Agassiz has collected at Cambridge a museum of such things as natural philosophers delight to show, which I am told is all but invaluable. As my ignorance on all such matters is of a depth which the Professor can hardly imagine, and which it would have shocked him to behold, I did not visit the museum. Taking the University of Harvard College as a whole, I should say that it is most remarkable in this,—that it does really give to its pupils that education which it professes to give. Of our own Universities other good things may be said, but that one special good thing cannot always be said.

Cambridge boasts itself as the residence of four or five men well known to fame on the American, and also on the European side of the ocean. President Felton's* name is very familiar to us, and wherever Greek scholarship is held in repute, that is known. So also is the name of Professor Agassiz, of whom I have spoken. Russell Lowell is one of the Professors of the College,—that Russell Lowell who sang of Bir-do'fredum Sawin, and whose Biglow Papers were edited with such an ardour of love by our Tom Brown. Birdo'fredum is worthy of all the ardour. Mr. Dana is also a Cambridge man,—he who was "two years before the mast," and who since that has written to us of Cuba. But Mr. Dana, though residing at Cambridge, is not of Cambridge, and, though a literary man, he does not belong to literature. He is,—could he help it?—a special attorney. I must not, however, degrade him, for in the States barristers and attorneys are all one. I cannot but think that he could help it, and that he should not give up to law what was meant for mankind. I fear, however, that successful law has caught him in her intolerant clutches, and that literature, who surely would be the nobler mistress, must wear the willow. Last and greatest is the poet-laureat of the West; for Mr. Longfellow also lives at Cambridge.

I am not at all aware whether the nature of the manufacturing corporation of Lowell is generally understood by Englishmen. I confess that until I made personal acquaintance with the plan, I was absolutely ignorant on the subject. I knew that Lowell was a manufacturing town at which cotton is made into calico, and at which calico is printed,—as is the case at Manchester; but I conceived this was done at Lowell, as it is done at Manchester, by individual enterprise,—that

* Since these words were written President Felton has died. I, as I returned on my way homewards, had the melancholy privilege of being present at his funeral. I feel bound to record here the great kindness with which Mr. Felton assisted me in obtaining such information as I needed respecting the Institution over which he presided.

I or any one else could open a mill at Lowell, and that the manufactur-
ers there were ordinary traders, as they are at other manufacturing
towns. But this is by no means the case.

That which most surprises an English visitor on going through the
mills at Lowell is the personal appearance of the men and women who
work at them. As there are twice as many women as there are men, it is
to them that the attention is chiefly called. They are not only better
dressed, cleaner, and better mounted in every respect than the girls
employed at manufactories in England, but they are so infinitely
superior as to make a stranger immediately perceive that some very
strong cause must have created the difference. We all know the class of
young women whom we generally see serving behind counters in the
shops of our larger cities. They are neat, well dressed, careful, especially
about their hair, composed in their manner, and sometimes a little
supercilious in the propriety of their demeanour. It is exactly the same
class of young women that one sees in the factories at Lowell. They are
not sallow, nor dirty, nor ragged, nor rough. They have about them no
signs of want, or of low culture. Many of us also know the appearance
of those girls who work in the factories in England; and I think it will
be allowed that a second glance at them is not wanting to show that
they are in every respect inferior to the young women who attend our
shops. The matter, indeed, requires no argument. Any young woman
at a shop would be insulted by being asked whether she had worked at
a factory. The difference with regard to the men at Lowell is quite as
strong, though not so striking. Working men do not show their status
in the world by their outward appearance as readily as women; and, as
I have said before, the number of the women greatly exceeded that of
the men.

One would of course be disposed to say that the superior condition
of the workers must have been occasioned by superior wages; and this,
to a certain extent, has been the cause. But the higher payment is not
the chief cause. Women's wages, including all that they receive at the
Lowell factories, average about 14s. a week, which is, I take it, fully a
third more than women can earn in Manchester, or did earn before the
loss of the American cotton began to tell upon them. But if wages at
Manchester were raised to the Lowell standard, the Manchester
women would not be clothed, fed, cared for, and educated like the
Lowell women. The fact is, that the workmen and the workwomen at
Lowell are not exposed to the chances of an open labour market. They
are taken in, as it were, to a philanthropical manufacturing college,
and then looked after and regulated more as girls and lads at a great

seminary, than as hands by whose industry profit is to be made out of capital. This is all very nice and pretty at Lowell, but I am afraid it could not be done at Manchester.

There are at present twelve different manufactories at Lowell, each of which has what is called a separate corporation. The Merrimack manufacturing company was incorporated in 1822, and thus Lowell was commenced. The Lowell machine-shop was incorporated in 1845, and since that no new establishment has been added. In 1821 a certain Boston manufacturing company, which had mills at Waltham, near Boston, was attracted by the water-power of the river Merrimack, on which the present town of Lowell is situated. A canal, called the Pawtucket Canal, had been made for purposes of navigation from one reach of the river to another, with the object of avoiding the Pawtucket Falls; and this canal, with the adjacent water-power of the river, was purchased for the Boston Company. The place was then called Lowell, after one of the partners in that company.

It must be understood that water-power alone is used for preparing the cotton and working the spindles and looms of the cotton mills. Steam is applied in the two establishments in which the cottons are printed, for the purposes of printing, but I think nowhere else. When the mills are at full work, about two-and-a-half million yards of cotton goods are made every week, and nearly a million pounds of cotton are consumed per week (*i.e.* 842,000 lbs.), but the consumption of coal is only 30,000 tons in the year. This will give some idea of the value of the water-power. The Pawtucket Canal was, as I say, bought, and Lowell was commenced. The town was incorporated in 1826, and the railway between it and Boston was opened in 1835, under the superintendence of Mr. Jackson, the gentleman by whom the purchase of the canal had in the first instance been made. Lowell now contains about 40,000 inhabitants.

The following extract is taken from the hand-book to Lowell:— "Mr. F. C. Lowell had in his travels abroad observed the effect of large manufacturing establishments on the character of the people, and in the establishment at Waltham the founders looked for a remedy for these defects. They thought that education and good morals would even enhance the profit, and that they could compete with Great Britain by introducing a more cultivated class of operatives. For this purpose they built boarding-houses, which, under the direct super-vision of the agent, were kept by discreet matrons"—I can answer for the discreet matrons at Lowell—"mostly widows, no boarders being allowed except operatives. Agents and overseers of high moral character were selected; regulations were adopted at the mills and boarding-houses, by which only respectable girls were employed. The mills were nicely painted and swept,"—I can also answer for the painting and sweeping at Lowell,—"trees set out in the yards and along the streets, habits of neatness and cleanliness encouraged; and the result justified the expenditure. At Lowell the same policy has been adopted and extended; more spacious mills and elegant boarding-houses have been erected;"—as to the elegance, it may be a matter of taste, but as to the comfort there is no question,—"the same care as to the classes employed; more capital has been expended for cleanliness and decoration; a hospital has been established for the sick, where, for a small price, they have an experienced physician and skilful nurses. An institute, with an extensive library, for the use of the mechanics, has been endowed. The agents have stood forward in the support of schools, churches, lectures, and lyceums, and their influence contributed highly to the elevation of the moral and intellectual character of the operatives. Talent has been encouraged, brought forward, and recommended."—For some considerable time the young women wrote, edited, and published a newspaper among themselves, called the Lowell Offering.—"And Lowell has supplied agents and mechanics for the later manufacturing places who have given tone to society, and extended the beneficial influence of Lowell through the United States. Girls from the country, with a true Yankee spirit of independence, and confident in their own powers, pass a few years here, and then return to get married with a dower secured by their exertions, with more enlarged ideas and extended means of information, and their places are supplied by younger relatives. A larger proportion of the female population of New England has been employed at some time in manufacturing establishments, and they are not on this account less good wives, mothers, or educators of families." Then the account goes on to tell how the health of the girls has been improved by their attendance at the mills, how they put money into the savings-banks, and buy railway shares and farms; how there are thirty churches in Lowell, a library, banks, and insurance offices; how there is a cemetery, and a park, and how everything is beautiful, philanthropic, profitable, and magnificent.

Thus Lowell is the realization of a commercial Utopia. Of all the statements made in the little book which I have quoted I cannot point out one which is exaggerated, much less false. I should not call the place elegant, in other respects I am disposed to stand by the book. Before I had made any inquiry into the cause of the apparent comfort, it struck me at once that some great effort at excellence was being made. I went into one of the discreet matrons' residences; and perhaps may give but an indifferent idea of her discretion when I say that she allowed me to go into the bedrooms. If you want to ascertain the inner ways or habits of life of any man, woman, or child, see, if it be practicable to do so, his or her bedroom. You will learn more by a minute's glance round that holy of holies, than by any conversation. Looking-glasses and such like, suspended dresses, and toilet-belongings if taken without notice, cannot lie or even exaggerate. The discreet matron at first showed me rooms only prepared for use, for at the period of my visit Lowell was by no means full; but she soon became more intimate with me, and I went through the upper part of the house. My report must be altogether in her favour and in that of Lowell. Everything was cleanly, well-ordered, and feminine. There was not a bed on which any woman need have hesitated to lay herself if occasion required it. I fear that this cannot be said of the lodgings of the manufacturing classes at Manchester. The boarders all take their meals together. As a rule, they have meat twice a-day. Hot meat for dinner is with them as much a matter of course, or probably more so, than with any English man or woman who may read this book. For in the States of America regulations on this matter are much more rigid than with us. Cold meat is rarely seen, and to live a day without meat would be as great a privation as to pass a night without bed.

The rules for the guidance of these boarding-houses are very rigid. The houses themselves belong to the corporations or different manufacturing establishments, and the tenants are altogether in the power of the managers. None but operatives are to be taken in. The tenants are answerable for improper conduct. The doors are to be closed at ten o'clock. Any boarders who do not attend divine worship are to be reported to the managers. The yards and walks are to be kept clean, and snow removed at once; and the inmates must be vaccinated, &c., &c., &c. It is expressly stated by the Hamilton Company,—and I believe by all the companies,—that no one shall be employed who is habitually absent from public worship on Sunday, or who is known to be guilty of immorality. It is stated that the average wages of the women are two dollars, or eight shillings, a week, besides their board. I found when I was there that from three dollars to three-and-a-half a week were paid to the women, of which they paid one dollar and twenty-five cents for their board. As this would not fully cover the expense of their keep, twenty-five cents a week for each was also paid to the boarding-house keepers by the mill agents. This substantially came to the same thing, as it left the two dollars a week, or eight shillings, with the girls over and above their cost of living. The board included washing, lights, food, bed, and attendance,—leaving a surplus of eight shillings a week for clothes and saving. Now let me ask any one acquainted with Manchester and its operatives, whether that is not Utopia realized. Factory girls, for whom every comfort of life is secured, with 21 *l.* a year over for saving and dress! One sees the failing, however, at a moment. It is Utopia. Any Lady Bountiful can tutor three or four peasants and make them luxuriously comfortable. But no Lady Bountiful can give luxurious comfort to half-a-dozen parishes. Lowell is now nearly forty years old, and contains but 40,000 inhabitants. From the very nature of its corporations it cannot spread itself. Chicago, which has grown out of nothing in a much shorter period, and which has no factories, has now 120,000 inhabitants. Lowell is a very wonderful place and shows what philanthropy can do; but I fear it also shows what philanthropy cannot do.

There are, however, other establishments, conducted on the same principle as those at Lowell, which have had the same amount, or rather the same sort, of success. Lawrence is now a town of about 15,000 inhabitants, and Manchester of about 24,000,—if I remember rightly;—and at those places the mills are also owned by corporations and conducted as are those at Lowell. But it seems to me that as New England takes her place in the world as a great manufacturing country—which place she undoubtedly will take sooner or later—she must abandon the hot-house method of providing for her operatives with which she has commenced her work. In the first place, Lowell is not open as a manufacturing town to the capitalists even of New England at large. Stock may, I presume, be bought in the corporations, but no interloper can establish a mill there. It is a close manufacturing community, bolstered up on all sides, and has none of that capacity for providing employment for a thickly-growing population which belongs to such places as Manchester and Leeds. That it should under its present system have been made in any degree profitable reflects great credit on the managers; but the profit does not reach an amount which in America can be considered as remunerative. The total capital invested by the twelve corporations is thirteen million and a half of dollars, or about two million seven hundred thousand pounds. In only one of the corporations, that of the Merrimack Company, does the profit amount to 12 per cent. In one, that of the Boott Company, it falls below 7 per cent. The average profit of the various establishments is something below 9 per cent. I am of course speaking of Lowell as it was previous to the war. American capitalists are not, as a rule, contented with so low a rate of interest as this.

The States in these matters have had a great advantage over England. They have been able to begin at the beginning. Manufactories have grown up among us as our cities grew;—from the necessities and chances of the times. When labour was wanted it was obtained in the ordinary way; and so when houses were built they were built in the ordinary way. We had not the experience, and the results either for good or bad, of other nations to guide us. The Americans, in seeing and resolving to adopt our commercial successes, have resolved also, if possible, to avoid the evils which have attended those successes. It would be very desirable that all our factory girls should read and write, wear clean clothes, have decent beds, and eat hot meat every day. But that is now impossible. Gradually, with very up-hill work, but still I trust with sure work, much will be done to improve their position and render their life respectable; but in England we can have no Lowells. In our thickly populated island any commercial Utopia is out of the question. Nor can, as I think, Lowell be taken as a type of the future manufacturing towns of New England. When New England employs millions in her factories, instead of thousands,—the hands employed at Lowell, when the mills are at full work, are about 11,000,—she must cease to provide for them their beds and meals, their church-going proprieties and orderly modes of life. In such an attempt she has all the experience of the world against her. But nevertheless I think she will have done much good. The tone which she will have given will not altogether lose its influence. Employment in a factory is now considered reputable by a farmer and his children, and this idea will remain. Factory work is regarded as more respectable than domestic service, and this prestige will not wear itself altogether out. Those now employed have a strong conception of the dignity of their own social position, and their successors will inherit much of this, even though they may find themselves excluded from the advantages of the present Utopia. The thing has begun well, but it can only be regarded as a beginning. Steam, it may be presumed, will become the motive power of cotton mills in New England as it is with us; and when it is so, the amount of work to be done at any one place will not be checked by any such limit as that which now prevails at Lowell. Water-power is very cheap, but it cannot be extended; and it would seem that no place can become large as a manufacturing town which has to depend chiefly upon water. It is not improbable that steam may be brought into general use at Lowell, and that Lowell may spread itself. If it should spread itself widely, it will lose its Utopian characteristics.

One cannot but be greatly struck by the spirit of philanthropy in which the system of Lowell was at first instituted. It may be presumed that men who put their money into such an undertaking did so with the object of commercial profit to themselves; but in this case that was not their first object. I think it may be taken for granted that when Messrs. Jackson and Lowell went about their task, their grand idea was to place factory work upon a respectable footing,—to give employment in mills which should not be unhealthy, degrading, demoralizing, or hard in its circumstances. Throughout the northern States of America the same feeling is to be seen. Good and thoughtful men have been active to spread education, to maintain health, to make work compatible with comfort and personal dignity, and to divest the ordinary lot of man of the sting of that curse which was supposed to be uttered when our first father was ordered to eat his bread in the sweat of his brow. One is driven to contrast this feeling, of which on all sides one sees such ample testimony, with that sharp desire for profit, that anxiety to do a stroke of trade at every turn, that acknowledged necessity of being smart, which we must own is quite as general as the nobler propensity. I believe that both phases of commercial activity may be attributed to the same characteristic. Men in trade in America are not more covetous than tradesmen in England, nor probably are they more generous or philanthropical. But that which they do, they are more anxious to do thoroughly and quickly. They desire that every turn taken shall be a great turn,—or at any rate that it shall be as great as possible. They go ahead either for bad or good with all the energy they have. In the institutions at Lowell I think we may allow that the good has very much prevailed.

I went over two of the mills, those of the Merrimack corporation, and of the Massachusetts. At the former the printing establishment only was at work; the cotton mills were closed. I hardly know whether it will interest any one to learn that something under half-a-million yards of calico are here printed annually. At the Lowell bleachery fifteen million yards are dyed annually. The Merrimack cotton-mills were stopped, and so had the other mills at Lowell been stopped, till some short time before my visit. Trade had been bad, and there had of course been a lack of cotton. I was assured that no severe suffering had been created by this stoppage. The greater number of hands had returned into the country,—to the farms from whence they had come; and though a discontinuance of work and wages had of course produced hardship, there had been no actual privation,—no hunger and want. Those of the workpeople who had no homes out of Lowell to which to betake themselves, and no means at Lowell of living, had received relief before real suffering had begun. I was assured, with something of a smile of contempt at the question, that there had been nothing like hunger. But, as I said before, visitors always see a great deal of rose colour, and should endeavour to allay the brilliancy of the tint with the proper amount of human shading. But do not let any visitor mix in the browns with too heavy a hand!

At the Massachusetts cotton-mills they were working with about two-thirds of their full number of hands, and this, I was told, was about the average of the number now employed throughout Lowell. Working at this rate they had now on hand a supply of cotton to last them for six months. Their stocks had been increased lately, and on asking from whence, I was informed that that last received had come to them from Liverpool. There is, I believe, no doubt but that a considerable quantity of cotton has been shipped back from England to the States since the civil war began. I asked the gentleman, to whose care at Lowell I was consigned, whether he expected to get cotton from the South,—for at that time Beaufort in South Carolina had just been taken by the naval expedition. He had, he said, a political expectation of a supply of cotton, but not a commercial expectation. That at least was the gist of his reply, and I found it to be both intelligent and intelligible. The Massachusetts mills, when at full work, employ 1300 females and 400 males, and turn out 540,000 yards of calico per week.

On my return from Lowell in the smoking car, an old man came and squeezed in next to me. The place was terribly crowded, and as the old man was thin and clean and quiet I willingly made room for him, so as to avoid the contiguity of a neighbour who might be neither thin, nor clean, nor quiet. He began talking to me in whispers about the war, and I was suspicious that he was a Southerner and a Secessionist. Under such circumstances his company might not be agreeable, unless he could be induced to hold his tongue. At last he said, "I come from Canada, you know, and you,—you're an Englishman, and therefore I can speak to you openly;" and he gave me an affectionate grip on the knee with his old skinny hand. I suppose I do look more like an Englishman than an American, but I was surprised at his knowing me with such certainty. "There is no mistaking you," he said, "with your round face and your red cheeks. They don't look like that here," and he gave me another grip. I felt quite fond of the old man, and offered him a cigar.

XVIII

The Rights of Women

WE all know that the subject which appears above as the title of this chapter is a very favourite subject in America. It is, I hope, a very favourite subject in England also, and I am inclined to think has been so for many years past. The rights of women, as contradistinguished from the wrongs of women, has perhaps been the most precious of the legacies left to us by the feudal ages. How amidst the rough darkness of old Teuton rule women began to receive that respect which is now their dearest right, is one of the most interesting studies of history. It came, I take it, chiefly from their own conduct. The women of the old classic races seem to have enjoyed but a small amount of respect or of rights, and to have deserved as little. It may have been very well for one Cæsar to have said that his wife should be above suspicion; but his wife was put away, and therefore either did not have her rights, or else had justly forfeited them. The daughter of the next Cæsar lived in Rome the life of a Messalina, and did not on that account seem to have lost her "position in society," till she absolutely declined to throw any veil whatever over her propensities. But as the Roman empire fell, chivalry began. For a time even chivalry afforded but a dull time to the women. During the musical period of the troubadours, ladies, I fancy, had but little to amuse them save the music. But that was the beginning, and from that time downwards the rights of women have progressed very favourably. It may be that they have not yet all that should belong to them. If that be the case, let the men lose no time in making up the difference. But it seems to me that the women who are now making their claims may perhaps hardly know when they are well off. It will be an ill movement if they insist on throwing away any of the advantages they have won. As for the women in America especially, I must confess that I think they have a "good time." I make them my compliments on their sagacity, intelligence, and attractions, but I utterly refuse to them any sympathy for supposed wrongs. *O fortunatas sua si bona nôrint!* Whether or no, were I an American married man and father of a family, I should not go in for the rights of man—that is altogether another question.

This question of the rights of women divides itself into two heads,—one of which is very important, worthy of much consideration, capable perhaps of much philanthropic action, and at any rate affording matter for grave discussion. This is the question of women's work; how far the work of the world, which is now borne chiefly by men, should be thrown open to women further than is now done. The other seems to me to be worthy of no consideration, to be capable of no action, to admit of no grave discussion. This refers to the political rights of women; how far the political working of the world, which is now entirely in the hands of men, should be divided between them and women. The first question is being debated on our side of the Atlantic as keenly perhaps as on the American side. As to that other question, I do not know that much has ever been said about it in Europe.

"You are doing nothing in England towards the employment of females," a lady said to me in one of the States soon after my arrival in America. "Pardon me," I answered, "I think we are doing much, perhaps too much. At any rate we are doing something." I then explained to her how Miss Faithfull had instituted a printing establishment in London; how all the work in that concern was done by females, except such heavy tasks as those for which women could not be fitted, and I handed to her one of Miss Faithfull's cards. "Ah," said my American friend, "poor creatures! I have no doubt their very flesh will be worked off their bones." I thought this a little unjust on her part; but nevertheless it occurred to me as an answer not unfit to be made by some other lady,—by some woman who had not already advocated the increased employment of women. Let Miss Faithfull look to that. Not that she will work the flesh off her young women's bones, or allow such terrible consequences to take place in Coram-street; not that she or that those connected with her in that enterprise will do aught but good to those employed therein. It will not even be said of her individually, or of her partners, that they have worked the flesh off women's bones; but may it not come to this, that when the tasks now done by men have been shifted to the shoulders of women, women themselves will so complain. May it not go further, and come even to this, that women will have cause for such complaint. I do not think that such a result will come, because I do not think that the object desired by those who are active in the matter will be attained. Men, as a general rule among civilized nations, have elected to earn their own bread and the bread of the women also, and from this resolve on their part I do not think that they will be beaten off.

We know that Mrs. Dall, an American lady, has taken up this subject, and has written a book on it, in which great good sense and honesty of purpose are shown. Mrs. Dall is a strong advocate for the increased employment of women, and I, with great deference, disagree with her. I allude to her book now because she has pointed out, I think very strongly, the great reason why women do not engage themselves advantageously in trade pursuits. She by no means overpraises her own sex, and openly declares that young women will not consent to place themselves in fair competition with men. They will not undergo the labour and servitude of long study at their trades. They will not give themselves up to an apprenticeship. They will not enter upon their tasks as though they were to be the tasks of their lives. They may have the same physical and mental aptitudes for learning a trade as men, but they have not the same devotion to the pursuit, and will not bind themselves to it thoroughly as men do. In all which I quite agree with Mrs. Dall; and the English of it is,—that the young women want to get married.

God forbid that they should not so want. Indeed God has forbidden in a very express way that there should be any lack of such a desire on the part of women. There has of late years arisen a feeling among masses of the best of our English ladies that this feminine propensity should be checked. We are told that unmarried women may be respectable, which we always knew; that they may be useful, which we also acknowledge,—thinking still that if married they would be more useful; and that they may be happy, which we trust,—feeling confident however that they might in another position be more happy. But the question is not only as to the respectability, usefulness, and happiness of womankind, but as to that of men also. If women can do without marriage, can men do so? And if not, how are the men to get wives if the women elect to remain single?

It will be thought that I am treating the subject as though it were simply jocose, but I beg to assure my reader that such is not my intention. It certainly is the fact that that disinclination to an apprenticeship and unwillingness to bear the long training for a trade, of which Mrs. Dall complains on the part of young women, arise from the fact, that they have other hopes with which such apprenticeships would jar; and it is also certain that if such disinclination be overcome on the part of any great number, it must be overcome by the destruction or banishment of such hopes. The question is, whether would good or evil result from such a change? It is often said that whatever difficulty a woman may have in getting a husband, no man need encounter difficulty in finding a wife. But in spite of this seeming fact, I think it must be allowed that if women are withdrawn from the marriage market, men must be withdrawn from it also to the same extent.

In any broad view of this matter we are bound to look, not on any individual case, and the possible remedies for such cases, but on the position in the world occupied by women in general; on the general happiness and welfare of the aggregate feminine world, and perhaps also a little on the general happiness and welfare of the aggregate male world. When ladies and gentlemen advocate the right of women to employment, they are taking very different ground from that on which stand those less extensive philanthropists who exert themselves for the benefit of distressed needlewomen, for instance, or for the alleviation of the more bitter misery of governesses. The two questions are in fact absolutely antagonistic to each other. The rights-of-women advocate is doing his best to create that position for women, from the possible misfortunes of which the friend of the needlewomen is struggling to relieve them. The one is endeavouring to throw work from off the shoulders of men onto the shoulders of women, and the other is striving to lessen the burden which women are already bearing. Of course it is good to relieve distress in individual cases. That Song of the Shirt, which I regard as poetry of the immortal kind, has done an amount of good infinitely wider than poor Hood ever ventured to hope. Of all such efforts I would speak not only with respect, but with loving admiration. But of those whose efforts are made to spread work more widely among women, to call upon them to make for us our watches, to print our books, to sit at our desks as clerks, and to add up our accounts; much as I may respect the individual operators in such a movement, I can express no admiration for their judgment.

I have seen women with ropes round their necks drawing a harrow over ploughed ground. No one will, I suppose, say that they approve of that. But it would not have shocked me to see men drawing a harrow. I should have thought it slow, unprofitable work, but my feelings would not have been hurt. There must, therefore, be some limit; but if we men teach ourselves to believe that work is good for women, where is the limit to be drawn, and who shall draw it? It is true that there is now no actually defined limit. There is much work that is commonly open to both sexes. Personal domestic attendance is so, and the attendance in shops. The use of the needle is shared between men and women, and few, I take it, know where the sempstress ends and where the tailor begins. In many trades a woman can be, and very often is, the owner and manager of the business. Painting is as much open to women as to men; as also is literature. There can be no defined limit; but nevertheless there is at present a quasi limit, which the rights-of-women advocates wish to move, and so to move that women shall do more work and not less. A woman now could not well be a cab-driver in London; but are these advocates sure that no woman will be a cab-driver when success has attended their efforts? And would they like to see a woman driving a cab? For my part I confess I do not like to see a woman acting as road-keeper on a French railway. I have seen a woman acting as ostler at a public stage in Ireland. I knew the circumstances,—how her husband had become ill and incapable, and how she had been allowed to earn the wages; but nevertheless the sight was to me disagreeable, and seemed, as far as it went, to degrade the sex. Chivalry has been very active in raising women from the hard and hardening tasks of the world, and through this action they have become soft, tender, and virtuous. It seems to me that they of whom I am now speaking are desirous of undoing what chivalry has done.

The argument used is of course plain enough. It is said that women are left destitute in the world,—destitute unless they can be self-dependent, and that to women should be given the same open access to wages that men possess, in order that they may be as self-dependent as men. Why should a young woman, for whom no father is able to provide, not enjoy those means of provision which are open to a young man so circumstanced? But I think the answer is very simple. The young man under the happiest circumstances which may befall him is bound to earn his bread. The young woman is only so bound when happy circumstances do not befall her. Should we endeavour to make the recurrence of unhappy circumstances more general or less so? What does any tradesman, any professional man, any mechanic wish for his children? Is it not this, that his sons shall go forth and earn their bread, and that his daughters shall remain with him till they are married? Is not that the mother's wish? Is it not notorious that such is the wish of us all as to our daughters? In advocating the rights of women it is of other men's girls that we think, never of our own.

But, nevertheless, what shall we do for those women who must earn their bread by their own work? Whatever we do, do not let us wilfully increase their number. By opening trades to women, by making them printers, watchmakers, accountants, or what not, we shall not simply relieve those who must now earn their bread by some such work or else starve. It will not be within our power to stop ourselves exactly at a certain point; to arrange that those women who under existing circumstances may now be in want, shall be thus placed beyond want, but that no others shall be affected. Men, I fear, will be too willing to relieve themselves of some portion of their present burden, should the world's altered ways enable them to do so. At present a lawyer's clerk may earn perhaps his two guineas a week, and he with his wife lives on that in fair comfort. But if his wife, as well as he, has been brought up as a lawyer's clerk, he will look to her also for some amount of wages. I doubt whether the two guineas would be much increased, but I do not doubt at all that the woman's position would be injured.

It seems to me that in discussing this subject, philanthropists fail to take hold of the right end of the argument. Money returns from work are very good, and work itself is good, as bringing such returns and occupying both body and mind; but the world's work is very hard, and workmen are too often overdriven. The question seems to me to be this,—of all this work have the men got on their own backs too heavy a share for them to bear, and should they seek relief by throwing more of it upon women? It is the rights of man that we are in fact debating. These watches are weary to make, and this type is troublesome to set. We have battles to fight and speeches to make, and our hands altogether are too full. The women are idle,—many of them. They shall make the watches for us and set the type; and when they have done that, why should they not make nails as they do sometimes in Worcestershire, or clean horses, or drive the cabs? They have had an easy time of it for these years past, but we'll change that. And then it would come to pass that with ropes round their necks the women would be drawing harrows across the fields.

I don't think this will come to pass. The women generally do know when they are well off, and are not particularly anxious to accept the philanthropy proffered to them;—as Mrs. Dall says, they do not wish to bind themselves as apprentices to independent money-making. This cry has been louder in America than with us, but even in America it has not been efficacious for much. There is in the States, no doubt, a

sort of hankering after increased influence, a desire for that
prominence of position which men attain by loud voices and brazen
foreheads, a desire in the female heart to be up and doing something, if
the female heart only knew what; but even in the States it has hardly
advanced beyond a few feminine lectures. In many branches of work
women are less employed than in England. They are not so frequent
behind counters in the shops, and are rarely seen as servants in hotels.
The fires in such houses are lighted and the rooms swept by men. But
the American girls may say they do not desire to light fires and sweep
rooms. They are ambitious of the higher classes of work. But those
higher branches of work require study, apprenticeships, a devotion of
youth; and that they will not give. It is very well for a young man to
bind himself for four years, and to think of marrying four years after
that apprenticeship is over. But such a prospectus will not do for a girl.
While the sun shines the hay must be made, and her sun shines earlier
in the day than that of him who is to be her husband. Let him go
through the apprenticeship and the work, and she will have sufficient
on her hands if she looks well after his household. Under nature's
teaching she is aware of this, and will not bind herself to any other
apprenticeship, let Mrs. Dall preach as she may.

I remember seeing, either at New York or Boston, a wooden figure of
a neat young woman, as large as life, standing at a desk with a ledger
before her, and looking as though the beau ideal of human bliss were
realized in her employment. Under the figure there was some notice
respecting female accountants. Nothing could be nicer than the lady's
figure, more flowing than the broad lines of her drapery, or more
attractive than her auburn ringlets. There she stood at work, earning
her bread without any impediment to the natural operation of her
female charms, and adjusting the accounts of some great firm with as
much facility as grace. I wonder whether he who designed that figure
had ever sat or stood at a desk for six hours,—whether he knew the dull
hum of the brain which comes from long attention to another man's
figures; whether he had ever soiled his own fingers with the everlasting
work of office hours, or worn his sleeves threadbare as he leaned weary
in body and mind upon his desk? Work is a grand thing,—the grandest
thing we have; but work is not picturesque, graceful, and in itself
alluring. It sucks the sap out of men's bones, and bends their backs,
and sometimes breaks their hearts; but though it be so, I for one would
not wish to throw any heavier share of it on to a woman's shoulders. It
was pretty to see those young women with spectacles at the Boston
library, but when I heard that they were there from eight in the

morning till nine at night, I pitied them their loss of all the softness of home, and felt that they would not willingly be there if necessity were less stern.

Say that by advocating the rights of women, philanthropists succeed in apportioning more work to their share, will they eat more, wear better clothes, lie softer, and have altogether more of the fruits of work than they do now? That some would do so there can be no doubt, but as little that some would have less. If on the whole they would not have more, for what good result is the movement made? The first question is, whether at the present time they have less than their proper share. There are, unquestionably, terrible cases of female want, and so there are also of want among men. Alas! do we not all feel that it must be so, let the philanthropists be ever so energetic? And if a woman be left destitute, without the assistance of father, brother, or husband, it would be hard if no means of earning subsistence were open to her. But the object now sought is not that of relieving such distress. It has a much wider tendency, or at any rate a wider desire. The idea is that women will ennoble themselves by making themselves independent, by working for their own bread instead of eating bread earned by men. It is in that that these new philosophers seem to me to err so greatly. Humanity and chivalry have succeeded after a long struggle in teaching the man to work for the woman; and now the woman rebels against such teaching,—not because she likes the work, but because she desires the influence which attends it. But in this I wrong the woman,—even the American woman. It is not she who desires it, but her philanthropical philosophical friends who desire it for her.

If work were more equally divided between the sexes some women would, of course, receive more of the good things of the world. But women generally would not do so. The tendency then would be to force young women out upon their own exertions. Fathers would soon learn to think that their daughters should be no more dependent on them than their sons; men would expect their wives to work at their own trades; brothers would be taught to think it hard that their sisters should lean on them; and thus women, driven upon their own resources, would hardly fare better than they do at present.

After all it is a question of money, and a contest for that power and influence which money gives. At present men have the position of the Lower House of Parliament. They have to do the harder work, but they hold the purse. Even in England there has grown up a feeling that the old law of the land gives a married man too much power over the joint pecuniary resources of him and his wife, and in America this feeling is much stronger, and the old law has been modified. Why should a married woman be able to possess nothing? And if such be the law of the land, is it worth a woman's while to marry and put herself in such a position? Those are the questions asked by the friends of the rights of women. But the young women do marry, and the men pour their earnings into their wives' laps.

If little has as yet been done in extending the rights of women by giving them a greater share of the work of the world, still less has been done towards giving them their portion of political influence. In the States there are many men of mark, and women of mark also, who think that women should have votes for public elections. Mr. Wendell Phillips, the Boston lecturer who advocates abolition, is an apostle in this cause also; and while I was at Boston I read the provisions of a will lately left by a millionaire, in which he bequeathed some very large sums of money to be expended in agitation on this subject. A woman is subject to the law; why then should she not help to make the law? A child is subject to the law, and does not help to make it; but the child lacks that discretion which the woman enjoys equally with the man. That I take it is the amount of the argument in favour of the political rights of women. The logic of this is so conclusive, that I am prepared to acknowledge that it admits of no answer. I will only say that the mutual good relations between men and women, which are so indispensable to our happiness, require that men and women should not take to voting at the same time and on the same result. If it be decided that women shall have political power, let them have it all to themselves for a season. If that be so resolved, I think we may safely leave it to them to name the time at which they will begin.

I confess that in the States I have sometimes been driven to think that chivalry has been carried too far;—that there is an attempt to make women think more of the rights of their womanhood than is needful. There are ladies' doors at hotels, and ladies' drawing-rooms, ladies' sides on the ferry-boats, ladies' windows at the post office for the delivery of letters;—which, by-the-by, is an atrocious institution, as anybody may learn who will look at the advertisements called personal in some of the New York papers. Why should not young ladies have their letters sent to their houses, instead of getting them at a private window? The post-office clerks can tell stories about those ladies' windows. But at every turn it is necessary to make separate provision for ladies. From all this it comes to pass that the baker's daughter looks down from a great height on her papa, and by no means thinks her brother good enough for her associate. Nature, the great restorer, comes in and teaches her to fall in love with the butcher's son. Thus the evil is mitigated; but I cannot but wish that the young woman should not see herself denominated a lady so often, and should receive fewer lessons as to the extent of her privileges. I would save her if I could from working at the oven; I would give to her bread and meat earned by her father's care and her brother's sweat; but when she has received these good things, I would have her proud of the one and by no means ashamed of the other.

Let women say what they will of their rights, or men who think themselves generous say what they will for them, the question has all been settled both for them and for us men by a higher power. They are the nursing mothers of mankind, and in that law their fate is written with all its joys and all its privileges. It is for men to make those joys as lasting and those privileges as perfect as may be. That women should have their rights no man will deny. To my thinking neither increase of work nor increase of political influence are among them. The best right a woman has is the right to a husband, and that is the right to which I would recommend every young woman here and in the States to turn her best attention. On the whole, I think that my doctrine will be more acceptable than that of Mrs. Dall or Mr. Wendell Phillips.

XIX

Education and Religion

THE one matter in which, as far as my judgment goes, the people of the United States have excelled us Englishmen, so as to justify them in taking to themselves praise which we cannot take to ourselves or refuse to them, is the matter of Education. In saying this I do not think that I am proclaiming anything disgraceful to England, though I am proclaiming much that is creditable to America. To the Americans of the States was given the good fortune of beginning at the beginning. The French at the time of their revolution endeavoured to reorganize everything, and to begin the world again with new habits and grand theories; but the French as a people were too old for such a change, and the theories fell to the ground. But in the States, after their revolution, an Anglo-Saxon people had an opportunity of making a new State, with all the experience of the world before them; and to this matter of education they were from the first aware that they must look for their success. They did so; and unrivalled population, wealth, and intelligence have been the results; and with these, looking at the whole masses of the people,—I think I am justified in saying,—unrivalled comfort and happiness. It is not that you, my reader, to whom in this matter of education fortune and your parents have probably been bountiful, would have been more happy in New York than in London. It is not that I, who, at any rate, can read and write, have cause to wish that I had been an American. But it is this;—if you and I can count up in a day all those on whom our eyes may rest, and learn the circumstances of their lives, we shall be driven to conclude that nine-tenths of that number would have had a better life as Americans than they can have in their spheres as Englishmen. The States are at a discount with us now, in the beginning of this year of grace 1862; and Englishmen were not very willing to admit the above statement, even when the States were not at a discount. But I do not think that a man can travel through the States with his eyes open and not admit the fact. Many things will conspire to induce him to shut his eyes and admit no conclusion favourable to the Americans. Men and women will sometimes be impudent to him;—the better his coat, the greater the impudence. He will be pelted with the braggadocio of equality. The corns of his Old-World conservatism will be trampled on hourly by the purposely vicious herd of uncouth democracy. The fact that he is paymaster will go for nothing, and will fail to insure civility. I shall never forget my agony as I saw and heard my desk fall from a porter's hand on a railway station, as he tossed it from him seven yards off on to the hard pavement. I heard its poor weak intestines rattle in their death-struggle, and knowing that it was smashed I forgot my position on American soil and remonstrated. "It's my desk, and you have utterly destroyed it," I said. "Ha! ha! ha!" laughed the porter. "You've destroyed my property," I rejoined, "and it's no laughing matter." And then all the crowd laughed. "Guess you'd better get it glued," said one. So I gathered up the broken article and retired mournfully and crestfallen into a coach. This was very sad, and for the moment I deplored the ill-luck which had brought me to so savage a country. Such and such like are the incidents which make an Englishman in the States unhappy, and rouse his gall against the institutions of the country;—these things and the continued appliance of the irritating ointment of American braggadocio with which his sores are kept open. But though I was badly off on that railway platform,—worse off than I should have been in England,—all that crowd of porters round me were better off than our English porters. They had a "good time" of it. And this, O my English brother who hast travelled through the States and returned disgusted, is the fact throughout. Those men whose familiarity was so disgusting to you are having a good time of it. "They might be a little more civil," you say, "and yet read and write just as well." True; but they are arguing in their minds that civility to you will be taken by you for subservience, or for an acknowledgment of superiority; and looking at your habits of life,—yours and mine together,—I am not quite sure that they are altogether wrong. Have you ever realized to yourself as a fact that the porter who carries your box has not made himself inferior to you by the very act of carrying that box? If not, that is the very lesson which the man wishes to teach you.

If a man can forget his own miseries in his journeyings, and think of the people he comes to see rather than of himself, I think he will find himself driven to admit that education has made life for the million in the northern States better than life for the million is with us. They have begun at the beginning, and have so managed that every one may learn to read and write,—have so managed that almost every one does learn to read and write. With us this cannot now be done. Population had come upon us in masses too thick for management before we had as yet acknowledged that it would be a good thing that these masses should be educated. Prejudices, too, had sprung up, and habits, and strong sectional feelings, all antagonistic to a great national system of education. We are, I suppose, now doing all that we can do; but comparatively it is little. I think I saw some time since that the cost for gratuitous education, or education in part gratuitous, which had fallen upon the nation had already amounted to the sum of 800,000*l.*; and I think also that I read in the document which revealed to me this fact, a very strong opinion that Government could not at present go much further. But if this matter were regarded in England as it is regarded in Massachusetts,—or rather, had it from some prosperous beginning been put upon a similar footing, 800,000*l.* would not have been esteemed a great expenditure for free education simply in the city of London. In 1857 the public schools of Boston cost 70,000*l.*, and these schools were devoted to a population of about 180,000 souls. Taking the population of London at two-and-a-half millions, the whole sum now devoted to England would, if expended in the metropolis, make education there even cheaper than it is in Boston. In Boston during 1857 there were above 24,000 pupils at these public schools, giving more than one-eighth of the whole population. But I fear it would not be practicable for us to spend 800,000*l.* on the gratuitous education of London. Rich as we are, we should not know where to raise the money. In Boston it is raised by a separate tax. It is a thing understood, acknowledged, and made easy by being habitual,—as is our national debt. I do not know that Boston is peculiarly blessed, but I quote the instance as I have a record of its schools before me. At the three high schools in Boston at which the average of pupils is 526, about 13*l.* per head is paid for free education. The average price per annum of a child's schooling throughout these schools in Boston is about 3*l.* per annum. To the higher schools any boy or girl may attain without any expense, and the education is probably as good as can be given, and as far advanced. The only question is, whether it is not advanced further than may be necessary. Here, as at New York, I was almost startled by the amount of knowledge around me, and listened, as I might have done, to an examination in theology among young Brahmins. When a young lad explained in my hearing all the properties of the different levers as exemplified by the bones of the human body, I bowed my head before him in unaffected humility. We, at our English schools, never got beyond the use of those bones which he described with such accurate scientific knowledge. In one of the girls' schools they were reading Milton, and when we entered were discussing the nature of the pool in which the Devil is described as wallowing. The question had been raised by one of the girls. A pool, so called, was supposed to contain but a small amount of water, and how could the Devil, being so large, get into it? Then came the origin of the word pool,—from "palus," a marsh, as we were told, some dictionary attesting to the fact,—and such a marsh might cover a large expanse. The 'Palus Mæotis' was then quoted. And so we went on till Satan's theory of political liberty,

Better to reign in hell than serve in heaven,

was thoroughly discussed and understood. These girls of sixteen and seventeen got up one after another and gave their opinions on the subject,—how far the Devil was right and how far he was manifestly wrong. I was attended by one of the directors or guardians of the schools, and the teacher, I thought, was a little embarrassed by her position. But the girls themselves were as easy in their demeanour as though they were stitching handkerchiefs at home.

It is impossible to refrain from telling all this, and from making a little innocent fun out of the super-excellencies of these schools; but the total result on my mind was very greatly in their favour. And indeed the testimony came in both ways. Not only was I called on to form an opinion of what the men and women would become from the education which was given to the boys and girls, but also to say what must have been the education of the boys and girls from what I saw of the men and women. Of course it will be understood that I am not here speaking of those I met in society, or of their children, but of the working people,—of that class who find that a gratuitous education for their children is needful, if any considerable amount of education is to be given. The result is to be seen daily in the whole intercourse of life. The coachman who drives you, the man who mends your window, the boy who brings home your purchases, the girl who stitches your wife's dress,—they all carry with them sure signs of education, and show it in every word they utter.

It will of course be understood that this is, in the separate States, a matter of State law; indeed I may go further and say that it is in most of the States a matter of State constitution. It is by no means a matter of Federal constitution. The United States as a nation takes no heed of the education of its people. All that is left to the judgment of the separate States. In most of the thirteen original States provision is made in the written constitution for the general education of the people; but this is not done in all. I find that it was more frequently done in the northern or Freesoil States than in those which admitted slavery,—as might have been expected. In the constitutions of South Carolina and Virginia I find no allusion to the public provision for education, but in those of North Carolina and Georgia it is enjoined. The forty-first section of the constitution for North Carolina enjoins that "schools shall be established by the legislature for the convenient instruction of youth, with such salaries to the masters, paid by the public, as may enable them to instruct *at low prices*;" showing that the intention here was to assist education, and not provide it altogether gratuitously. I think that provision for public education is enjoined in the constitutions of all the States admitted into the Union since the first federal knot was tied, except in that of Illinois. Vermont was the first so admitted, in 1791, and Vermont declares that "a competent number of schools ought to be maintained in each town for the convenient instruction of youth." Ohio was the second, in 1802, and Ohio enjoins that "the general assembly shall make such provisions by taxation or otherwise as, with the income arising from the school trust fund, will secure a thorough and efficient system of common schools throughout the State; but no religious or other sect or sects shall ever have any exclusive right or control of any part of the school funds of this State." In Indiana, admitted in 1816, it is required that "the general assembly shall provide by law for a general and uniform system of common schools." Illinois was admitted next, in 1818; but the constitution of Illinois is silent on the subject of education. It enjoins, however, in lieu of this, that no person shall fight a duel or send a challenge! If he do he is not only to be punished, but to be deprived for ever of the power of holding any office of honour or profit in the State. I have no reason, however, for supposing that education is neglected in Illinois, or that duelling has been abolished. In Maine it is demanded that the towns—the whole country is divided into what are called towns—shall make suitable provision at their own expense for the support and maintenance of public schools.

Some of these constitutional enactments are most magniloquently worded, but not always with precise grammatical correctness. That for the famous Bay State of Massachusetts runs as follows:— "Wisdom and knowledge, as well as virtue, diffused generally among the body of the people, being necessary for the preservation of their rights and liberties, and as these depend on spreading the opportunities and advantages of education in the various parts of the country, and among the different orders of the people, it shall be the duty of the legislatures and magistrates, in all future periods of this commonwealth, to cherish the interest of literature and the sciences, and of all seminaries of them, especially the University at Cambridge, public schools, and grammar schools in the towns; to encourage private societies and public institutions, by rewards, and immunities for the promotion of agriculture, arts, sciences, commerce, trades, manufactures, and a natural history of the country; to countenance and inculcate the principles of humanity and general benevolence, public and private charity, industry and frugality, honesty and punctuality in all their dealings; sincerity, good humour, and all social affections and generous sentiments among the people." I must confess, that had the words of that little constitutional enactment been made known to me before I had seen its practical results, I should not have put much faith in it. Of all the public schools I have ever seen,—by public schools I mean schools for the people at large maintained at public cost,—those of Massachusetts are, I think, the best. But of all the educational enactments which I ever read, that of the same State is, I should say, the worst. In Texas now, of which as a State the people of Massachusetts do not think much, they have done it better. "A general diffusion of knowledge being essential to the preservation of the rights and liberties of the people, it shall be the duty of the legislature of this State to make suitable provision for the support and maintenance of public schools." So say the Texians; but then the Texians had the advantage of a later experience than any which fell in the way of the constitution-makers of Massachusetts.

There is something of the magniloquence of the French style,—of the liberty, equality, and fraternity mode of eloquence in the preambles of most of these constitutions, which, but for their success, would have seemed to have prophesied loudly of failure. Those of New York and Pennsylvania are the least so, and that of Massachusetts by far the most violently magniloquent. They generally commence by thanking

God for the present civil and religious liberty of the people, and by declaring that all men are born free and equal. New York and Pennsylvania, however, refrain from any such very general remarks.

I am well aware that all these constitutional enactments are not likely to obtain much credit in England. It is not only that grand phrases fail to convince us, but that they carry to our senses almost an assurance of their own inefficiency. When we hear that a people have declared their intention of being henceforward better than their neighbours, and going upon a new theory that shall lead them direct to a terrestrial paradise, we button up our pockets and lock up our spoons. And that is what we have done very much as regards the Americans. We have walked with them and talked with them, and bought with them and sold with them; but we have mistrusted them as to their internal habits and modes of life, thinking that their philanthropy was pretentious and that their theories were vague. Many cities in the States are but skeletons of towns, the streets being there, and the houses numbered,—but not one house built out of ten that have been so counted up. We have regarded their institutions as we regard those cities, and have been specially willing so to consider them because of the fine language in which they have paraded before us. They have been regarded as the skeletons of philanthropical systems, to which blood and flesh and muscle, and even skin are wanting. But it is at least but fair to inquire how far the promise made has been carried out. The elaborate wordings of the constitutions made by the French politicians in the days of their great revolution have always been to us no more than so many written grimaces; but we should not have continued so to regard them had the political liberty which they promised followed upon the promises so magniloquently made. As regards education in the States,—at any rate in the northern and western States,—I think that the assurances put forth in the various written constitutions have been kept. If this be so, an American citizen, let him be ever so arrogant, ever so impudent if you will, is at any rate a civilized being, and on the road to that cultivation which will sooner or later divest him of his arrogance. *Emollit mores*. We quote here our old friend the Colonel again. If a gentleman be compelled to confine his classical allusions to one quotation, he cannot do better than hang by that.

But has education been so general, and has it had the desired result? In the city of Boston, as I have said, I found that in 1857 about one-eighth of the whole population were then on the books of the free public schools as pupils, and that about one-ninth of the population formed the average daily attendance. To these numbers of course must be added all pupils of the richer classes,—those for whose education their parents chose to pay. As nearly as I can learn, the average duration of each pupil's schooling is six years, and if this be figured out statistically, I think it will show that education in Boston reaches a very large majority—I must almost say the whole—of the population. That the education given in other towns of Massachusetts is not so good as that given in Boston I do not doubt, but I have reason to believe that it is quite as general.

I have spoken of one of the schools of New York. In that city the public schools are apportioned to the wards, and are so arranged that in each ward of the city there are public schools of different standing for the gratuitous use of the children. The population of the city of New York in 1857 was about 650,000, and in that year it is stated that there were 135,000 pupils in the schools. By this it would appear that one person in five throughout the city was then under process of education,—which statement, however, I cannot receive with implicit credence. It is, however, also stated that the daily attendances averaged something less than 50,000 a day—and this latter statement probably implies some mistake in the former one. Taking the two together for what they are worth, they show, I think, that school teaching is not only brought within the reach of the population generally, but is used by almost all classes. At New York there are separate free schools for coloured children. At Philadelphia I did not see the schools, but I was assured that the arrangements there were equal to those at New York and Boston. Indeed I was told that they were infinitely better;—but then I was so told by a Philadelphian. In the State of Connecticut the public schools are certainly equal to those in any part of the Union. As far as I could learn, education—what we should call advanced education—is brought within the reach of all classes in the northern and western States of America,—and, I would wish to add here, to those of the Canadas also.

So much for the schools, and now for the results. I do not know that anything impresses a visitor more strongly with the amount of books sold in the States, than the practice of selling them as it has been adopted in the railway cars. Personally the traveller will find the system very disagreeable,—as is everything connected with these cars. A young man enters during the journey,—for the trade is carried out while the cars are travelling, as is also a very brisk trade in lollipops, sugar-candy, apples, and ham sandwiches,—the young tradesman enters the car firstly with a pile of magazines or of novels bound like magazines. These are chiefly the 'Atlantic,' published at Boston,

'Harper's Magazine,' published at New York, and a cheap series of
novels published at Philadelphia. As he walks along he flings one at
every passenger. An Englishman, when he is first introduced to this
manner of trade, becomes much astonished. He is probably reading,
and on a sudden he finds a fat, fluffy magazine, very unattractive in its
exterior, dropped on to the page he is perusing. I thought at first that it
was a present from some crazed philanthropist, who was thus endeavouring to disseminate literature. But I was soon undeceived. The
bookseller, having gone down the whole car and the next, returned,
and beginning again where he had begun before, picked up either his
magazine or else the price of it. Then, in some half-hour, he came
again, with an armful or basket of books, and distributed them in the
same way. They were generally novels, but not always. I do not think
that any endeavour is made to assimilate the book to the expected
customer. The object is to bring the book and the man together, and in
this way a very large sale is effected. The same thing is done with
illustrated newspapers. The sale of political newspapers goes on so
quickly in these cars that no such enforced distribution is necessary. I
should say that the average consumption of newspapers by an American must amount to about three a day. At Washington I begged the
keeper of my lodgings to let me have a paper regularly,—one American newspaper being much the same to me as another,—and my host
supplied me daily with four.

But the numbers of the popular books of the day, printed and sold,
afford the most conclusive proof of the extent to which education is
carried in the States. The readers of Tennyson, Thackeray, Dickens,
Bulwer, Collins, Hughes, and—Martin Tupper, are to be counted by
tens of thousands in the States, to the thousands by which they may be
counted in our own islands. I do not doubt that I had fully fifteen
copies of the 'Silver Cord' thrown at my head in different railway cars
on the continent of America. Nor is the taste by any means confined to
the literature of England. Longfellow, Curtis, Holmes, Hawthorne,
Lowell, Emerson,—and Mrs. Stowe, are almost as popular as their
English rivals. I do not say whether or no the literature is well chosen,
but there it is. It is printed, sold, and read. The disposal of ten
thousand copies of a work is no large sale in America of a book
published at a dollar; but in England it is a large sale of a book brought
out at five shillings.

I do not remember that I ever examined the rooms of an American
without finding books or magazines in them. I do not speak here of the
houses of my friends, as of course the same remark would apply as

strongly in England, but of the houses of persons presumed to earn their bread by the labour of their hands. The opportunity for such examination does not come daily; but when it has been in my power I have made it, and have always found signs of education. Men and women of the classes to which I allude talk of reading and writing as of arts belonging to them as a matter of course, quite as much as are the arts of eating and drinking. A porter or a farmer's servant in the States is not proud of reading and writing. It is to him quite a matter of course. The coachmen on their boxes and the boots as they sit in the halls of the hotels, have newspapers constantly in their hands. The young women have them also, and the children. The fact comes home to one at every turn, and at every hour, that the people are an educated people. The whole of this question between North and South is as well understood by the servants as by their masters, is discussed as vehemently by the private soldiers as by the officers. The politics of the country and the nature of its constitution are familiar to every labourer. The very wording of the Declaration of Independence is in the memory of every lad of sixteen. Boys and girls of a younger age than that know why Slidell and Mason were arrested, and will tell you why they should have been given up, or why they should have been held in durance. The question of the war with England is debated by every native paviour and hodman of New York.

I know what Englishmen will say in answer to this. They will declare that they do not want their paviours and hodmen to talk politics; that they are as well pleased that their coachmen and cooks should not always have a newspaper in their hands; that private soldiers will fight as well, and obey better, if they are not trained to discuss the causes which have brought them into the field. An English gentleman will think that his gardener will be a better gardener without than with any excessive political ardour; and the English lady will prefer that her housemaid shall not have a very pronounced opinion of her own as to the capabilities of the cabinet ministers. But I would submit to all Englishmen and Englishwomen who may look at these pages whether such an opinion or feeling on their part bears much, or even at all, upon the subject. I am not saying that the man who is driven in the coach is better off because his coachman reads the paper, but that the coachman himself who reads the paper is better off than the coachman who does not and cannot. I think that we are too apt, in considering the ways and habits of any people, to judge of them by the effect of those ways and habits on us, rather than by their effects on the owners of them. When we go among garlic-eaters, we condemn them because they are offensive to us; but to judge of them properly we should ascertain whether or no the garlic be offensive to them. If we could imagine a nation of vegetarians hearing for the first time of our habits as flesh-eaters, we should feel sure that they would be struck with horror at our blood-stained banquets; but when they came to argue with us, we should bid them inquire whether we flesh-eaters did not live longer and do more than the vegetarians. When we express a dislike to the shoeboy reading his newspaper, I fear we do so because we fear that the shoeboy is coming near our own heels. I know there is among us a strong feeling that the lower classes are better without politics, as there is also that they are better without crinoline and artificial flowers; but if politics and crinoline and artificial flowers are good at all, they are good for all who can honestly come by them and honestly use them. The political coachman is perhaps less valuable to his master as a coachman than he would be without his politics, but he with his politics is more valuable to himself. For myself, I do not like the Americans of the lower orders. I am not comfortable among them. They tread on my corns and offend me. They make my daily life unpleasant. But I do respect them. I acknowledge their intelligence and personal dignity. I know that they are men and women worthy to be so called; I see that they are living as human beings in possession of reasoning faculties; and I perceive that they owe this to the progress that education has made among them.

After all, what is wanted in this world? Is it not that men should eat and drink, and read and write, and say their prayers? Does not that include everything, providing that they eat and drink enough, read and write without restraint, and say their prayers without hypocrisy? When we talk of the advances of civilization, do we mean anything but this, that men who now eat and drink badly shall eat and drink well, and that those who cannot read and write now shall learn to do so,—the prayers following, as prayers will follow upon such learning? Civilization does not consist in the eschewing of garlic or the keeping clean of a man's finger-nails. It may lead to such delicacies, and probably will do so. But the man who thinks that civilization cannot exist without them imagines that the church cannot stand without the spire. In the States of America men do eat and drink, and do read and write.

But as to saying their prayers? That, as far as I can see, has come also, though perhaps not in a manner altogether satisfactory, or to a degree which should be held to be sufficient. Englishmen of strong religious feeling will often be startled in America by the freedom with which religious subjects are discussed, and the ease with which the matter is treated; but he will very rarely be shocked by that utter absence of all knowledge on the subject,—that total darkness, which is still so common among the lower orders in our own country. It is not a common thing to meet an American who belongs to no denomination of Christian worship, and who cannot tell you why he belongs to that which he has chosen.

"But," it will be said, "all the intelligence and education of this people have not saved them from falling out among themselves and their friends, and running into troubles by which they will be ruined. Their political arrangements have been so bad, that in spite of all their reading and writing they must go to the wall." I venture to express an opinion that they will by no means go to the wall, and that they will be saved from such a destiny, if in no other way, then by their education. Of their political arrangements, as I mean before long to rush into that perilous subject, I will say nothing here. But no political convulsions, should such arise,—no revolution in the constitution, should such be necessary,—will have any wide effect on the social position of the people to their serious detriment. They have the great qualities of the Anglo-Saxon race,—industry, intelligence, and self-confidence; and if these qualities will no longer suffice to keep such a people on their legs, the world must be coming to an end.

I have said that it is not a common thing to meet an American who belongs to no denomination of Christian worship. This I think is so; but I would not wish to be taken as saying that religion on that account stands on a satisfactory footing in the States. Of all subjects of discussion, this is the most difficult. It is one as to which most of us feel that to some extent we must trust to our prejudices rather than our judgments. It is a matter on which we do not dare to rely implicitly on our own reasoning faculties, and therefore throw ourselves on the opinions of those whom we believe to have been better men and deeper thinkers than ourselves. For myself, I love the name of State and Church, and believe that much of our English well-being has depended on it. I have made up my mind to think that union good, and not to be turned away from that conviction. Nevertheless I am not prepared to argue the matter. One does not always carry one's proofs at one's finger-ends.

But I feel very strongly that much of that which is evil in the structure of American politics is owing to the absence of any national religion, and that something also of social evil has sprung from the same cause. It is not that men do not say their prayers. For aught I know, they may do so as frequently and as fervently, or more frequently and more fervently, than we do; but there is a rowdiness, if I may be allowed to use such a word, in their manner of doing so which robs religion of that reverence which is, if not its essence, at any rate its chief protection. It is a part of their system that religion shall be perfectly free, and that no man shall be in any way constrained in that matter. Consequently, the question of a man's religion is regarded in a free-and-easy way. It is well, for instance, that a young lad should go somewhere on a Sunday; but a sermon is a sermon, and it does not much concern the lad's father whether his son hear the discourse of a freethinker in the music-hall, or the eloquent but lengthy outpouring of a preacher in a Methodist chapel. Everybody is bound to have a religion, but it does not much matter what it is.

The difficulty in which the first fathers of the Revolution found themselves on this question, is shown by the constitutions of the different States. There can be no doubt that the inhabitants of the New England States were, as things went, a strictly religious community. They had no idea of throwing over the worship of God, as the French had attempted to do at their Revolution. They intended that the new nation should be pre-eminently composed of a God-fearing people; but they intended also that they should be a people free in everything,—free to choose their own forms of worship. They intended that the nation should be a Protestant people; but they intended also that no man's conscience should be coerced in the matter of his own religion. It was hard to reconcile these two things, and to explain to the citizens that it behoved them to worship God,—even under penalties for omission; but that it was at the same time open to them to select any form of worship that they pleased, however that form might differ from the practices of the majority. In Connecticut it is declared that it is the duty of all men to worship the Supreme Being, the Creator and Preserver of the universe, but that it is their right to render that worship in the mode most consistent with the dictates of their consciences. And then a few lines further down the article skips the great difficulty in a manner somewhat disingenuous, and declares that each and every society of Christians in the State shall have and enjoy the same and equal privileges. But it does not say whether a Jew shall be divested of those privileges, or, if he be divested, how that treatment of him is to be reconciled with the assurance that it is every man's right to worship the Supreme Being in the mode most consistent with the dictates of his own conscience.

In Rhode Island they were more honest. It is there declared that every man shall be free to worship God according to the dictates of his own conscience, and to profess and by argument to maintain his opinion in matters of religion; and that the same shall in nowise diminish, enlarge, or affect his civil capacity. Here it is simply presumed that every man will worship a God, and no allusion is made even to Christianity.

In Massachusetts they are again hardly honest. "It is the right," says the constitution, "as well as the duty of all men in society publicly and at stated seasons to worship the Supreme Being, the great Creator and Preserver of the universe." And then it goes on to say that every man may do so in what form he pleases; but further down it declares that "every denomination of Christians, demeaning themselves peaceably and as good subjects of the commonwealth, shall be equally under the protection of the law." But what about those who are not Christians? In New Hampshire it is exactly the same. It is enacted that— "Every individual has a natural and unalienable right to worship God according to the dictates of his own conscience and reason." And that—"Every denomination of Christians, demeaning themselves quietly and as good citizens of the State, shall be equally under the protection of the law." From all which it is, I think, manifest that the men who framed these documents, desirous above all things of cutting themselves and their people loose from every kind of trammel, still felt the necessity of enforcing religion,—of making it to a certain extent a matter of State duty. In the first constitution of North Carolina it is enjoined,—"That no person who shall deny the being of God, or the truth of the Protestant religion, shall be capable of holding any office or place of trust or profit." But this was altered in the year 1836, and the words "Christian religion" were substituted for "Protestant religion."

In New England the Congregationalists are, I think, the dominant sect. In Massachusetts, and I believe in the other New England States, a man is presumed to be a Congregationalist if he do not declare himself to be anything else; as with us the Church of England counts all who do not specially have themselves counted elsewhere. The Congregationalist, as far as I can learn, is very near to a Presbyterian. In New England I think the Unitarians would rank next in number; but a Unitarian in America is not the same as a Unitarian with us. Here, if I understand the nature of his creed, a Unitarian does not recognize the divinity of our Saviour. In America he does do so, but throws over the doctrine of the Trinity. The Protestant Episcopalians muster strong in all the great cities, and I fancy that they would be regarded as taking the lead of the other religious denominations in New York. Their tendency is to high-church doctrines. I wish they had not found it necessary to alter the forms of our prayer-book in so many little matters, as to which there was no national expediency for such changes. But it was probably thought necessary that a new people should show their independence in all things. The Roman Catholics have a very strong party—as a matter of course—seeing how great has been the immigration from Ireland; but here, as in Ireland—and as indeed is the case all the world over—the Roman Catholics are the hewers of wood and drawers of water. The Germans, who have latterly flocked into the States in such swarms that they have almost German-ized certain States, have of course their own churches. In every town there are places of worship for Baptists, Presbyterians, Methodists, Anabaptists, and every denomination of Christianity; and the meeting-houses prepared for these sects are not, as with us, hideous buildings contrived to inspire disgust by the enormity of their ugliness, nor are they called Salem, Ebenezer, and Sion, nor do the ministers within them look in any way like the Deputy-Shepherd. The churches belonging to those sects are often handsome. This is especially the case in New York; and the pastors are not unfrequently among the best educated and most agreeable men whom the traveller will meet. They are for the most part well paid; and are enabled by their outward position to hold that place in the world's ranks which should always belong to a clergyman. I have not been able to obtain information from which I can state with anything like correctness what may be the average income of ministers of the Gospel in the northern States, but that it is much higher than the average income of our parish clergy-men, admits, I think, of no doubt. The stipends of clergymen in the American towns are higher than those paid in the country. The opposite to this, I think as a rule, is the case with us.

I have said that religion in the States is rowdy. By that I mean to imply that it seems to me to be divested of that reverential order and strictness of rule which, according to our ideas, should be attached to matters of religion. One hardly knows where the affairs of this world end, or where those of the next begin. When the holy men were had in at the lecture, were they doing stage-work or church-work? On hearing sermons, one is often driven to ask oneself whether the discourse from the pulpit be in its nature political or religious. I heard an Episcopa-lian Protestant clergyman talk of the scoffing nations of Europe,— because at that moment he was angry with England and France about Slidell and Mason. I have heard a chapter of the Bible read in Con-gress at the desire of a member, and very badly read. After which the chapter itself and the reading of it became the subject of a debate,

partly jocose and partly acrimonious. It is a common thing for a
clergyman to change his profession and follow any other pursuit. I
know two or three gentlemen who were once in that line of life, but
have since gone into other trades. There is, I think, an unexpressed
determination on the part of the people to abandon all reverence, and
to regard religion from an altogether worldly point of view. They are
willing to have religion, as they are willing to have laws; but they
choose to make it for themselves. They do not object to paying for it,
but they like to have the handling of the article for which they pay. As
the descendants of Puritans and other godly Protestants, they will
submit to religious teaching, but as Republicans they will have no
priestcraft. The French at their Revolution had the latter feeling
without the former, and were therefore consistent with themselves in
abolishing all worship. The Americans desire to do the same thing
politically, but infidelity has had no charms for them. They say their
prayers, and then seem to apologize for doing so, as though it were
hardly the act of a free and enlightened citizen, justified in ruling
himself as he pleases. All this to me is rowdy. I know no other word by
which I can so well describe it.

Nevertheless the nation is religious in its tendencies, and prone to
acknowledge the goodness of God in all things. A man there is expected to belong to some church, and is not, I think, well looked on if
he profess that he belongs to none. He may be a Swedenborgian, a
Quaker, a Muggletonian;—anything will do. But it is expected of him
that he shall place himself under some flag, and do his share in
supporting the flag to which he belongs. This duty is, I think, generally
fulfilled.

XX

From Boston to Washington

FROM Boston, on the 27th of November, my wife returned to England, leaving me to prosecute my journey southward to Washington by myself. I shall never forget the political feeling which prevailed in Boston at that time, or the discussions on the subject of Slidell and Mason, in which I felt myself bound to take a part. Up to that period I confess that my sympathies had been strongly with the northern side in the general question; and so they were still, as far as I could divest the matter of its English bearings. I had always thought, and do think, that a war for the suppression of the southern rebellion could not have been avoided by the North without an absolute loss of its political prestige. Mr. Lincoln was elected President of the United States in the autumn of 1860, and any steps taken by him or his party towards a peaceable solution of the difficulties which broke out immediately on his election, must have been taken before he entered upon his office. South Carolina threatened secession as soon as Mr. Lincoln's election was known, while yet there were four months left of Mr. Buchanan's Government. That Mr. Buchanan might, during those four months, have prevented secession, few men, I think, will doubt when the history of the time shall be written. But instead of doing so he consummated secession. Mr. Buchanan is a northern man, a Pennsylvanian; but he was opposed to the party which had brought in Mr. Lincoln, having thriven as a politician by his adherence to southern principles. Now, when the struggle came, he could not forget his party in his duty as President. General Jackson's position was much the same when Mr. Calhoun, on the question of the tariff, endeavoured to produce secession in South Carolina thirty years ago, in 1832,—excepting in this, that Jackson was himself a southern man. But Jackson had a strong conception of the position which he held as President of the United States. He put his foot on secession and crushed it, forcing Mr. Calhoun, as senator from South Carolina, to vote for that compromise as to the tariff which the Government of the day proposed. South Carolina was as eager in 1832 for secession as she was in 1859–1860; but the Government was in the hands of a strong man and an honest one. Mr. Calhoun would have been hung had he carried out his threats. But Mr. Buchanan had neither the power nor the honesty of General Jackson, and thus secession was in fact consummated during his Presidency.

But Mr. Lincoln's party, it is said—and I believe truly said—might have prevented secession by making overtures to the South, or accepting overtures from the South, before Mr. Lincoln himself had been inaugurated. That is to say,—if Mr. Lincoln and the band of politicians who with him had pushed their way to the top of their party, and were about to fill the offices of State, chose to throw overboard the political convictions which had bound them together and insured their success,—if they could bring themselves to adopt on the subject of slavery the ideas of their opponents,—then the war might have been avoided, and secession also avoided. I do believe that had Mr. Lincoln at that time submitted himself to a compromise in favour of the Democrats, promising the support of the Government to certain acts which would in fact have been in favour of slavery, South Carolina would again have been foiled for the time. For it must be understood, that though South Carolina and the Gulf States might have accepted certain compromises, they would not have been satisfied in so accepting them. They desired secession, and nothing short of secession would, in truth, have been acceptable to them. But in doing so Mr. Lincoln would have been the most dishonest politician even in America. The North would have been in arms against him; and any true spirit of agreement between the cotton-growing slave States and the manufacturing States of the North, or the agricultural States of the West, would have been as far off and as improbable as it is now. Mr. Crittenden, who proffered his compromise to the Senate in December 1860, was at that time one of the two senators from Kentucky, a slave State. He now sits in the Lower House of Congress as a member from the same State. Kentucky is one of those border

States which has found it impossible to secede, and almost equally impossible to remain in the Union. It is one of the States into which it was most probable that the war would be carried;—Virginia, Kentucky, and Missouri being the three States which have suffered the most in this way. Of Mr. Crittenden's own family, some have gone with secession and some with the Union. His name had been honourably connected with American politics for nearly forty years, and it is not surprising that he should have desired a compromise. His terms were in fact these,—a return to the Missouri compromise, under which the Union pledged itself that no slavery should exist north of 36.30 N. lat. except where it had so existed prior to the date of that compromise; a pledge that Congress would not interfere with slavery in the individual States,—which under the constitution it cannot do; and a pledge that the Fugitive Slave Law should be carried out by the northern States. Such a compromise might seem to make very small demand on the forbearance of the Republican party, which was now dominant. The repeal of the Missouri compromise had been to them a loss, and it might be said that its re-enactment would be a gain. But since that compromise had been repealed, vast territories south of the line in question, had been added to the Union, and the re-enactment of that compromise would hand those vast regions over to absolute slavery, as had been done with Texas. This might be all very well for Mr. Crittenden in the slave State of Kentucky—for Mr. Crittenden, although a slave-owner, desired to perpetuate the Union; but it would not have been well for New England or for the West. As for the second proposition, it is well understood that under the constitution Congress cannot interfere in any way in the question of slavery in the individual States. Congress has no more constitutional power to abolish slavery in Maryland than she has to introduce it into Massachusetts. No such pledge, therefore, was necessary on either side. But such a pledge given by the North and West would have acted as an additional tie upon them, binding them to the finality of a constitutional enactment to which, as was of course well known, they strongly object. There was no question of Congress interfering with slavery, with the purport of extending its area by special enactment, and therefore by such a pledge the North and West could gain nothing; but the South would in prestige have gained much.

But that third proposition as to the Fugitive Slave Law and the faithful execution of that law by the northern and western States would, if acceded to by Mr. Lincoln's party, have amounted to an unconditional surrender of everything. What! Massachusetts and

Connecticut carry out the Fugitive Slave Law! Ohio carry out the Fugitive Slave Law after the 'Dred Scot' decision and all its consequences! Mr. Crittenden might as well have asked Connecticut, Massachusetts, and Ohio to introduce slavery within their own lands. The Fugitive Slave Law was then, as it is now, the law of the land; it was the law of the United States as voted by Congress and passed by the President, and acted on by the Supreme Judge of the United States' Court. But it was a law to which no free State had submitted itself, or would submit itself. "What!" the English reader will say,— "sundry States in the Union refuse to obey the laws of the Union,— refuse to submit to the constitutional action of their own Congress!" Yes. Such has been the position of this country! To such a dead lock has it been brought by the attempted but impossible amalgamation of North and South. Mr. Crittenden's compromise was moonshine. It was utterly out of the question that the free States should bind themselves to the rendition of escaped slaves,—or that Mr. Lincoln, who had just been brought in by their voices, should agree to any compromise which should attempt so to bind them. Lord Palmerston might as well attempt to re-enact the Corn Laws.

Then comes the question whether Mr. Lincoln or his Government could have prevented the war after he had entered upon his office in March 1861? I do not suppose that any one thinks that he could have avoided secession and avoided the war also;—that by any ordinary effort of Government he could have secured the adhesion of the Gulf States to the Union after the first shot had been fired at Fort Sumter. The general opinion in England is, I take it, this,—that secession then was manifestly necessary, and that all the bloodshed and money-shed, and all this destruction of commerce and of agriculture might have been prevented by a graceful adhesion to an indisputable fact. But there are some facts, even some indisputable facts, to which a graceful adherence is not possible. Could King Bomba have welcomed Garibaldi to Naples? Can the Pope shake hands with Victor Emmanuel? Could the English have surrendered to their rebel colonists peaceable possession of the colonies? The indisputability of a fact is not very easily settled while the circumstances are in course of action by which the fact is to be decided. The men of the northern States have not believed in the necessity of secession, but have believed it to be their duty to enforce the adherence of these States to the Union. The American Governments have been much given to compromises, but had Mr. Lincoln attempted any compromise by which any one southern State could have been let out of the Union, he would have been impeached. In all probability the whole constitution would have gone to ruin, and the presidency would have been at an end. At any rate, his presidency would have been at an end. When secession, or in other words, rebellion was once commenced, he had no alternative but the use of coercive measures for putting it down;—that is, he had no alternative but war. It is not to be supposed that he or his ministry contemplated such a war as has existed,—with 600,000 men in arms on one side, each man with his whole belongings maintained at a cost of 150*l.* per annum, or ninety millions sterling per annum for the army. Nor did we, when we resolved to put down the French revolution, think of such a national debt as we now owe. These things grow by degrees, and the mind also grows in becoming used to them; but I cannot see that there was any moment at which Mr. Lincoln could have stayed his hand and cried Peace! It is easy to say now that acquiescence in secession would have been better than war, but there has been no moment when he could have said so with any avail. It was incumbent on him to put down rebellion, or to be put down by it. So it was with us in America in 1776.

I do not think that we in England have quite sufficiently taken all this into consideration. We have been in the habit of exclaiming very loudly against the war, execrating its cruelty and anathematizing its results, as though the cruelty were all superfluous and the results unnecessary. But I do not remember to have seen any statement as to what the northern States should have done,—what they should have done, that is, as regards the South, or when they should have done it. It seems to me that we have decided as regards them that civil war is a very bad thing, and that therefore civil war should be avoided. But bad things cannot always be avoided. It is this feeling on our part that has produced so much irritation in them against us,—reproducing, of course, irritation on our part against them. They cannot understand that we should not wish them to be successful in putting down a rebellion; nor can we understand why they should be outrageous against us for standing aloof, and keeping our hands, if it be only possible, out of the fire.

When Slidell and Mason were arrested, my opinions were not changed, but my feelings were altered. I seemed to acknowledge to myself that the treatment to which England had been subjected, and the manner in which that treatment was discussed, made it necessary that I should regard the question as it existed between England and the States, rather than in its reference to the North and South. I had always felt that as regarded the action of our Government we had been sans reproche; that in arranging our conduct we had thought neither of money nor political influence, but simply of the justice of the case,— promising to abstain from all interference and keeping that promise faithfully. It had been quite clear to me that the men of the North, and the women also, had failed to appreciate this, looking, as men in a quarrel always do look, for special favour on their side. Everything that England did was wrong. If a private merchant, at his own risk, took a cargo of rifles to some southern port, that act to northern eyes was an act of English interference,—of favour shown to the South by England as a nation; but twenty shiploads of rifles sent from England to the North merely signified a brisk trade and a desire for profit. The 'James Adger,' a northern man-of-war, was refitted at Southampton as a matter of course. There was no blame to England for that. But the 'Nashville,' belonging to the Confederates, should not have been allowed into English waters! It was useless to speak of neutrality. No Northerner would understand that a rebel could have any mutual right. The South had no claim in his eyes as a belligerent, though the North claimed all those rights which he could only enjoy by the fact of there being a recognized war between him and his enemy the South. The North was learning to hate England, and day by day the feeling grew upon me that, much as I wished to espouse the cause of the North, I should have to espouse the cause of my own country. Then Slidell and Mason were arrested, and I began to calculate how long I might remain in the country. "There is no danger. We are quite right," the lawyers said. "There are Vattel and Puffendorff and Stowell and Phillimore and Wheaton," said the ladies. "Ambassadors are contraband all the world over,—more so than gunpowder; and if taken in a neutral bottom, &c." I wonder why ships are always called bottoms when spoken of with legal technicality? But neither the lawyers nor the ladies convinced me. I know that there are matters which will be read not in accordance with any written law, but in accordance with the bias of the reader's mind. Such laws are made to be strained any way. I knew how it would be. All the legal acumen of New England declared the seizure of Slidell and Mason to be right. The legal acumen of Old England has declared it to be wrong; and I have no doubt that the ladies of Old England can prove it to be wrong out of Vattel, Puffendorff, Stowell, Phillimore, and Wheaton.

"But there's Grotius," I said, to an elderly female at New York, who had quoted to me some half-dozen writers on international law, thinking thereby that I should trump her last card. "I've looked into Grotius too," said she, "and as far as I can see," &c. &c. &c. So I had to fall back again on the convictions to which instinct and common sense had brought me. I never doubted for a moment that those convictions would be supported by English lawyers.

I left Boston with a sad feeling at my heart that a quarrel was imminent between England and the States, and that any such quarrel must be destructive to the cause of the North. I had never believed that the States of New England and the Gulf States would again become parts of one nation, but I had thought that the terms of separation would be dictated by the North, and not by the South. I had felt assured that South Carolina and the Gulf States, across from the Atlantic to Texas, would succeed in forming themselves into a separate confederation; but I had still hoped that Maryland, Virginia, Kentucky, and Missouri might be saved to the grander empire of the North, and that thus a great blow to slavery might be the consequence of this civil war. But such ascendancy could only fall to the North by reason of their command of the sea. The northern ports were all open, and the southern ports were all closed. But if this should be reversed. If by England's action the southern ports should be opened, and the northern ports closed, the North could have no fair expectation of success. The ascendancy in that case would all be with the South. Up to that moment,—the Christmas of 1861,—Maryland was kept in subjection by the guns which General Dix had planted over the city of Baltimore. Two-thirds of Virginia were in active rebellion, coerced originally into that position by her dependence for the sale of her slaves on the cotton States. Kentucky was doubtful, and divided. When the federal troops prevailed, Kentucky was loyal; when the Confederate troops prevailed, Kentucky was rebellious. The condition in Missouri was much the same. Those four States, by two of which the capital, with its district of Columbia, is surrounded, might be gained, or might be lost. And these four States are susceptible of white labour,—as much so as Ohio and Illinois,—are rich in fertility, and rich also in all associations which must be dear to Americans. Without Virginia, Maryland, and Kentucky, without the Potomac, the Chesapeake, and Mount Vernon, the North would indeed be shorn of its glory! But it seemed to be in the power of the North to say under what terms secession should take place, and where should be the line. A senator from South Carolina could never again sit in the same chamber with one from Massachusetts; but there need be no such bar against the border States. So much might at any rate be gained, and might stand hereafter as the product of all that money spent on 600,000 soldiers. But if the Northerners should now elect to throw themselves into a

quarrel with England, if in the gratification of a shameless braggadocio they should insist on doing what they liked, not only with their
own, but with the property of all others also, it certainly did seem as
though utter ruin must await their cause. With England, or one might
say with Europe, against them, secession must be accomplished, not
on northern terms, but on terms dictated by the South. The choice was
then for them to make; and just at that time it seemed as though they
were resolved to throw away every good card out of their hand. Such
had been the ministerial wisdom of Mr. Seward. I remember hearing
the matter discussed in easy terms by one of the United States senators.
"Remember, Mr. Trollope," he said to me, "we don't want a war with
England. If the choice is given to us, we had rather not fight England.
Fighting is a bad thing. But remember this also, Mr. Trollope—that if
the matter is pressed on us, we have no great objection. We had rather
not, but we don't care much one way or the other." What one individual may say to another is not of much moment, but this senator was
expressing the feelings of his constituents, who were the legislature of
the State from whence he came. He was expressing the general idea on
the subject of a large body of Americans. It was not that he and his
State had really no objection to the war. Such a war loomed terribly
large before the minds of them all. They knew it to be fraught with the
saddest consequences. It was so regarded in the mind of that senator.
But the braggadocio could not be omitted. Had he omitted it, he would
have been untrue to his constituency.

When I left Boston for Washington nothing was as yet known of
what the English Government or the English lawyers might say. This
was in the first week in December, and the expected voice from
England could not be heard till the end of the second week. It was a
period of great suspense, and of great sorrow also to the more sober-
minded Americans. To me the idea of such a war was terrible. It
seemed that in these days all the hopes of our youth were being
shattered. That poetic turning of the sword into a sickle, which glad-
dened our hearts ten or twelve years since, had been clean banished
from men's minds. To belong to a peace-party was to be either a
fanatic, an idiot, or a driveller. The arts of war had become everything.
Armstrong guns, themselves indestructible, but capable of destroying
everything within sight, and most things out of sight, were the only
recognized results of man's inventive faculties. To build bigger, stronger, and more ships than the French was England's glory. To hit a
speck with a rifle bullet at 800 yards' distance was an Englishman's
first duty. The proper use for a young man's leisure hours was the

practice of drilling. All this had come upon us with very quick steps, since the beginning of the Russian war. But if fighting must needs be done, one did not feel special grief at fighting a Russian. That the Indian mutiny should be put down was a matter of course. That those Chinese rascals should be forced into the harness of civilization was a good thing. That England should be as strong as France,—or perhaps, if possible, a little stronger,—recommended itself to an Englishman's mind as a State necessity. But a war with the States of America! In thinking of it I began to believe that the world was going backwards. Over sixty millions sterling of stock—railway stock and such like—are held in America by Englishmen, and the chances would be that before such a war could be finished the whole of that would be confiscated. Family connections between the States and the British isles are almost as close as between one of those islands and another. The commercial intercourse between the two countries has given bread to millions of Englishmen, and a break in it would rob millions of their bread. These people speak our language, use our prayers, read our books, are ruled by our laws, dress themselves in our image, are warm with our blood. They have all our virtues; and their vices are our own too, loudly as we call out against them. They are our sons and our daughters, the source of our greatest pride, and as we grow old they should be the staff of our age. Such a war as we should now wage with the States would be an unloosing of hell upon all that is best upon the world's surface. If in such a war we beat the Americans, they with their proud stomachs would never forgive us. If they should be victors, we should never forgive ourselves. I certainly could not bring myself to speak of it with the equanimity of my friend the senator.

I went through New York to Philadelphia and made a short visit to the latter town. Philadelphia seems to me to have thrown off its Quaker garb, and to present itself to the world in garments ordinarily assumed by large cities; by which I intend to express my opinion that the Philadelphians are not in these latter days any better than their neighbours. I am not sure whether in some respects they may not perhaps be worse. Quakers,—Quakers absolutely in the very flesh of close bonnets and brown knee-breeches,—are still to be seen there; but they are not numerous, and would not strike the eye if one did not specially look for a Quaker at Philadelphia. It is a large town, with a very large hotel,—there are no doubt half-a-dozen large hotels, but one of them is specially great,—with long straight streets, good shops and markets, and decent comfortable-looking houses. The houses of Philadelphia generally are not so large as those of other great cities in the States. They are more modest than those of New York, and less commodious than those of Boston. Their most striking appendage is the marble steps at the front doors. Two doors as a rule enjoy one set of steps, on the outer edges of which there is generally no parapet or raised curb-stone. This, to my eye, gave the houses an unfinished appearance,—as though the marble ran short, and no further expenditure could be made. The frost came when I was there, and then all these steps were covered up in wooden cases.

The city of Philadelphia lies between the two rivers, the Delaware and the Schuylkill. Eight chief streets run from river to river, and twenty-four cross-streets bisect the eight at right angles. The long streets are, with the exception of Market Street, called by the names of trees,—chestnut, walnut, pine, spruce, mulberry, vine, and so on. The cross-streets are all called by their numbers. In the long streets the numbers of the houses are not consecutive, but follow the numbers of the cross-streets; so that a person living in Chestnut Street between Tenth Street and Eleventh Street, and ten doors from Tenth Street, would live at No. 1010. The opposite house would be No. 1011. It thus follows that the number of the house indicates the exact block of houses in which it is situated. I do not like the right-angled building of these towns, nor do I like the sound of Twentieth Street and Thirtieth Street; but I must acknowledge that the arrangement in Philadelphia has its convenience. In New York I found it by no means an easy thing to arrive at the desired locality.

They boast in Philadelphia that they have half a million inhabitants. If this be taken as a true calculation, Philadelphia is in size the fourth city in the world,—putting out of the question the cities of China, as to which we have heard so much and believe so little. But in making this calculation the citizens include the population of a district on some sides ten miles distant from Philadelphia. It takes in other towns connected with it by railway, but separated by large spaces of open country. American cities are very proud of their population, but if they all counted in this way, there would soon be no rural population left at all. There is a very fine bank at Philadelphia,—and Philadelphia is a town somewhat celebrated in its banking history. My remarks here, however, apply simply to the external building, and not to its internal honesty and wisdom, or to its commercial credit.

In Philadelphia also stands the old house of Congress,—the house in which the Congress of the United States was held previous to 1800, when the Government, and the Congress with it, were moved to the new city of Washington. I believe, however, that the first Congress, properly so called, was assembled at New York in 1789, the date of the inauguration of the first President. It was, however, here, in this building at Philadelphia, that the independence of the Union was declared in 1776, and that the constitution of the United States was framed.

Pennsylvania, with Philadelphia for its capital, was once the leading State of the Union,—leading by a long distance. At the end of the last century it beat all the other States in population, but has since been surpassed by New York in all respects,—in population, commerce, wealth, and general activity. Of course it is known that Pennsylvania was granted to William Penn, the Quaker, by Charles II. I cannot completely understand what was the meaning of such grants—how far they implied absolute possession in the territory, or how far they confirmed simply the power of settling and governing a colony. In this case a very considerable property was confirmed, as the claims made by Penn's children after Penn's death were bought up by the commonwealth of Pennsylvania for 130,000*l*.; which in those days was a large price for almost any landed estate on the other side of the Atlantic.

Pennsylvania lies directly on the borders of slave land, being immediately north of Maryland. Mason and Dixon's line, of which we hear so often, and which was first established as the division between slave soil and free soil, runs between Pennsylvania and Maryland. The little State of Delaware, which lies between Maryland and the Atlantic, is also tainted with slavery; but the stain is not heavy nor indelible. In a population of a hundred and twelve thousand there are not two thousand slaves, and of these the owners generally would willingly rid themselves if they could. It is, however, a point of honour with these owners, as it is also in Maryland, not to sell their slaves; and a man who cannot sell his slaves must keep them. Were he to enfranchise them and send them about their business, they would come back upon his hands. Were he to enfranchise them and pay them wages for work, they would get the wages but he would not get the work. They would get the wages, but at the end of three months they would still fall back upon his hands in debt and distress, looking to him for aid and comfort as a child looks for it. It is not easy to get rid of a slave in a slave State. That question of enfranchising slaves is not one to be very readily solved.

In Pennsylvania the right of voting is confined to free white men. In New York the coloured free men have the right to vote, providing they have a certain small property qualification, and have been citizens for three years in the State;—whereas a white man need have been a citizen but for ten days, and need have no property qualification; from which it is seen that the position of the negro becomes worse, or less like that of a white man, as the border of slave land is more nearly reached. But in the teeth of this embargo on coloured men, the constitution of Pennsylvania asserts broadly that all men are born equally free and independent. One cannot conceive how two clauses can have found their way into the same document so absolutely contradictory to each other. The first clause says that white men shall vote, and that black men shall not, which means that all political action shall be confined to white men. The second clause says that all men are born equally free and independent!

In Philadelphia I for the first time came across live secessionists,—secessionists who pronounced themselves to be such. I will not say that I had met in other cities men who falsely declared themselves true to the Union; but I had fancied, in regard to some, that their words were a little stronger than their feelings. When a man's bread,—and much more, when the bread of his wife and children—depends on his professing a certain line of political conviction, it is very hard for him to deny his assent to the truth of the argument. One feels that a man under such circumstances is bound to be convinced, unless he be in a position which may make a stanch adherence to opposite politics a matter of grave public importance. In the North I had fancied that I could sometimes read a secessionist tendency under a cloud of unionist protestations. But in Philadelphia men did not seem to think it necessary to have recourse to such a cloud. I generally found in mixed society, even there, that the discussion of secession was not permitted; but in society that was not mixed, I heard very strong opinions expressed on each side. With the unionists nothing was so strong as the necessity of keeping Slidell and Mason. When I suggested that the English Government would probably require their surrender, I was talked down and ridiculed. "Never that; come what may." Then, within half an hour, I would be told by a secessionist that England must demand reparation if she meant to retain any place among the great nations of the world; but he also would declare that the men would not be surrendered. "She must make the demand," the secessionist would say, "and then there will be war; and after that we shall see whose ports will be blockaded!" The Southerner has ever looked to England for some breach of the blockade, quite as strongly as the North has looked to England for sympathy and aid in keeping it.

The railway from Philadelphia to Baltimore passes along the top of Chesapeake Bay and across the Susquehanna river; at least the railway cars do so. On one side of that river they are run on to a huge ferryboat, and are again run off at the other side. Such an operation would seem to be one of difficulty to us under any circumstances; but as the Susquehanna is a tidal river, rising and falling a considerable number of feet, the natural impediment in the way of such an enterprise would, I think, have staggered us. We should have built a bridge costing two or three millions sterling, on which no conceivable amount of traffic would pay a fair dividend. Here, in crossing the Susquehanna, the boat is so constructed that its deck shall be level with the line of the railway at half tide, so that the inclined plane from the shore down to the boat, or from the shore up to the boat, shall never exceed half the amount of the rise or fall. One would suppose that the most intricate machinery would have been necessary for such an arrangement; but it was all rough and simple, and apparently managed by two negroes. We should employ a small corps of engineers to conduct such an operation, and men and women would be detained in their carriages under all manner of threats as to the peril of life and limb; but here everybody was expected to look out for himself. The cars were dragged up the inclined plane by a hawser attached to an engine, which hawser, had the stress broken it, as I could not but fancy probable, would have flown back and cut to pieces a lot of us who were standing in front of the car. But I do not think that any such accident would have caused very much attention. Life and limbs are not held to be so precious here as they are in England. It may be a question whether with us they are not almost too precious. Regarding railways in America generally, as to the relative safety of which, when compared with our own, we have not in England a high opinion, I must say that I never saw any accident or in any way became conversant with one. It is said that large numbers of men and women are slaughtered from time to time on different lines; but if it be so, the newspapers make very light of such cases. I myself have seen no such slaughter, nor have I even found myself in the vicinity of a broken bone. Beyond the Susquehanna we passed over a creek of Chesapeake Bay on a long bridge. The whole scenery here is very pretty, and the view up the Susquehanna is fine. This is the bay which divides the State of Maryland into two parts, and which is blessed beyond all other bays by the possession of canvas-back ducks. Nature has done a great deal for the State of Maryland, but in nothing more than in sending thither these web-footed birds of Paradise.

Nature has done a great deal for Maryland; and Fortune also has done much for it in these latter days in directing the war from its territory. But for the peculiar position of Washington as the capital, all that is now being done in Virginia would have been done in Maryland, and I must say that the Marylanders did their best to bring about such a result. Had the presence of the war been regarded by the men of Baltimore as an unalloyed benefit, they could not have made a greater struggle to bring it close to them. Nevertheless fate has so far spared them.

As the position of Maryland and the course of events as they took place in Baltimore on the commencement of secession had considerable influence both in the North and in the South, I will endeavour to explain how that State was affected, and how the question was affected by that State. Maryland, as I have said before, is a slave State lying immediately south of Mason and Dixon's line. Small portions both of Virginia and of Delaware do run north of Maryland, but practically Maryland is the frontier State of the slave States. It was therefore of much importance to know which way Maryland would go in the event of secession among the slave States becoming general; and of much also to ascertain whether it could secede if desirous of doing so. I am inclined to think that as a State it was desirous of following Virginia, though there are many in Maryland who deny this very stoutly. But it was at once evident that if loyalty to the North could not be had in Maryland of its own free will, adherence to the North must be enforced upon Maryland. Otherwise the city of Washington could not be maintained as the existing capital of the nation.

The question of the fidelity of the State to the Union was first tried by the arrival at Baltimore of a certain Commissioner from the State of Mississippi, who visited that city with the object of inducing secession. It must be understood that Baltimore is the commercial capital of Maryland, whereas Annapolis is the seat of Government and the legislature—or is, in other terms, the political capital. Baltimore is a city containing 230,000 inhabitants, and is considered to have as strong and perhaps as violent a mob as any city in the Union. Of the above number 30,000 are negroes and 2000 are slaves. The Commissioner made his appeal, telling his tale of southern grievances, declaring, among other things, that secession was not intended to break up the Government but to perpetuate it, and asked for the assistance and sympathy of Maryland. This was in December 1860. The Commissioner was answered by Governor Hicks, who was placed in a somewhat difficult position. The existing legislature of the State was presumed to be secessionist, but the legislature was not sitting, nor in the ordinary course of things would that legislature have been called on to sit again. The legislature of Maryland is elected every other year, and in the ordinary course sits only once in the two years. That session had been held, and the existing legislature was therefore exempt from further work,—unless specially summoned for an extraordinary session. To do this is within the power of the Governor. But Governor Hicks, who seems to have been mainly anxious to keep things quiet, and whose individual politics did not come out strongly, was not inclined to issue the summons. "Let us show moderation as well as firmness," he said; and that was about all he did say to the Commissioner from Mississippi. The Governor after that was directly called on to convene the legislature; but this he refused to do, alleging that it would not be safe to trust the discussion of such a subject as secession to—"excited politicians, many of whom having nothing to lose from the destruction of the Government, may hope to derive some gain from the ruin of the State!" I quote these words, coming from the head of the executive of the State and spoken with reference to the legislature of the State, with the object of showing in what light the political leaders of a State may be held in that very State to which they belong! If we are to judge of these legislators from the opinion expressed by Governor Hicks, they could hardly have been fit for their places. That plan of governing by the little men has certainly not answered. It need hardly be said that Governor Hicks having expressed such an opinion of his State's legislature, refused to call them to an extraordinary session.

On the 18th of April 1860, Governor Hicks issued a proclamation to the people of Maryland, begging them to be quiet, the chief object of which, however, was that of promising that no troops should be sent out from their State, unless with the object of guarding the neighbouring city of Washington,—a promise which he had no means of fulfilling, seeing that the President of the United States is the Commander-in-Chief of the army of the nation and can summon the militia of the several States. This proclamation by the Governor to the State was immediately backed up by one from the Mayor of Baltimore to the city, in which he congratulates the citizens on the Governor's promise that none of their troops are to be sent to another State; and then he tells them that they shall be preserved from the horrors of civil war.

But on the very next day the horrors of civil war began in Baltimore. By this time President Lincoln was collecting troops at Washington for the protection of the capital; and that army of the Potomac, which has ever since occupied the Virginian side of the river, was in course of construction. To join this, certain troops from Massachusetts were sent down by the usual route, *viâ* New York, Philadelphia, and Baltimore; but on their reaching Baltimore by railway, the mob of that town refused to allow them to pass through,—and a fight began. Nine citizens were killed and two soldiers, and as many more were wounded. This, I think, was the first blood spilt in the civil war; and the attack was first made by the mob of the first slave city reached by the northern soldiers. This goes far to show, not that the border States desired secession, but that, when compelled to choose between secession and union,—when not allowed by circumstances to remain neutral,—their sympathies were with their sister slave States rather than with the North.

Then there was a great running about of official men between Baltimore and Washington, and the President was besieged with entreaties that no troops should be sent through Baltimore. Now this was hard enough upon President Lincoln, seeing that he was bound to defend his capital, that he could get no troops from the South, and that Baltimore is on the high road from Washington, both to the West and to the North; but, nevertheless, he gave way. Had he not done so, all Baltimore would have been in a blaze of rebellion, and the scene of the coming contest must have been removed from Virginia to Maryland, and Congress and the Government must have travelled from Washington north to Philadelphia. "They shall not come through Baltimore," said Mr. Lincoln. "But they shall come through the State of Maryland. They shall be passed over Chesapeake Bay by water to Annapolis, and shall come up by rail from thence." This arrangement was as distasteful to the State of Maryland as the other; but Annapolis is a small town without a mob, and the Marylanders had no means of preventing the passage of the troops. Attempts were made to refuse the use of the Annapolis branch railway, but General Butler had the arranging of that. General Butler was a lawyer from Boston, and by no means inclined to indulge the scruples of the Marylanders who had so roughly treated his fellow-citizens from Massachusetts. The troops did therefore pass through Annapolis, much to the disgust of the State. On the 27th of April Governor Hicks, having now had a sufficiency of individual responsibility, summoned the legislature of which he had expressed so bad an opinion; but on this occasion he omitted to repeat that opinion, and submitted his views in very proper terms to the wisdom of the senators and representatives. He entertained, as he said, an honest conviction that the safety of Maryland lay in preserving a neutral position between the North and the South. Certainly, Governor Hicks, if it were only possible! The legislature again went to work to prevent, if it might be prevented, the passage of troops through their State; but luckily for them, they failed. The President was bound to defend Washington, and the Marylanders were denied their wish of having their own fields made the fighting ground of the civil war.

That which appears to me to be the most remarkable feature in all this is the antagonism between United States law and individual State feeling. Through the whole proceeding the Governor and the State of Maryland seemed to have considered it legal and reasonable to oppose the constitutional power of the President and his Government. It is argued in all the speeches and written documents that were produced in Maryland at the time, that Maryland was true to the Union; and yet she put herself in opposition to the constitutional military power of the President! Certain commissioners went from the State legislature to Washington, in May, and from their report, it appears that the President had expressed himself of opinion that Maryland might do this or that, as long "as she had not taken and was not about to take a hostile attitude to the Federal Government!" From which we are to gather that a denial of that military power given to the President by the constitution was not considered as an attitude hostile to the Federal Government. At any rate, it was direct disobedience of federal law. I cannot but revert from this to the condition of the fugitive slave law. Federal law, and indeed the original constitution, plainly declare that fugitive slaves shall be given up by the free-soil States. Massachusetts proclaims herself to be specially a federal, law-loving State. But every man in Massachusetts knows that no judge, no sheriff, no magistrate, no policeman in that State would at this time, or then, when that civil war was beginning, have lent a hand in any way to the rendition of a fugitive slave. The Federal law requires the State to give up the fugitive, but the State law does not require judge, sheriff, magistrate, or policeman to engage in such work, and no judge, sheriff, or magistrate will do so; consequently that Federal law is dead in Massachusetts, as it is also in every free-soil State,—dead, except inasmuch as there was life in it to create ill-blood as long as the North and South remained together, and would be life in it for the same effect if they should again be brought under the same flag.

On the 10th of May the Maryland legislature, having received the report of their Commissioners above-mentioned, passed the following resolution:—

"Whereas the war against the Confederate States is unconstitutional and repugnant to civilization, and will result in a bloody and shameful overthrow of our constitution, and whilst recognizing the obligations of Maryland to the Union, we sympathize with the South in the struggle for their rights; for the sake of humanity, we are for peace and reconciliation, and solemnly protest against this war, and will take no part in it.

"Resolved,—That Maryland implores the President, in the name of God, to cease this unholy war, at least until Congress assembles"—a period of above six months. "That Maryland desires and consents to the recognition of the independence of the Confederate States. The military occupation of Maryland is unconstitutional and she protests against it, though the violent interference with the transit of the Federal troops is discountenanced. That the vindication of her rights be left to time and reason, and that a convention under existing circumstances is inexpedient."

From which it is plain that Maryland would have seceded as effectually as Georgia seceded, had she not been prevented by the interposition of Washington between her and the Confederate States,—the happy intervention, seeing that she has thus been saved from becoming the battle-ground of the contest. But the legislature had to pay for its rashness. On the 13th of September thirteen of its members were arrested, as were also two editors of newspapers presumed to be secessionists. A member of Congress was also arrested at the same time, and a candidate for Governor Hicks's place, who belonged to the secessionist party. Previously, in the last days of June and beginning of July, the chief of the police at Baltimore and the member of the Board of Police had been arrested by General Banks, who then held Baltimore in his power.

I should be sorry to be construed as saying that republican institutions, or what may more properly be called democratic institutions, have been broken down in the States of America. I am far from thinking that they have broken down. Taking them and their work as a whole, I think that they have shown, and still show, vitality of the best order. But the written constitution of the United States and of the several States, as bearing upon each other, are not equal to the requirements made upon them. That, I think, is the conclusion to which a spectator should come. It is in that doctrine of finality that our friends have broken down,—a doctrine not expressed in their constitutions, and indeed expressly denied in the constitution of the United States, which provides the mode in which amendments shall be made—but appearing plainly enough in every word of self-gratulation which comes from them. Political finality has ever proved a delusion,—as has the idea of finality in all human institutions. I do not doubt but that the republican form of government will remain and make progress in North America; but such prolonged existence and progress must be based on an acknowledgment of the necessity for change, and must in part depend on the facilities for change which shall be afforded.

I have described the condition of Baltimore as it was early in May 1861. I reached that city just seven months later, and its condition was considerably altered. There was no question then whether troops should pass through Baltimore, or by an awkward round through Annapolis, or not pass at all through Maryland. General Dix, who had succeeded General Banks, was holding the city in his grip, and martial law prevailed. In such times as those, it was bootless to inquire as to that promise that no troops should pass southward through Baltimore. What have such assurances ever been worth in such days! Baltimore was now a military depôt in the hands of the northern army, and General Dix was not a man to stand any trifling. He did me the honour to take me to the top of Federal Hill, a suburb of the city, on which he had raised great earthworks and planted mighty cannons, and built tents and barracks for his soldiery, and to show me how instantaneously he could destroy the town from his exalted position. "This hill was made for the very purpose," said General Dix; and no doubt he thought so. Generals when they have fine positions and big guns and prostrate people lying under their thumbs, are inclined to think that God's providence has specially ordained them and their points of vantage. It is a good thing in the mind of a general so circumstanced that 200,000 men should be made subject to a dozen big guns. I confess that to me, having had no military education, the matter appeared in a different light, and I could not work up my enthusiasm to a pitch which would have been suitable to the General's courtesy. That hill, on which many of the poor of Baltimore had lived, was desecrated in my eyes by those columbiads. The neat earthworks were ugly, as looked upon by me; and though I regarded General Dix as energetic, and no doubt skilful in the work assigned to him, I could not sympathize with his exultation.

Previously to the days of secession Baltimore had been guarded by Fort MacHenry, which lies on a spit of land running out into the bay just below the town. Hither I went with General Dix, and he explained to me how the cannon had heretofore been pointed solely towards the sea; that, however, now was all changed, and the mouths of his bombs and great artillery were turned all the other way. The commandant of the fort was with us, and other officers, and they all spoke of this martial tenure as a great blessing. Hearing them, one could hardly fail to suppose that they had lived their forty, fifty, or sixty years of life in full reliance on the powers of a military despotism. But not the less were they American republicans, who, twelve months since, would have dilated on the all-sufficiency of their republican institutions, and on the absence of any military restraint in their country, with that peculiar pride which characterizes the citizens of the States. There are, however, some lessons which may be learned with singular rapidity!

Such was the state of Baltimore when I visited that city. I found, nevertheless, that cakes and ale still prevailed there. I am inclined to think that cakes and ale prevail most freely in times that are perilous, and when sources of sorrow abound. I have seen more reckless joviality in a town stricken by pestilence than I ever encountered elsewhere. There was General Dix seated on Federal Hill with his cannon; and there, beneath his artillery, were gentlemen hotly professing themselves to be secessionists, men whose sons and brothers were in the southern army, and women!—alas whose brothers would be in one army, and their sons in another. That was the part of it which was most heart-rending in this border land. In New England and New York men's minds at any rate were bent all in the same direction,—as doubtless they were also in Georgia and Alabama. But here fathers were divided from sons, and mothers from daughters. Terrible tales were told of threats uttered by one member of a family against another. Old ties of friendship were broken up. Society had so divided itself, that one side could hold no terms of courtesy with the other. "When this is over," one gentleman said to me, "every man in Baltimore will have a quarrel to the death on his hands with some friend whom he used to love." The complaints made on both sides were eager and open-mouthed against the other.

Late in the autumn an election for a new legislature of the State had taken place, and the members returned were all supposed to be unionist. That they were prepared to support the Government is certain. But no known or presumed secessionist was allowed to vote without first taking the oath of allegiance. The election therefore, even if the numbers were true, cannot be looked upon as a free election. Voters were stopped at the poll and not allowed to vote unless they would take an oath which would , on their parts, undoubtedly have been false. It was also declared in Baltimore that men engaged to promote the northern party were permitted to vote five or six times over, and the enormous number of votes polled on the Government side gave some colouring to the statement. At any rate an election carried under General Dix's